# FoxTales:
# Scenes at F

CW00822197

## *Kerry Nietz*

## *Hentzenwerke Publishing*

Published by:
Hentzenwerke Publishing
980 East Circle Drive
Whitefish Bay WI 53217 USA

Hentzenwerke Publishing books are available through booksellers and directly
from the publisher. Contact Hentzenwerke Publishing at:
414.332.9876
414.332.9463 (fax)
www.hentzenwerke.com
books@hentzenwerke.com

FoxTales: Behind the Scenes at Fox Software
    By   Kerry Nietz
    Copy Editor: Nicole McNeish
    Cover Art: "You Allocate Some Memory" by Todd Gnacinski,
Milwaukee, WI

ISBN: 1-930919-50-6

Manufactured in the United States of America.

# About the Author

## Kerry Nietz

Kerry Nietz graduated with honors from Bowling Green State University with a degree in Computer Science. He was employed by Fox Software as a software developer for four years where he worked on FoxPro 1.0 and 2.0. Following the Fox/Microsoft merger he became employee #29754 of Microsoft for nearly seven years. At Microsoft he worked on FoxPro version 2.5 and 3.0 for both Windows and Mac before leaving the pack to work briefly on Expedia and then on Microsoft's online bill payment system, TransPoint. Kerry currently makes his home in northwest Ohio with his wife, a dog, a cat, and whatever varmit is living in the crawlspace this week. Kerry can be reached at FoxTales@Nietz.com.

# Acknowledgements

Wow, this is a lot like being at the Oscars...so many to thank, so many to thank....

First, to Marlene Troxel, now deceased, for taking a high school sophomore to work with her. Thanks for living beyond yourself.

Many thanks to David Chilson, for a job recommendation that opened a can of wombats.

And to my parents, Rex and Helen, for allowing my path to find me (and for not sending me to military school). You're the best.

And to my wife, Leah, for her love, prayers and perpetual support. I guess I **will** be published before I die, Sweetie.

And to Whil, my publisher, for taking a serious chance on a random piece of e-mail. This book would've been really boring without you. May you be blessed a hundredfold.

And to Nicole McNeish for her copy editing skills. I'm sorry I use the words 'pretty', 'then' and 'had' so much.

And to Mike Feltman, Toni Feltman and the Heindel-man for proofreading and keeping a secret.

And to the rest of the Fox gang for being a part of the stories I can't stop telling. You're all virtuoso stunt-men (and women) to me.

And many thanks to Dave Fulton. Though at times the narrative may make it **seem** like I don't appreciate everything you did in those long ago days, I do. Aside from taking a chance on me, you took hundreds of risks and made thousands of "right" decisions in order to create a "lyrical" product and build a company into something that Microsoft paid serious dough for. Few people can say that. I see some things differently now than I did fresh out of school.

And my ultimate thanks to the God who works in the circumstances....

Nuff said!
Kerry Nietz
2003

# List of Chapters

# Prologue
# Morning

There's been no phone call yet, but that doesn't mean anything. It's still early.

The overhead lights came on only a few minutes ago, signaling that Howard, the head of Tech Support, has made it in. He's a real business-as-usual guy. Always wears a button down shirt.

But, I'm not. I never turn the lights on when I come in. The florescence is too bright, especially in the morning. In fact, most of us in the outer circle removed bulbs from our overheads. Too much glare on the computer screen.

I like it when it's still a little dark in here. It's usually quiet and you can get some good coding done without fear of interruption. After nine, you never know what's going to happen.

My machine is compiling my latest change, so I glance around my office, my fortress of privacy. Within its off-white walls are glimpses of what my life has become.

On one wall hangs a picture of a space shuttle taking off. It's an early morning launch, so the scene is really an explosion of light and activity from a place of solitude and darkness. *Sort of like this place after nine*, I think with a smile.

I look behind me. I have a table with a small collection of CDs and a semi-usable Sony Discman. It doesn't work very well since the Marketing guy unknowingly checked it for me at the airport. Sometimes it makes a loud humming sound.

Next to that is my window. It's a perk of my position—I can view the outside world. All I can really see, though, is the roof of the adjoining building and the dumpsters in the back. But, it's something that only a handful of us have, so I'm not complaining. Beyond the dumpsters and the few buildings that mark the edge of town, is the beginning of Ohio's farm country. I grew up on one of those farms. It's comforting to know it's still out there. I reach out and adjust the blinds slightly. Of course, I'm allergic to everything that grows, which is part of the reason I'm here.

I glance back at the screen. *Still compiling.* I look at the top of the monitor where Snippet-Man tremors slightly. He's just a little metal spring guy who holds a tennis racquet, a knickknack someone gave me.

I dressed him in his first bit of clothing recently—a wrapper from some candy named 'Snippets'. They taste a lot like Tootsie Rolls, but the name has significance to me now. The wrapper draped around the little guy makes him Snippet-Man. Visitors who are in on the joke think he's funny. And he is, and that's good. Things have been really tense here lately, and we all need a little more laughter.

On the front wall of my office, just below the Plexiglas portion, is a bookshelf with a small selection of computer books and manuals in it. Just next to that is a poster of two bikini-clad women Heindel and Eric (or his alter ego Skippy) hung up for me. It's their way of harassing the single guy. Everyone else on the staff, except my next-door neighbor Sally, is married. I'm the proverbial nice guy who never has a date. *But hey, I'm only twenty-three!* I don't know why I'm not hitched (or even have a girlfriend). But I don't think it's all my fault. Things just never work out. Besides, management fired my last girlfriend. *And, here's a thought, maybe if I had my weekends back...*

I frown. Still no phone call. Maybe I'm home free today. It would be great not to have to take *The Walk*. I have a lot of things to do.

I look at the top of my bookshelf. The previous version of our product rests there. It's a white box with the outline of a fox's head. The head appears to be looking to its right and behind it is a purplish-red rainbow of color. The fox gives the product a friendly feel, as if it's something for the kids. But it isn't, and I know. The fox is nimble and the fox is driven, but often the head is downright mean.

I hear a sound, a distant booming footfall. *Uh, oh.* There won't be any phone calls today. He's coming on his own. Things are bad. *Still, he may not be coming for me.*

He's moving steadily, but quickly. Boom, boom, boom. The floor reverberates. He's past Bill and Eric's office already. Still coming...but maybe he'll stop to see Heindel or Chris. They get to take 'The Walk' often. *Please let it be READ,* I pray, *please let it be READ....*

No such luck. Sally is next in line, but she isn't working on anything that's a hot button. A pain starts in my gut.

There are offices past mine, of course. He could be on his way to talk to Janet. That happens sometimes. Snippet-Man is jiggling. I focus on my computer screen. It's finished compiling now. I click a few keys to open up my editor and look busy. *Things will be fine.*

The footfalls stop. I try to concentrate on my code, but I can't. I know what's going to happen next. I hear tapping on the Plexiglas and look up. Just to the left of the door I see his face glowering in at me. He doesn't look pleased. His finger appears and curls itself toward him. He wants me. *It's me again.*

I frown, stand up, and circle around the desk. I have a walk to take, and I bet it's not going to make me happy.

# Chapter 1
# Fox Den

I was in my room at my parents' house, when the phone rang.

"Kerry!" my mother yelled up the stairs, a little softer than she normally would. "It's for you!"

I dropped my textbook on the bed and made for the door. Finals week was approaching and I still had a lot to ingest. To get an A in a Computer Science class at Bowling Green you needed at least a 93. If I got all A's that semester I would graduate with honors and that would mean a lot. *I may not have a job, but at least I'll make a good show of it.*

I walked to the phone in the hall. My short, spectacled mother was still at the foot of the stairs. She looked up at me and smiled.

"Who is it?" I asked.

"It's for you," she said, still smiling.

I frowned and picked up the receiver. As much as I liked talking to my friends (and I had the same three my whole life) this would have to be short. I had work to do. "Hello," I said.

"Ah, Kerry," the jovial-sounding voice on the phone said. "I think I'm going to make you happy."

I recognized the voice. It was someone I met only a few days before.

"I'm going to offer you a position with us," he continued, "—with Fox Software."

I smiled and glanced down at my Mom. *Finally. Just when I'd nearly given up. An offer, finally.*

*      *      *

I like to think of it as God working in the circumstances, a string of seemingly unrelated events that sent my life down a path. But, whatever you call it, it was a diversion from the norm.

I grew up on a farm in Ohio. My father was a farmer, his father was a farmer, and—if you get right to it—the first Nietz that stepped off the boat, was probably, a farmer. So, when I was born, it was assumed that I too would be a farmer; the corn doesn't fall far from the stalk in Wood County.

It came as a surprise to all involved when, at an early age, I was diagnosed with an incurable condition—one that would jeopardize my future career. I was allergic to farms. Well, maybe not farms themselves, but nearly everything growing on or around them, especially Ragweed.

So, the question became what should I be? When asked, I usually said "fireman," but I really had no idea. The only thing I liked to do— aside from hanging out with my three friends—was read. However, if you check the phone book, there aren't too many "professional readers" listed. In general, people won't pay you to do something they wish they could be doing themselves. My only other interest— "creative doodling"—wasn't an acceptable occupation either. My parents frequently threatened me with military school.

\*        \*        \*

A turning point came when a family friend took a friend and I to her workplace. It was 1981 and I was a sophomore in high school. The computer industry was well established by then, but most useful computers still filled a room.

Marlene, the family friend, worked at the top of a ten-story bank building in downtown Toledo. Just outside her office was the room-filling computer her company used. That night she let my friend, Rusty, and I try our best at the text adventure games loaded on the machine. We weren't so good.

"I died again," I said, shaking my head. "The troll caught the knife and threw it back at me."

Marlene laughed. "Hey Kerry, look at this," she said.

I turned in her direction. She held an armful of green-striped paper in her hands.

"What's that?"

She nodded toward my terminal. "It's the code to that game you guys are playing."

"What?" I said, squinting at the mass of green. "All that?"

She laughed again. "Well…yeah…isn't that something?"

I glanced at Rusty. His eyebrows were high, hidden beneath blonde locks. "Dang," he said. "That's a lot of typing."

And it was, but it was something else too. It planted a seed. To me, playing the game was almost like reading a book. Maybe, aside from enjoying the game, I could help write it, or something like it. Maybe.

\*        \*        \*

The first personal computers came out in the years that followed. Before I graduated high school, my parents— realizing I needed something to do during allergy season beyond reading and doodling— bought one for the family. It had only 16K of memory and read programs from a tape recorder, but I thought it was great. Aside from the games I played, I learned a little about programming. It was another piece of the puzzle.

In addition, I needed something to make me special. As a 6 foot, 145-pound teenage boy, I didn't fit into much of my high school's scene. I was too lanky (and uncommitted) for sports. I played in band, but only because my Dad said, "You have to do something!", and girls...well, girls were something my friends and I watched from a distance and talked about. Like deer sprinting across a field.

At my school, if you weren't a jock, a doper, or a member of the FFA (Future Farmers of America) you didn't have a group. I was none of the above. Couple that with the fact my mom taught there, my slight physique, and it isn't hard to see why I was an easy target for bullies.

For me, high school was four years spent waiting for graduation.

$$*\qquad*\qquad*$$

Senior year was when I met my first career challenge. I had already decided I was going to try this thing called "Computer Programming" and fortunately within twenty minutes of my parents' home was a university with courses in that very thing—Bowling Green State University (BGSU, for short). In a few months, I could send in an application.

As it happened, my class took a field trip to BGSU to help us with our future career choices. As part of our campus tour, we stopped at the college's Placement Office. Housed in a building shaped like a slide projector, it was the office that—if we attended the school—would one day help us find a job. One of the resident "Placement Officers" took time away from her busy schedule to answer our career inquiries.

"I have a question," one of my classmates said, waving a hand in the air.

"Yes?" the immaculately-dressed lady said.

The questioning classmate excelled at sports in high school, but was offered few scholarships. I knew he was searching for direction. "Yeah," he said, smiling respectfully. "I was wondering what you think about a career in computers?"

The Officer frowned and placed her hands on her hips. "In my honest opinion," she said, "I don't see much hope for a long term career in programming."

My classmate looked as stunned as I felt. "Why?" he asked.

"I just think eventually we will get to the point where computers will program themselves. Human programmers won't be needed."

My classmate's face wilted. His direction changed entirely.

I frowned and shook my head. *Well, someone's going to have to write the program that makes those computers program themselves*, I thought. *I'll write that.*

Challenge accepted.

\* \* \*

So, I enrolled at BGSU in Computer Science, not knowing if the computers themselves would be competing with me for a job when I got out, and really not knowing whether I'd like to program or not. I'd written a few programs at home, but they were trivial. At college, it would be for real.

But after only one class, I knew I liked it. It tapped into the imaginative aspects of my personality, just like reading and doodling, and it was something I could actually do for a living. As the semesters went by, more and more of my colleagues left the major, but I stayed with it. And, despite leaving little time for a social life (or perhaps providing me with a convenient excuse), my academic career went remarkably well.

Being good in school is one thing, though. Finding a job that uses those new skills is something else entirely.

\* \* \*

The closing weeks of my senior year found me waiting for some company (any company) to make me an offer. I had no clue as to where I would work following graduation and it was beginning to seem like I might not be working at all. But, not for lack of trying.

Through the same Placement Office that once tried to harpoon my career choice, my peers and I were able to interview with many reputable companies—all with positions to fill. We dressed our best and took our shot. We smiled, we answered, we questioned, and we corresponded. However, for whatever reason, one of my peers always got the offer to fill those positions. Never me, and the time until graduation was growing short.

On more than one occasion, the head of the CS department invited me to her office. She was a pleasant person with dark curly hair who taught a class on Operating Systems. But our office get-togethers weren't about coursework.

"Your grades are certainly high enough to garner an offer or two," she said, smiling politely. "What are you doing wrong?"

Then came the interviewing skills review. Was I smiling enough? Was I answering thoroughly? Was I dressing appropriately? Were my questions well researched? Just what was the problem?

But I had few answers. I was following the checklist perfectly...at least I thought I was. I interviewed a lot...and I wrote many "letters of appreciation" to those who interviewed me. If I was breaking one of the "rules of interviewing", it wasn't obvious.

After a few of her pep talks, though, I began to wonder if in some strange way the department's reputation wasn't squarely on my back.

"Students who have the sort of grades you have do not fail to find a job," she said. "Not BGSU grads anyway. So, what's the problem?"

Each meeting made the load feel a little heavier.

Deep down, though, I had a good idea of what the hitch was. All the programming positions I interviewed for, attractive as they were, were mainframe work—work that would find me locked in a huge lab somewhere with only the drone of disk drives to keep me company. It was the land of bean counters, propeller heads, and dark suits worn all day. None of that was on the list of things I wanted in a job.

No. In my heart, I wanted to work on small machines, on the personal computers. I wanted to program on the same sort of machines and write the same sort of (software) code I'd used ever since I first sat at my 16K machine. I wanted a job where you could physically carry your work home if you had to. I wanted a place where everyone knew my name, not just the number on my ID badge. I wanted to make an impact!

\*       \*       \*

One afternoon, while I was working at my part time job for the University's Office of Admissions, the phone rang.

"This is Dr. Chilson," the voice in my ear said. Dr. Chilson was my favorite instructor in the CS department and probable the most methodical of any. When he lectured, he'd first tell you what he was going to tell you, next he would tell you 'it' (whatever it was), and then he'd tell you what he just told you. There were never any tricks on his tests. Just attend the lectures, study the notes, and you would do fine. Consequently, I did well in his classes.

He had three questions for me. "Do you like the C programming language?" Dr. Chilson asked.

I had only one class that touched on C, but it was enough to know I liked it. I was hoping to code in C someday. "Yes," I said.

"Do you like database work?" he said. "My database course last semester, did you like that?"

Any class that I got an A in, I liked. "Sure," I said. "Of course."

"OK," he said. "Have you taken the 408 course?"

CS 408 was the Operating Systems course taught by the head of the department. "Yeah," I said. "I took it."

"Good," he said. "How would you like to interview with a small company in Perrysburg. It's called Fox Software."

"Fox?"

Dr. Chilson went on to explain that the owner of Fox Software— Dr. Dave Fulton—used to teach with him at Bowling Green. Dr Chilson had done a little backdoor recruiting for the company for a number of years. "They write database software that runs on PCs," he said. "Would you be interested in that type of work?"

*They make software for PCs? No way!* "I'd be interested in that," I said, trying not to sound too excited.

If Dr. Chilson noticed any emotion, he didn't let on. "You want me to set up an interview then?"

*They work in C and I could go down to the local software store and point to their product on the shelf? Are you kidding?* "Can you?" I said. "That'd be great."

"Will do," he said, and then hung up the phone.

I smiled. *Maybe I won't have to work on the farm after all.*

                    *         *         *

With a scheduled interview in hand, I thought it wise to do a little research. I needed to know if Fox Software was everything I hoped it was. I made a stop at the college library. It was located in a building that looked like an upright stack of books.

The magazine articles I found told me Fox Software, which employed around thirty people, was started by four programmers like myself. They designed a database product called FoxBASE+ that ran on personal computers and had gained a respectable amount of success. This success was largely because it was a 'workalike' of the industry's leading database product named *dBASE*.

I knew little about dBASE, but in the eighties, workalike products were prevalent. A workalike was a program built to look, act, and feel exactly like another company's (often highly successful) product. The three most successful products of the day—WordPerfect (a word processor), Lotus 1-2-3 (a spreadsheet) and dBASE—each had workalikes. In fact, some had more than one. dBASE had two reasonably successful workalikes—FoxBASE+ and another called Clipper by Nantucket—and a few others that were marginally successful.

These workalikes (later called 'clones') survived because the software market was large enough to allow them. They made their niche by being a cheaper version of their cloned rivals. They also tended to have fewer bugs, be more responsive to user requests, and sometimes—as was reported to be the case with FoxBASE+—they performed better.

Their legality, however, was still a point of contention. Even though the clones looked nothing like the products they were duplicating on the inside (at the level a programmer would see them), on the outside (at the level a user would see) they were designed to look and act identical to the product they were cloning. At the time I was leaving college, allowing the 'look and feel' similarity or not was an issue the courts had not yet fully decided.

I dug deeper, hoping to find more specific information about the origins of Fox Software and its products. I found some, but some I didn't learn until later. It was a history that really revolved around one person—Dave Fulton.

Sometime prior to the formation of Fox, Dave co-owned (with his first wife) another company named DACOR. During his ownership of DACOR he managed to hire three of his former BGSU students—Bill Ferguson, Eric Christensen, and Amy Chapman (who later became Amy Fulton) as programmers.

DACOR was in the business of writing custom software, and in 1983 they were hired to write a manufacturing application. While investigating the right tools to use, they happened upon the dBASE product from Ashton-Tate. The feature set of dBASE suited their needs, but in trying to develop their application they kept running into problems or inconsistencies in dBASE that made completing the project next to impossible. This eventually led them to write their own product—one with the same functionality as dBASE, but without all the problems. When the 'clone' product was done, they used it to finish their original manufacturing application. Unfortunately, after completing the original application they found the market for it had dried up. It was a near-tragic turn—and one that threatened the future of DACOR as a company.

At that point, a handful of factors came into play. First, Dave was having relationship difficulties with his wife (and DACOR's co-owner). Second, the company itself was now having financial difficulties and would have to downsize severely to stay viable. And finally, Dave's small development team had constructed a working dBASE clone—a product that just **might** be marketable.

The eventual outcome was Dave divorced his wife—selling his share of DACOR to her—and with his three favorite programmers in tow, started a new venture. So was born Fox Software, and FoxBASE, its first product.

The story hinted at an aspect of dBASE (and its clones) that I found interesting. dBASE was unique from other software programs because it was really two products in one. In one respect it was a database program a user could interact with through its interface and use to manipulate their personal data, much like someone might use a word processor to manipulate their words. But, dBASE also had a built in language, known as the dBASE (and later xBASE) language, which users could create and run programs against, much like I as a programmer was hoping to do with a language called C. So, dBASE was both an interactive user program and a language program.

Because it was a language program, dBASE could be used as a developer tool. This gave rise to a group of highly sophisticated users known as 'dBASE developers'. These developers made their livelihood by creating customized applications using the dBASE language. In general, their applications could run on dBASE or any of its clones.

What those developers found, and what gave Fox its early success, was when they ran their applications on FoxBASE, they ran more efficiently. Their databases could be accessed quicker and sorted faster. Their interface was more responsive. In command-by-command comparisons, FoxBASE performed better than Ashton-Tate's product, with little exception. Usually the difference between the two products was remarkable. Fox essentially created a better dBASE than dBASE, with only a small support staff and a Cracker Jack team of C developers.

Few still-unemployed college grads would want to miss that. It was a chance for significance and an opportunity to work on personal computers for a living. It was the job I wanted. Now all that remained was to convince the Fox people of it.

\*       \*       \*

When the day of my interview arrived, I donned my interview "blues" and set off for the town of Perrysburg.

Perrysburg is a quiet, little suburb of Toledo located just down Highway 25 from Bowling Green. The city's most notable feature is Fort Meigs, a large wooden fort on the west side of town constructed by General (and later President) William Henry Harrison. Situated on the Maumee River, Fort Meigs played a vital defensive role in the War of 1812.

Likewise, Perrysburg played a vital role in the history of Fox Software. It served as Fox's home since the company's inception and in 1988, their dwelling was a retooled bank building set near one of Perrysburg's main thoroughfares, West South Boundary.

Upon arriving at the address I was given, I was thrown off initially by the fact that the two-story brick structure also housed the office of a pediatrician. I searched the exterior for some time before finally locating a glass door with a red Fox logo on it. I walked in and was greeted by a receptionist who promptly directed me up the stairs. At the top of the stairs were two doors—an unmarked one and one that read "Dave Fulton."

I knocked on the latter and was soon greeted by a round, nearly bald man about forty years old. "Ah, you must be Kerry," he said, smiling pleasantly. "I'm Dave Fulton. Come in, come in." Dave gave my hand a firm shake and indicated a small, circular table. "Have a seat. I'll gather the rest." He bustled out through another door.

As I waited, I examined his office. On the wall to my right was a white marking board with little written on it, and to my left, near the window, was an L-shaped wooden desk. Sitting on the desk were two computers. A Macintosh (a type II model—new at the time) near the center of the L and another DOS-based machine sat to one side. Racked nearby was a sizable collection of music CDs—still a novelty medium. I was jealous.

Dave returned with three people in tow. One of them, a petite woman with short, dark hair came around the table and shook my hand. "This is my wife, Amy," Dave said. Amy smiled politely and sat down to my right.

A stocky man with salted black hair and a thick mustache came forward next. "Bill Ferguson," Dave informed me. Following a quick handshake, Bill methodically pulled out the seat across from me.

"And this is Eric Christensen," Dave said. A taller, thinner man with sandy-colored hair stuck out a hand, and then slid into the seat between Bill and Amy.

*I'm about to be gang-interviewed by the founding quartet of developers*, I thought, and immediately began to feel nervous. Adding to my anxiety was the fact that in all the other interviews I'd been in, I was never quite sure what I did wrong. I thought I acted appropriately, but I still always came up empty. "Be confident and enthusiastic," the department head had coached me. *OK, here we go...*

From there the interview progressed along normal lines. They asked me about the programming projects I did at school and at home. They asked whether I had coded in C before (their programming language of choice) and they asked about what I wanted in a job.

Nerves aside, that portion of the interview went well. The founding four seemed like nice, normal people who enjoyed their work. They exuded a passion for their product, but Dave emphasized, "We all have lives outside of work as well." In addition, their appearance made it clear the dress code at Fox Software was something on the order of jeans and a clean t-shirt—a detail that appealed to me strongly. I was getting a rash from all the polyester I had to wear for interviews.

The dialogue finally reached a point where Dave seemed to want to question my resolve. "We have a top notch team here," he said.

Bill Ferguson cradled his chin is his hand, yet managed to nod once slowly. "Yes," he said. "We work to the edge of our abilities."

Eric covered a smile with his hand and Dave frowned slightly. "I don't know about that," he said. "But we do work some extra hours close to release." He studied me intently. "Do you think you can do that?" he asked. All eyes were on me.

I had never been asked a question like that in an interview before. Every other interviewer seemed to only rely on their own tests and intuition to determine whether I could do the job or not. They never just asked me.

*Confidence and enthusiasm.* "Yes," I answered, nodding my head once firmly.

The room remained serious. Only Amy, who had a slight grin on her face the entire time, seemed relaxed. She could tell I was nervous.

"That means an occasional Saturday," Dave continued. "Not regularly, but sometimes. Just whatever it takes to get the product out. Can you handle that?"

I stayed serious too. "Yes," I said again.

There were slow nods from around the table, and then the mood relaxed. The benefit of free pop in the refrigerator was mentioned, along with the flexible hours and casual dress style. We finished with handshakes and I left, hoping I made a good impression. If I didn't, I wasn't sure what I would do next.

*    *    *

Dave called the following week. "So, do you want to join us?" he asked, speaking rapidly. I wondered if he had to use the restroom.

"Well, when would you want me to start?" I asked. I still had a couple weeks of school left. After that, I was hoping for a little time to catch my breath.

"As soon as you can," he said. "So, are you with us?"

Now, in my heart, I knew I wanted to work for Fox. The work was close to home, it seemed like an exciting challenge, they had free pop in the refrigerator, and I wouldn't even have to wear a suit! There was literally no downside.

Still, the Placement Office advised us seniors always to take some time in making our decision. You shouldn't look too anxious, they said. Any reputable company would gladly give us time to think through such a major decision.

"I'd like some time to think about it," I said.

Dave seemed startled. "Think about it?" he said. "Well, for how long?"

"A week?"

"A week! Well, that's a long time...."

*OK*, I thought, *I'm not going to lose this chance because of the Placement Office. The computers may have the jobs soon, after all.* "How about two days?" I said.

"All right, two days," Dave said. "We'll hear from you then."

"In two days," I repeated. I smiled and hung up the phone. I had a couple days, but I didn't know why. I didn't even need two minutes. It wasn't like there were any other offers on the table. The path had led to this, and it seemed right.

After my two days of thinking about it, I called back to accept. I would walk through graduation on May 7th, and walk into Fox Software on May 9th. No sense wasting time, I had work to do.

# Chapter 2
# Introductions

Next came the first day of work. Dr. Dave told me that everyone got in around eight o'clock in the morning. I wanted to make a good impression, so I showed up about a quarter 'til.

The front door was still locked. All I could see inside was a darkened room with a few boxes on the floor. *Now what?*

A few seconds later a young man with dark, curly hair came to the front door and picked up one of the boxes. He saw me standing there, and with a puzzled expression on his face, stepped forward and opened the door.

"You look like you need something," he said.

I glanced at the box he held—a new computer. "Well…this is my first day," I said. "And I don't have a key."

He smiled. "Come on." He nodded at another box on the floor. "Could you give me a hand?"

"Ah…sure." I stooped to pick up a large box—a monitor—and then turned left to follow him up the stairs.

The man's name was Kevin and he told me he wore two hats at the company. When he wasn't selling the product over the phone, he was busy setting up employee machines and solving network problems. He was a busy guy.

Kevin reached the unmarked door at the top of the stairs and waited for me to catch up. "So, what are you going to be doing here?" he asked.

I checked my feet.  "Programming," I said. "Working on the product."

Kevin's eyes widened. "You're going to be a developer?" he said. "Wow! How did you get hired as a developer?"

I shrugged. I was a little unclear on the factors that led to my hiring too. "One of my instructors set up an interview," I said.

Kevin gave me another long look. He was young, but I was a few years younger. Finally, he tipped his head. "Well, most of 'dev' doesn't get in until closer to nine. I think Eric is here, though. I'll show you around." He leaned back to leverage his box against his body, and then opened the door.

As I entered the top floor, the most evident feature was the corral of yellow-walled cubicles—offices for over a dozen people—that filled the central portion of the room. The rectangle of the corral began just beyond the door, and created a bounding hall that ran around the outside of the building. On the opposite side of that hall—the 'right side' as you moved counter clockwise through the building—was the floor's "walled and windowed" offices.

Kevin followed the hall that ran straight-ahead of us from the door, the southern hall. As I followed, I noticed the names on the doors of the exterior offices. They were all names I knew—the names of the developers who interviewed me.

Kevin led me to the room at the easternmost point of the hall. It was empty except for a few boxes. He stowed his box on the floor, and so did I. I glanced at the door. It read "Dick LaValley."

"Who's Dick LaValley?" I asked.

Kevin glanced at the name on the door. "Dick LaValley? Oh, he's one of the company owners."

It was the first time I heard the company had another owner aside from Dave Fulton. "What does he do here?" I asked.

Kevin shrugged. "He has a legal firm downtown," he said. "He's not really here that much. I think he's officially the company's CFO or something." He indicated the boxes on the floor. "They let me use the room for putting machines together." He moved back to the door. "Come on, I'll show you around."

Kevin took me on a brisk tour of the building. While we walked, he alternated between prying me for details on my background and experience, and lauding Fox and its products. "Fox is the best database product ever," he said. "No one is as fast as Fox. We're hundreds of times faster." It didn't take long to see why Kevin was a salesman. He would have been my pick for company cheerleader, were the position available.

His tour revealed that the top floor housed offices for development, technical support, sales people, and other support personnel. The bottom floor had a small receptionist desk in front, and behind was…

"…the production facility," Kevin said as we walked into the largest room in the building. The room had a number of machines in it. One in particular had Saran-wrap material running through it. "The shrink-wrap machine," Kevin told me. The facility was the place where the product was put into a box and shrink-wrapped for sale.

"How many work here?" I asked.

"In production? Maybe seven."

"The whole company?"

"Thirty to forty. Something like that."

It wasn't quite a software house in a garage, but Fox was still a small, family-run software business. *I can make an impact here*, I thought. *I was hired while the company is still small.*

Kevin's tour also validated his assertion that few made it in before nine. "Pretty empty here, yet," I said.

Kevin smiled. "Yep," he said. "Come on. I'll take you to Eric."

\*         \*         \*

Eric Christensen's office was actually one of the offices we passed on our way to Dick LaValley's. We arrived to find him seated in a black office chair in the center of the room with a rolling computer stand in front of him. On the stand was a Macitosh computer. On one side of the room was a longer white desk with a DOS machine on it. There were a number of boxes in the office as well.

"What're you working on?" I asked Eric after Kevin had gone.

Eric glanced at his computer screen. "Oh…speeding up the Mac product," he said, frowning. "Trying to, anyway." Eric spoke softly and his manner was relaxed, but there was a glint of something—impishness, maybe—in his eyes.

"How do you do that?" I asked. "Speed up the product." We didn't much care how fast our programs ran in college, as long as they worked.

I saw the glint in Eric's eyes again. "Well," he said, crossing his legs, "you find the slow parts, and you take them out."

"I see," I said, forcing a smile. I wasn't sure if he was picking on me or not.

I didn't know it yet, but Eric was a bona-fide computer genius. He could almost breathe code—and not just any code, but code that would run twice as fast as anyone else's. His job was to make Fox products faster, and he was exceptionally good at it. He was master of 'taking out the slow parts'.

I was hoping to be master of something too. "Do you know what I'll be working on?" I asked.

Eric stretched out both hands and raised his shoulders. "I don't know."

"Well, do you know where my office will be?"

Eric raised his shoulders again. "I don't know. They don't tell me anything." He nodded at another black chair. "You can wait here if you want."

I seated myself and Eric turned back to study his computer screen. He went on to tell me that, although **he** usually got in at seven-thirty, most of the rest of 'dev' didn't get in until closer to nine. He let me hang out in his office until someone came in who knew what to do with me, which, as predicted, was nearly an hour later.

However, from that morning forward, I took Eric's seven-thirty starting time as my own.

*    *    *

When everything was finally sorted out, the office they found me was in the central corral, adjacent to another of Fox's young programmers—a guy named Marty Sedluk.

Marty's cube was empty that first morning, but after lunch I heard someone shuffle into it and the chiming sound of a Mac being turned on. A short time later there was a friendly "Huh-low" from behind me.

Marty was a head shorter than me with bushy, brown hair. In appearance and temperament he most closely resembled the actor who plays Sam Gamgee in the movie "The Lord of the Rings." He even had the large feet relative to their size typical of hobbits. Marty's defense of that condition was, "Well, I was supposed to be tall."

After Marty and I got through exchanging pleasantries, I asked him what he was working on. He motioned me toward his cubicle, so I stood up and looked over the side.

On Marty's screen was an open window that looked similar to most painting and drawing programs I'd seen. It had a column of small pictures along the left side (a 'palette') and a design surface with a pattern of dotted 'grid lines' on it.

"It's a Screen Painter for our Mac product," Marty said. He then proceeded to give me a demonstration of his work.

His Screen Painter was the coolest thing I'd ever seen. It allowed users to fashion interactive input screens by placing and moving different objects (such as pictures, lines, and text) on a design surface. They could visually compose a 'What You See Is What You Get' interface to incorporate later in their application. In the process, they saved themselves from typing hundreds of lines of code.

"How long have you been working here, Marty?" I asked.

"Oh, about six months."

"Six months?" I couldn't imagine creating such a thing in half a year. I wouldn't even know where to begin. My projects in college hadn't even come close to that level of complexity.

"Yeah, but I'm only in part-time," Marty said. "I'm still finishing school at UT (University of Toledo)."

I was amazed someone still in college was working on such a crucial component, part-time. "Wow," I said. "How did you get hired?"

"They demoed FoxBASE+/Mac at my Mac-users group in Toledo," Marty said. He smiled and puffed out his chest. "Yeah, they decided they needed my help." He chuckled a little.

Marty joked about it, but what he said wasn't far from the truth. During a demonstration of an early version of FoxBASE+/Mac, Marty so beleaguered the Fox people with statements to the effect of "we don't do it like that on the Mac" they finally realized they needed someone with his firm ideals and tenacity to make their product truly 'Mac-like'. Consequently, they offered Marty a job. He was the company's resident Macintosh-whiz.

*I'm part of a talented group*, I thought, returning to my seat. *The company might be called Fox Software, but I'm going to be running with wolves.*

*          *          *

That first day was the start of about a month of reading manuals, looking at code and learning about Fox products. As it happened, even though the Fox staff found me an office, there still weren't any spare computers available. So, while they spent weeks trying to find me one, I spent time in the office of someone named Dave Heindel—another developer. He was out on vacation, so having me occupy his space seemed (to the Fultons) like the best way to keep me out of everyone's way. Because of this, one morning found me sitting at the desk with my back to the door.

"Go away for a few days and they give away your office," a voice behind me said.

Startled, I turned to see a boyish face grinning at me.

"See if I take a vacation again," the man said.

"Um…sorry," I said.

He gave a little wave. "That's OK. You must be the new guy. I'm another one of the Daves." He extended a hand. (I later found out that there were three people named Dave at the company, the third being a writer).

I wasn't sure what to say next.

"So, you're a BG grad, huh?" Heindel asked, still smiling.

I nodded my head.

"Me too," he said.

"Really?" I said. I stood up to give Heindel back his chair.

"Yeah, a few years ago. Is your degree in Computer Science?"

I smiled. "Yep."

Heindel took his seat. "Did you know your boss started the CS department at BG?" he said. He leaned back in his chair some.

"**Dave** did?"

Heindel nodded. "Yep, he started it. His degree was in Statistics or something. Before him, there was no Computer Science major at BG."

"Hmm…" Now I knew why my professor recruited for Fox. Dave's connection with the CS department was huge. "Is your degree in CS too?" I asked.

Heindel nodded again. "With a minor in Journalism."

"Journalism?" It was an unusual minor for a CS student. Most of us had little time for a minor so disparate. A minor of 'Science' was the easiest path.

"Yeah, they hired me to code **and** write," Heindel said, smiling. "But they've kept me in development ever since they found out how much I suck at writing." Heindel laughed.

I smiled and shook my head. Someone else with a double title. *Fox employees are flexible.*

The next twenty minutes were filled with countless "me toos." Heindel and I both grew up in Ohio, graduated from the same university, loved sports (while **none** of the other developers could tell a goal line from a foul line), and we shared a lot of views—socially, politically and spiritually. It was the beginning of a long friendship.

Heindel's current task was to complete an upgrade to FoxBASE+, Fox Software's DOS product. Designated "version 2.10," this upgrade would supply users of the 2.0 product with some new standalone applications.

One of them was a code generation program called CodeGen that Fox purchased from an outside developer named Luis Castro. The other was called FoxCentral and it was a front-end program for FoxBASE+ that would make doing tedious operations in the product a little easier to accomplish.

Soon after meeting Heindel, Dr. Fulton made the decision to put me under Heindel's supervision. So, along with my continued studies, testing FoxCentral became one of my assignments.

Already I'd been given two jobs.

*     *     *

My first real coding project didn't come until a few weeks later, around the middle of June.

I was in my cubicle one morning, studying the manual from the Mac product. My office space was now stocked with the standard equipment for a cube-dweller at Fox. Positioned along the wall opposite the cubicle opening (my "door") I had a beige metal desk with a brown, faux-wood surface. On the desk, I had my own Mac II computer, oriented to the left. I also had a small, hanging bookshelf. It gripped the wall just above the Mac. In it was the box from my complimentary copy of Fox's Mac product and a few of my programming books from school. Over my desk to the right, was a picture of the space shuttle taking off. That wasn't standard issue—I just liked the way it looked. The other object in my cube that wasn't typical for everyone was the large rectangular building support that ran just in front of the right edge of my desk. It occupied a good chunk of my space, but it was something I could prop my feet against when I felt the need to "kick back."

I was kicked back with the manual on my lap when I heard a deep baritone voice to my right.

"So…," the voice said, and then nothing else.

I swiveled in my chair. Bill Ferguson stood at the entrance to my cube. "Bill," I said.

Bill was dressed in a short-sleeve button down and shorts. His hands were balled and he swung them a little as he spoke. "So…," he said again.

I already knew that Bill chewed on his words before spitting them out. He was deliberate to a fault. "Yeah?" I said, smiling.

Another pause while the hands swung. "Are you ready to do a little C programming?" he said finally.

After weeks of studying, trying out Fox products, and testing I was more than ready to code. I threw the Mac manual on my desk. "You bet!" I said.

Bill nodded again. "Ohh…kay."

I shrugged. "Well, what am I going to do?" I asked.

"Well…we need the strings taken out of the Mac product," he said. "That's what we thought we'd have you work on next."

Every C programmer knows what a string is. In fact, there was one in the first program I wrote in my college C course. That program looked like this:

```c
#include <stdio.h>

main()
{
printf ("Hello World!\n");
}
```

Its purpose was to print the words "Hello World!" on a computer screen. The first line ("#include <stdio.h>") just made the C language's standard output routines available. The second line ("main()") signaled the start of a C program and the braces (the first '{' and the final '}') set the program boundaries.

The third line was where the magic happened, though. That line printed the string "Hello World!" to the screen by calling a routine (printf())included in the first step.

So, the definition of a string in the C language was essentially anything contained within quotation marks. "Hello World\n" was the only string in that college example, but in a product like FoxBASE+/Mac there were thousands. Every error message, every bit of text in the menus, every prompt in every dialog—all of them, were strings.

Bill explained that part of my job was to replace each string I found in the code, with a call to a routine that would load that string from a separate file. There were a number of reasons to make such a change, but the primary advantage was that it got all the strings in one place so that our groups working in other countries (called "localizers") could replace the English text with strings from whatever language they were translating. With that separate string file available, they wouldn't have to touch our C code at all—just the file the strings were in. When they got through, there would be a German, or French, or Spanish version of FoxBASE+/Mac.

There wasn't much C coding in that portion of the project, though.

"You'll need to write a string compiler too," Bill said, nodding as if the meaning of "string compiler" was obvious.

"A string what?" In programming, most things with the word "compiler" in their name were very, very difficult to write. The program that took my C code and turned it into the numbers necessary for the computer to understand it was called a "compiler."

Bill smiled briefly. "Follow me back to my place. I'll explain."

I followed, and Bill explained.

The string compiler was to be a small application that would take strings from the separate string file and place them in the portion of the Mac product called "the resource fork." I had never heard of a "resource fork" before, but apparently every Macintosh application had one. Each Mac application file was composed of two parts—a "code fork" and a "resource fork"—and different portions of the application resided in each part. DOS applications—like the stuff I worked on with Heindel—typically had only one file for everything. On the Mac, though, the resource fork was where things like pictures and strings were supposed to live.

"And the compiler needs to be relatively fast," Bill said. "This is something that will be getting used a lot."

*My trial by fire*, I thought, nodding. *I get it*. The string compiler was a chance to show what I was made of.

It wasn't clear, though, why I was given a new supervisor. I liked working with Heindel, and I learned a lot.

I got the answer a few days later.

"Heindel's a good programmer," Dave Fulton said to me in passing, "but he's sort of a nine-to-fiver."

*A nine-to-fiver?* I thought. *What's wrong with that?* "Yeah?" I said.

Dave nodded. "We thought it'd be best for Bill to watch over you for awhile."

*     *     *

My time with Bill did nothing to exercise any "nine-to-fiver" traits I picked up from Heindel. I did learn a few things about my new mentor, though.

Bill was a problem solver. To the uninformed it might **seem** like he didn't have a solution because he was slow in expressing himself, but more often than not he **did** have a solution. The lag between the time Bill knew, and the time he let you know, was just because he was mulling it over in his head a little more.

As a fortunate side effect of his deliberate nature, Bill was patient to a fault. He had no problem explaining something more than once, nor did he expect a quick answer to a question he asked. He was a fitting coach for someone still trying to learn the ropes.

And with his guidance, I made swift progress. In only a few short weeks I had the strings all in a separate file (which meant I touched nearly every one of the hundreds of files in the product and changed thousands of lines of code...though trivially) and I was putting the finishing touches on the string compiler.

Finally, I went into Bill's office holding a floppy disk that contained—what I thought—was the finished compiler. The final decision was up to him, though. "I think I've got it," I said as I entered.

"OK..." Bill said slowly. "Let me see it." He reached out and took the disk, slipped it into his machine, and double-clicked the icon to start my compiler. "I want to check the speed," he said. Speed was the Fox thing, after all.

As the program started, it prompted Bill for the names of two files: the separate string file, and the application to put the strings into. Bill filled in those two names, and the application immediately began to run. It ran for only a few seconds before it finished. The strings were all in their proper place.

Bill crossed his arms, and reached up to straighten his mustache. He looked at me then and gave a quick little nod. "That'll do," he said.

I smiled. *My first success.* I proved that I could write code near Fox Software standards and I did it in a relatively short amount of time. I felt confident, useful.

"One more thing," I said, still smiling. I leaned forward and went through the steps to run my program again. When it reached the point where it was doing its work, I pointed at the screen. "What do you think?" I asked.

Bill squinted and leaned close. "You mean the cursor?"

"Yeah!" On the Mac it was common for the cursor to appear as a wristwatch when an application was performing a task that would make you wait. I did something a little more creative, though.

"Is that a running fox?" Bill said.

"Yeah! A little running fox. What do ya think?"

Bill shook his head slowly. "Kids…" he said.

* * *

A few days later, Heindel and I were gathered outside Eric's office. Early on I had become a member of the 11:30 lunch crew. Typically it was composed of Eric, Heindel, Bill—and now—me.

"When's Brian starting?" Heindel asked Eric.

"Who's Brian?" I asked. I hadn't met any Brians yet. Plenty of Daves, but no Brians.

Heindel had a hand on the door-jam while he absently watched Eric. Eric checked his screen one last time, and then with a firm slap on his knees, he stood to join us. "Where're we going?" he asked. When he got to the door, the three of us turned and started down the floor's southern bounding hall.

"Who's Brian?" I asked again.

"A new developer Dave hired," Heindel said.

*Another new developer?* I thought. *Someone to be compared against **already**?* I began to have flashbacks of the swimming lessons my mother took me and a friend to growing up. The lessons were enjoyable until the year he was promoted to the next class and I wasn't. *I hope this Brian is as inexperienced as I am,* I thought. *Then I won't be the low man any more.*

We reached Bill's office and Bill quickly stood to join us.

"Where's he from?" I asked.

I lagged Heindel a few paces, so he turned back slightly to speak to me. "From Florida now, I think."

"Yeah, that's right," Eric said. "I think he starts this week."

"From Florida?" I said. "How'd he get hired?" If Brian was from that far away, he was probably as unknown a quantity as I was.

"He used to work with Eric and I back at Marathon," Heindel said.

Or not. Marathon was an oil company with its headquarters in a town fifty miles south of Perrysburg. Their software group was a land of suits and day-long coffee breaks. Heindel and Eric worked there prior to Fox (although Eric always worked for Dave on the side). That association was part of the reason Heindel was hired.

I was still the only developer without a prior connection, aside from Marty, and Marty was a guaranteed (and proven) specialist. I was the odd man out—the low man on the totem pole.

*Man, I do not like this.*

\*         \*         \*

I met Brian a few days later. He was hard to avoid because his cubicle was just outside the entrance to mine. He was about thirty years old, well manicured, and dressed a little better than the company standard.

And for some reason, I wanted not to like him. I wanted him to be hard to get along with, or aloof, or have some annoying quality; something to make me feel like I had a uniquely positive trait going for me—the only other new guy.

But Brian had few negatives. He was bright, friendly, and about as easygoing as they come. I couldn't even hope for programming incompetence. Brian's first project (which was similar in difficulty to mine) was finished in about half the time. I couldn't compete with him, and after a few weeks, I didn't want to. Brian was rock-solid in so many ways I couldn't help but respect him.

If I was going to become a respected team member, I'd have to do it on my own merit, and with my own abilities. I made that a motivating factor.

\*         \*         \*

While I sweated my place in the pecking order and the final details of my string compiler, Heindel succeeded in shipping the 2.10 version of the DOS product and moved over to work on the Mac. Surprisingly, 2.10 would be the last major release of the FoxBASE product—more surprising because we thought the next version was already on its way.

It was code-named *FireFox* and it was to be a souped-up version of FoxBASE+, with the addition of whatever language commands Ashton-Tate decided to put into their soon-to-be-released version of dBASE, dubbed dBASE IV. *FireFox* represented Fox's continued commitment to producing a less expensive and faster version of dBASE, and initially Eric was the only one working on it.

He was busy finding the slow parts—and taking them out.

# Chapter 3
# Evaluations

In August I was given a review form to fill out. My first review with Fox would be the following month and this was my one chance to speak my mind. The form itself was straightforward. It was a one-page list of multiple-choice questions covering different aspects of my job. To answer each question I just picked a value from a range of satisfaction. Probably everyone has taken such a test

Finding the appropriate answers was easy. I couldn't have been more satisfied with a job. I was doing the kind of work I wanted to do, the work I trained for. My colleagues were smart and our products were great. It was an exciting place to be, and I said as much on my form

Then there was one final question. It was a generic "Is there anything else that bothers you about your workplace?" question. I stared at that one for awhile. As I did so, I heard the salesman whose cubicle shared a wall with mine say, "This is John Walker…," for the hundredth time that day. Marty was to my right, but to my left I could hear the clamor of Tech Support. "This is Bart Hanline…this is Jackie Jaynes…this is Randy…" It was an unceasing din. It persisted all day, every day. It warred against my concentration. It made it difficult for me to code. For work, I liked silence.

I hesitated to mention the noise though. The exterior offices were filled already, and even if they weren't, I wouldn't ask for one. I was the new guy. I didn't want to be labeled a whiner.

I listened as the clamor continued. "This is John, this is Jackie, this is Bart…" Salutations repeated endlessly. *Alright, I'll mention it,* I thought. *But, I'll be as subtle as possible.* I put pen to paper.

"Sometimes, it's a little noisy in here," I wrote, and left it at that. I signed my name and turned in my form.

Two days later I heard Dave call from behind me. I turned to see him partially blocking the entrance to my cube. "Yeah?" I said, sounding respectfully curious.

Dave had a serious look, but as I turned, he gave a quick smile before getting serious again. "Ah yeah, Kerry, we're going to move Marty and you into the conference room."

*Wow,* I thought, *that's…incredible.* "OK," was all I said.

Marty was standing near the entrance to his cubicle, listening. He nodded his head slowly a few times.

Dave bounced backward a few paces. "We realize it's probably noisy out here so we're going to do what we can. Brian is moving in with Eric and we'll put you two in the conference room." He raised his eyebrows slightly. "Is that OK?"

"Fine with me," I said and Marty echoed.

By the end of that week the two of us were sharing the corner conference room (the building's only conference room). It had two large windows, one that overlooked the parking lot and one that overlooked South Boundary and the small brick houses that lined it. Marty set up his desk facing the back window. Mine faced the room's lone swinging door. Between us there was only a single cubicle divider.

The room was light, and big, and completely noiseless. It was heaven.

\*          \*          \*

Toward the end of the summer of 1988, Fox Software was gearing up to release an updated Mac product—version 1.10. By then, nearly all of the forty-some employees were using the product on their machines while they went about their normal day of selling, supporting, or writing.

This impromptu testing was the only in-house testing Fox products got. Unlike larger software companies, where dedicated testing departments were the norm, at Fox—just prior to the release of a product—everyone became a tester. Aside from a few external users who volunteered to test the product (called 'Beta' testers), the employees alone were responsible for finding any bugs that remained before FoxBASE+/Mac was shrink-wrapped and sent out the door.

The release date was in early October.

\*          \*          \*

Sometime in September the developer force was divided. Most of the team moved on to various *FireFox* tasks and from then on had little involvement with the Mac effort (aside from occasional consultation). Those that remained—Marty, Heindel, and I—were involved with a specific aspect of the product, called code generation, and were still busy with new development work. We were essentially "under the gun" and became regulars at Fox on the weekends.

Aside from fixing whatever bugs our *in-house testing* turned up, Marty was putting the finishing touches on his Screen Painter. It was the first step in the code generation process.

Heindel—after just finishing the 2.10 release of the DOS product—now had the task of moving the C code for the CodeGen application generator to the Mac product. In the DOS product this entity was a standalone product (one that ran separately from FoxBASE+) but on the Mac it would be completely integrated. It would be available via a menu item in the product. CodeGen's purpose was to give users (or more likely a dBASE developer) the ability to compose a specialized program called a 'template'.

There were three separate programming languages in play in this project. Marty and Heindel (and those working on *FireFox*) were programming (ie 'coding') in the language called C. It had been around for decades, and was considered the standard for software development.

The next language involved was commonly known as the 'dBASE' language. It was the language users of our product could write in, if they chose to. It was specifically geared toward database manipulation. A simple example might look like this:

```
USE mydata.dbf INDEX myindex.idx
SET RELATION TO name INTO moredata
```

That program would open a database file named 'mydata.dbf' with an index file named 'myindex.idx,' and then set a relationship between 'mydata.dbf' and another database file named 'moredata'.

The third language—the one Heindel was adding support for in the Mac product—was a 'template language'. The template language was sort of an extension of the dBASE language but our product handled it differently. It allowed users to write a generic dBASE application where some parts of it could be filled in later by CodeGen with values produced by Marty's Screen Painter. This generic application was called a 'template'. An example might look like this:

```
USE {dbfnam} INDEX {ndxnam}
SET RELATION TO {relexp} INTO {relals}
```

When used in conjunction with CodeGen and a screen designed in the Screen Painter, that program could produce a dBASE program that looked like this:

```
USE books.dbf INDEX books.idx
SET RELATION TO title INTO borrowed
```

Or like this...

```
USE employees.dbf INDEX employees.idx
SET RELATION TO lastname INTO to_fire
```

It was entirely dependent on the created screen (and the user's preference). A template program was a powerful tool. It wasn't exactly "the program that made the computer program itself," but it did give novice users the ability to write dBASE code without having to actually write code. Consequently, it was a huge timesaver. Creating sample templates was my part of the effort. I had wrestled with them since late July.

My task came with a good share of frustration, because I was trying to work with a product that was under construction. Everything I did was dependent on Marty and Heindel's work. I was using features they were adding **as** they were added. It was like trying to live in a house while it's being built, except the doors might move on you while you slept.

Yet, my template work progressed steadily through the summer months and as the release date approached, it was nearly complete. I had constructed two separate templates. The first, named Simple.GEN (a name Marty loved to proclaim at random points during the day), would produce dBASE code that presented the user's screen, just as they designed it. The second, Advanced.GEN, would generate a full-blown database application with the user's screen as its primary interface. This generated application allowed them to view their database, navigate through it, and even add and delete information.

The whole project was a fair amount of work in a language I had never seen before, but I was confident I'd finish on time—as long as Marty and Heindel did.

There was one extra complication in our push toward shipping, though.

For some unexplained reason, before Fox could actually release FoxBASE+/Mac, Apple required us to ship a few thousand copies of it to them. This meant the three of us, through no fault of our own, really had another deadline before the release deadline we were initially striving toward. As if our lives weren't complicated enough.

*     *     *

At the end of the day, on the Friday before production was to start duplicating product for Apple, Dave phoned my office. "I want a look at the templates before they go out," he said. "Could you bring them down?"

"Sure!" By that time I'd worked on the templates for months with little input so I was glad Dave was finally showing some interest. My only other major project—the string compiler—he didn't see at all. I was also happy with what I'd accomplished. As far as I knew, the templates were ready to go. They were doing everything they were supposed to do.

But, as I made my way to the corner office, I couldn't help feeling a little nervous. It was my first time to show Dave my work, and really, the first time I'd been in his office alone. He was the president and co-owner of the company where I enjoyed working. He had given me a shot at doing what I wanted to do when no one else would, and recently, he even gave me a quiet place to work. I respected Dave. I wanted to make a good impression.

Dave's office had two entrances. The one at the top of the stairs I used the day of my interview and another accessible from the top floor's southern bounding hall. As an insider, I could use the latter now, and I did.

Dave was staring at the color screen of his Macintosh when I entered. Color Mac monitors were a hot (and lusted after) commodity at Fox. There were maybe a half dozen in the whole building and developers used most of them. I had one loaned to me so I could test my templates in color and even that turned into a minor scandal. Someone (a non-developer) got jealous and made a stink.

"Here you go, Dave," I said, holding up the floppy disk I brought with me.

Dave took the disk. "Ah yes," he said. "Let's see, let's see."

After copying the templates to his machine, Dave started up the Mac product. The most noticeable indication of this was the rainbow-colored "splash" screen (a window of about 3" high by 5" wide) that opened. Superimposed on the rainbow was a white fox head that appeared to be looking to its right—the Fox trademark.

Dave walked his way through the code generation steps. He first navigated the menu system to open up the Screen Painter and create a simple screen that included a number of fields from his database. In this case, the database he used contained an inventory of a home movie collection, so the fields were things like "Title," "Description," and "Running Time." Following this, he selected a menu item that said "Generate From…" This item engaged Heindel's new Code Generator. The first thing the Generator did was present a dialog that prompted Dave for a template to use. The templates I created were available in the dialog's list, so he chose one—Advanced.GEN. He clicked a button labeled "Generate."

A new window opened up. Within the window, lines of text began to flow up the screen. This window was mostly for show; it presented the new dBASE code as it was generated. It wasn't something you could actually read though. The code was streaming by way too fast. It was just to illustrate that **something** was going on. It was flashier than a wristwatch cursor (or a running fox).

Earlier, Dave specified that his generated application be called "Video.prg," so when the window of flowing text went away, there was a program on his machine with that name. Dave selected the menu item to run that program.

From start to finish his walkthrough worked flawlessly. The application generated fine. The generated code ran fine. Dave could see his data, he could add records, and he could delete records. It was a work of art. I was quite proud.

Then he went through the entire process again. He reopened the screen he created and moved a couple of buttons around—a simple, innocuous change—and then generated the application "Video.prg" again. Once again, everything appeared to proceed as expected. *And why wouldn't it?*

Dave then ran the generated application....

And the bottom fell out. A string of error messages began to assault his screen. "NO DATABASE IN USE," a dialog screamed. "INDEX NOT FOUND! RELATION NOT SET!" The windowed chaos continued for a many seconds.

*This is not good*, I thought. I stared at the ceiling and tried to figure out where the error messages were coming from. I'd never seen this behavior before. When I tested it, everything worked flawlessly. Yet nothing about what Dave did was unusual. I glanced at the door. *I wish I could go back to my office and check....*

Dave remained still, quietly studying his computer screen.

*No doubt mulling over my fate*, I thought. I took a step toward the door. *I might still be able to get away.*

Dave noticed the motion and looked up, stopping me. "You know what the problem is?" he asked.

I felt lost. "Um...no," I said.

Dave's eyebrows lifted. "What!?!" he said. "It's your program and you don't know what the problem is?"

The answer was still "No." I shook my head and said nothing.

"Well, I'll tell you what the problem is," Dave said. "Go get Heindel and Marty."

I made for the door and power-walked my way to the opposite side of the building. I gathered the others—and together—we quickly returned.

After we seated ourselves, Dave ran through the entire offending scenario again. Every step produced the same results—and at the end—the same unknowing look was present on the faces of both Marty and Heindel.

"It's a flaw in the Screen Painter!" Dave proclaimed finally.

Marty slid back a little. "How, Dave?" he asked, sounding defensive.

Dave pushed his head forward. "Because, my friend…Kerry's generated application is closing the databases I used when it finishes."

There was silence for a time. "So, it shouldn't be doing that?" Heindel offered.

Dave shook his head. "No. That's what a properly written application should do. It's the Screen Painter that's wrong."

"The Screen Painter is performing as it was designed, Dave," Marty said calmly.

Dave looked at Marty. His face was stern. "These errors are 'as designed'?!"

Marty leaned forward. "Well, the Screen Painter was designed as sort of a standalone tool."

Dave straightened his back. "What?" he said. "It's a part of our product!"

"Yes," Marty said, nodding his head slowly. "But it could be used for other things."

Dave wasn't buying it. "You know how to fix this?" he said, pointed a finger in the air. "The Screen Painter should save a view file."

I had no idea what a view file was, but apparently Heindel did. His face got a few shades whiter.

"A view file?" Heindel shook his head. "I don't know, Dave. That's a big hammer."

They went on to discuss the contents of a view file. Apparently, there was a command in the language that saved a snapshot of the product's condition: what databases were open, what indexes were in effect (an "index" controlled how the database's information was presented), and a mass of other important data. It was a big hammer.

Marty face was expressionless and his voice still calm. "Now Dave, the Screen Painter was designed as a standalone tool…"

What followed was a meeting that lasted nearly an hour, with Dave heatedly stating that it was a "flaw in the Screen Painter" and Marty doggedly explaining that the Screen Painter was performing the way it was designed to, and that it should stay that way. It ended with the three of us schlepping off to make substantial changes to a product that was supposed to ship out to Apple the next day. The only in-house testing the product would get this time was whatever Marty, Heindel, and I did on our own machines.

But, in the end there were no serious repercussions (that we knew of). The product went out to Apple, and then finally to the rest of the world. The templates I wrote were a part of the Mac product for many years to come.

*        *        *

Any questions I had about my employment following the template debacle were laid to rest a few weeks later. I was in Dave's office again, but this time it was only he, Amy, and I. They were on one side of the round table—the side nearest the windows. I was on the other— the side nearest the door. They had the blinds on the windows closed, so the room seemed a little dim.

"We just wanted to let you know that we've decided to keep you on," Dave said. "That you made it through our probationary period…"

I nodded my head slowly. *Probationary period? No one told me there was a probationary period.* "Um…thanks," I said.

"Yes, and we wanted to say that we really appreciate your work," Amy added. "And your flexibility with the things you work on."

I couldn't help but smile. Her comments were the first direct input I'd received about my work, either positive or negative. I was used to doing whatever needed to be done. I grew up on a farm. *Glad to hear I was doing OK this time....*

Dave nodded. "A company this size, we need our people to have some elasticity in the things they will work on." He scratched his elbow. "The template stuff…well, that isn't really the work our developers normally do." Dave reached out to take his coffee cup from the table, balanced it on one knee. "But you took to it and did a laudable job…a better than adequate job, really."

"Thanks again," I said, still smiling.

"Yes, so, we decided to keep you on with us at Fox, and um…," he looked at Amy as if he'd forgotten something. Amy only smiled sweetly. "Oh yes, and we're giving you a raise," Dave said, turning to look at me again.

I was getting a raise after only four months. *Woohoo!* "Wow," I said. "Thanks!"

Dave gave a quick little smile. "Yes, well, thank you."

The review ended a few moments later. *Interesting work, a semi-private office, and a raise in four months. It doesn't get any better than this.* I left the room fired up for a new challenge.

I was officially a part of the team.

*       *       *

By the time the russet leaves beyond our windows began to fall, development work on *FireFox* was in full swing. Aside from being our dBASE IV workalike, the fact that it was designed for the DOS operating system (a much larger market than the Mac) meant it had the potential to be a big seller when it was finally released. We needed as many coders on it as possible.

So, Marty was left behind as the sole developer on the Mac product, and Heindel and I moved over. (Marty stayed busy adding something called a "Report Writer", part of a new release planned for the following year.)

My first task in *FireFox* was to duplicate the language syntax Ashton-Tate added to their product. There were essentially two parts to adding a new command to *FireFox*. The first portion was the syntax portion. It involved taking the text typed in by the user—'USE employees.dbf INDEX employees.idx', for instance—and checking to see if it was valid syntactically (i.e. the command was spelled correctly and everything about it made sense), and then translating that text into a more concise (symbolic) form. That was my part of the process. When my work was complete, any program written for dBASE IV could be run on FireFox without giving a syntax error. It still wouldn't do **anything**, but it wouldn't give an error.

The second portion—what we called the runtime portion—was semantic in nature. It involved taking the symbols my work generated, figuring out what they all meant, and performing the actions required—opening the database, creating the window, or clearing the screen—whatever it took to make the command do what it was supposed to do. Although my part was necessary, the runtime portion was where the real work came in. To be fully compatible with dBASE IV, there was a lot of this type of work to do.

Ashton-Tate's new product was touted to be the end-all of database software. From what we heard, nearly seventy programmers worked for years in creating it. They added hundreds of new commands to give users the ability to create interface elements like windows and menus. It also included a brand new Report Writer, a Screen Painter, and a vastly improved "user-friendly" interface. Ashton-Tate was calling dBASE IV their "clone killer."

Our mission, as Dave described it, was to get the SBT application running on *FireFox* before Comdex. SBT was a California-based company, and their application was a weighty accounting package specifically designed to run on dBASE IV. It showcased many of the newly added features. Comdex—as I had only recently found out—was the largest computer show in the world. It was held every November in Las Vegas and was the place where every computer company came to show their latest and greatest. If we got the SBT application working on *FireFox* we'd prove our product was still compatible with dBASE IV—and if we did it by Comdex, we'd have plenty of witnesses.

So, with the "SBT by Comdex" goal set firmly in our minds, we immersed ourselves in our tasks. Heindel worked on the new commands to create menus. Bill did the first cut of the windowing commands (which was later turned over to Brian Tallman). Amy and Eric identified and implemented the other miscellaneous commands used in SBT's code, and I put in the syntax for everyone as they needed it.

I was happy with my new chore. I had spent my first few months of employment working on ancillary things and felt a little ancillary myself. Now I was working on the product. Instead of being a stranger on the other side of the fence, I was holding the top rail and peering over.

And the more I worked on the product the more I realized how fast we were progressing toward our goal. The team was made up of really bright people and I felt lucky to be included (even just over the fence). Though we may not be "working to the edge of our abilities," we were working well together and there was a lot of natural ability on display. Everyone was creative and extremely motivated.

Consequently, we reached the goal by the beginning of November—only a few weeks before the start of Comdex. The product was complete enough to run the SBT application and those who were attending Comdex were busy preparing demos on it. Many of those demos showed *FireFox* ran code written for dBASE IV **much faster** than dBASE IV itself did—in some cases a hundred times faster—a fact that should guarantee us a good show.

So, when the week of Comdex finally arrived, Dave, Amy, Eric, Bill and a handful of sales and support staff flew off for Vegas. They promised to send us news as the week progressed.

\*       \*       \*

By the middle of the week we heard that the show was going extremely well. Most of our loyal customers had no idea we were so far along toward having a fully functioning dBASE IV clone and couldn't wait to get their hands on it. Our booth had constant visitors and one of our attendants even thought they saw the CEO of Ashton-Tate, Ed Esber, stop by to marvel at the product.

Back in Perrysburg, that rumor got more talk than any other. To see the leader of our biggest competition at our booth was considered a great honor. We made our living by eating the scraps that fell from Ashton-Tate's plate; it was a niche we lived comfortably in. We had never been enough competition to make them nervous, nor would we be.

Prior to dBASE IV, Ashton-Tate seemed content to let us have our niche. They viewed us and our fellow clones as add-on products— software you buy after already purchasing dBASE. They **owned** the PC database market and our quaint little products weren't going to change that.

If Ed Esber had visited our booth, we could only imagine what he must have thought when he saw *FireFox* running applications written for dBASE IV. We thought he'd be surprised, but we also hoped he'd be a little impressed.

Imitation is a sincere form of flattery, after all.

# Chapter 4
# Competition and
# Litigation

On the first Sunday night following the end of Comdex, Eric
Christensen called me at home. The call surprised me for two reasons.
First, prior to that night, I had never been called at home about
anything work related. Secondly, the fact it was Eric was odd because
he was the last person I expected to call. He valued time away from
work as much as any, and probably more than most.

But, as I brought the receiver to my ear, I was primarily concerned
I did something to screw the product up. If Eric noticed a problem he
might be forewarning me before hotter heads moved in. I could think
of no other reason he would call.

"Hey Kerry," Eric said, sounding as if he were smiling. "Heard
any good rumors lately?"

That was a weird way to start a scolding. "No…" I said. "Why?"

"Well…I have." He paused. "Dave wants a meeting with everyone
in the company tomorrow morning."

I felt my pulse accelerate. *Man, what did I do? Is there going to be
a public execution?* "Oh," I said. "Why?"

"Well…," Eric's voice was still smiling. "Last Friday Ashton-Tate
decided to sue us."

Relief came over me, only to be replaced by a feeling of
excitement. I asked a number of follow-up questions, but I could hardly
hear Eric's answers for the thoughts that were shouting in my mind.
What a story! Not more than six months before I studied about lawsuits
between software companies and now I was going to be smack-dab in
the middle of one!

I took a Computer Ethics course while in college. One of the
subjects we discussed was the various legal means computer firms used
to protect their software. The most common protection was to obtain a
copyright on the code. But, there were aspects of copyright protection
that made it inadequate for software. In general, copyrights only
protect the expression of an idea, not the idea itself. So, I might have
ownership of the phrase "I want to go buy ice cream" if it was part of a
poem I wrote, but the idea behind the phrase—the fact that I **really**

want a frozen treat—wouldn't be protected. With software though, usually what has more meaning are the ideas expressed in software code, not the code itself.

Copyrights weren't originally conceived with computers—or software—in mind, and it was only in the mid-eighties that companies began to test the limits of a copyright's legal protection. In a case settled only a few years before I graduated, a company actually won damages based, not on the literal code written, but on the program's "structure, sequence, and organization." That meant they won on how the software appeared to the user, or its "look and feel." Because of this, "look and feel" became a catch phrase in the industry and any company that wrote software that looked and acted like another company's program did so knowing they might be skating on thin legal ice.

I knew FoxBASE+ looked and felt **exactly** like dBASE III+, but I also knew it had done so for a number of years. I didn't know why Ashton-Tate hadn't made an issue of "look and feel" before, and I wasn't sure why they were doing so now.

I had a hard time sleeping that night. I couldn't wait to hear what Dave would say the next day. Would the developers be witnesses? Was I going to have to testify? What would happen next?

*       *       *

Morning came none too quickly. I arose at six-thirty, rushed around the house, jumped in the car, and was at the bank building by seven-thirty. There were quite a few more early risers than usual that morning. Even the sales manager—who usually didn't make it in before nine—had already arrived.

At around eight o'clock everyone made their way to the building's largest room, the production facility. While we waited, most of us milled around and looked nervous. In contrast, Dave looked jovial— almost giddy. After he surveyed the crowd enough to know that nearly everyone was present, he found a place near the center of the room.

"Well folks," he began, "it looks like Ashton-Tate has done for us by litigation what we, as of yet, could not do by competition. For the first time **ever** we were mentioned on the front page of the Wall Street Journal!" He smiled and chuckled briefly.

"You know, someone said they saw Ed Esber at our booth at Comdex last week. Well, it's apparent that whether he was there or not, he heard about what we were showing, because last Friday Ashton-Tate filed a lawsuit against us."

This brought a share of gasps and murmured questions. Apparently, not everyone had heard the same information I had.

Dave waved off the interruption. "Not to fear! Not to fear," he said, sounding confident. "We have every reason to believe we are in the right!" He paused, scanned the room. "You see, they claim they **own** the dBASE language and intend to defend that position in court. They also claim we infringed on their 'look and feel' copyrights with our FoxBASE+ product and they are trying to prevent us from selling it along with FoxBASE+/Mac and the product we've codenamed *FireFox*."

Dave panned the room again, undoubtedly still seeing concern on some faces. "Now, let's take a look at what they claim," he said. "We'll start with the issue of the language. Ashton-Tate is breaking new ground on that one because **nobody** has ever owned a language before. It's impossible! If it isn't, then I'll take ADA…" He motioned toward our sales manager. "Jeff here will take C, and someone else can have BASIC—or for that matter English! It's crazy! Nobody can own a language."

He gave a dismissive wave. "So that's a non-issue," he said. "That leaves only the issue of 'look and feel'…."

*The big one*, I knew. The one they might actually have a case over.

"Now, I don't know how many of you are aware of this," Dave said, "but there is an old statute of law that says if you encourage someone to do something for years and years, you cannot turn around and sue them for doing the very thing you encouraged them to do." His face gained some color. "At least, not and expect to get anything for your trouble. And that is **precisely** the case with the 'look and feel' of FoxBASE+. For years, Ashton-Tate allowed us, and even encouraged us to copy the 'look and feel' of dBASE III+, hoping our product— along with the other dBASE clones—would help grow the dBASE market." Dave brought his arms in and scratched an elbow. "So that's what we've done…and now they intend to sue us for it." He smiled. "Well, my friends, it just don't work that way!"

Dave panned the room again. The faces were a little less concerned; some were even smiling. "And while we're on the subject of 'look and feel'…there is no reason why they should be able to sue us for sales on our Mac product or our upcoming DOS product, *FireFox*. The Mac product doesn't look anything like dBASE III+, and *FireFox* hasn't even been released yet!"

He frowned. "However, if they can prove they own the language, then they do have a basis for a lawsuit against those products. Soooo, the language issue is the important part of the lawsuit. But, since no

one can own a language, it's hard to imagine them winning on
that alone."

Dave smiled again and raised a finger. "So, you may be asking
yourself, what is the purpose of the lawsuit, if they can't win?" He
paused to give us time to think. "Well, you see…the purpose of the
lawsuit, is to do by litigation what they couldn't do through
competition! Put an end to Fox Software!" He brought his finger up,
dagger-like. "And, a couple of years ago it may have worked!" The
finger lowered. Another room pan. "But we've gotten a little too big
for that now. We have absolutely no debt and our overhead is very
small. They are betting we are wracked with debt and don't have the
capital to defend ourselves, but I tell you what—we do, and we will.
My partner, Dick LaValley, is already gearing up his lawyer forces to
take it to 'em. So, be of good cheer!"

I glanced around the room. Most of the concerned faces were
gone, replaced by looks of intent. We were going to fight the giant.

Dave got serious then. "Now, you are all probably wondering how
this is going to affect your lives in the days to come. Well for the most
part, it won't. These things take a long time—years probably—and we
intend to fight it to the very end."

"It **is** the case, however, that those of you on the phones will be
asked a lot of questions about the lawsuit. We have prepared written
answers for you to some of the common questions." A mischievous
grin snuck onto his face. "Under **no** circumstance do I want anyone
making comments about Ed Esber having a substandard size penis!"
He paused, cackled softly. "Whether it is true or not." He cackled
louder and others joined him. He surveyed the room a final time.
"Now, are there any questions?"

Of course there were, and the questions that followed were all
predictable in scope; concerns over job security, clarifications of legal
matters, and then questions about the questions.

For me, though, it was a great way to start the week. Overnight,
my work at the little family-run software company took on new
meaning. I was part of a team that was now scowling at the schoolyard
bully. Would we back him down or would we flinch? Only time and
the legal process would tell.

*       *       *

Immediately following the company assembly, Dave called another
meeting *for developers only.* It was the first iteration of what we later
referred to as a "five year plan" meeting—an event that occurred
regularly during the coding phase of *FireFox.*

The basic meeting structure was simple. First we brought Dave up to date on the status of "things," next we discussed what remained to be done, and finally Dave would conclude with a discourse about the future of Fox Software and its products.

However, as the weeks went by, our future would change. So, every week we'd go in for a "five year plan" (FYP) meeting and come out with a different FYP—a frustrating situation for us developers. The last thing we wanted to hear, ever, was that everything was going to change again next week.

These meetings did have their advantages, though. Encapsulated within was the ability to change directions quickly. In a later meeting, Dave would say "the worst thing a software company could do was to make a FYP and stick to it." And he may have been right.

Guy Kawasaki, the CEO of a rival database company, when asked what he thought about Fox, once said, "their product might be fast, but dragsters can't turn." It was a nice allusion, but it didn't really fit the company I worked for. If Fox Software was a dragster, it was one that could not only turn, but also do 180's in the sand. The FYP meetings were the embodiment of that.

*     *     *

The initial FYP meeting was more significant than most, though.

"The Command Line is gone," Dave told the seven of us gathered around his small office table. "Instead we'll create a Command Window for *FireFox*," he said. "Just like we have in the Mac product."

The "Command Line" was FoxBASE+'s primary interface. Essentially, it was a one-character high line at the bottom of the screen users could type their commands into. The text output of those commands scrolled up to fill the rest of the screen. The rest of the screen—24 lines, each 80 characters across—was referred to as the "Desktop." This Command Line / Desktop interface was used by all prior versions of dBASE, and dBASE IV was using it as well.

However, that interface didn't work in the window-oriented, mouse-driven environment Macintosh users were accustomed to. So, for FoxBASE+/Mac, the team replaced the character-based Desktop and Command Line mechanism with two separate windows. One, called the Command Window, was for typing commands into. Any text output of those commands, was then sent to a separate "Desktop" window.

"We'll bring the ease-of-use of our Mac product to DOS," Dave said. "In the process we'll dodge the 'look and feel' portion of the lawsuit. The only area Ashton-Tate will be able to pursue us on with *FireFox* is the language. It's the only similarity *FireFox* will have!"

All leaned close and listened with rapt attention.

"This, of course, means we'll need to add mouse support to *FireFox*," Dave said.

Eric had a hand at his lips. His thinking position. "We can't count on people to have mice, though, Dave." He flipped up a hand. "On the Mac, everyone does."

Dave nodded his head. "Yes, we'll have to build in keyboard support for everything…" He thought for a moment. "Maybe we can work out a deal…throw in a low-cost mouse or something. We'll worry about those details later…."

It sounded simple, but Dave's proposal would mean an incredible amount of work for the development team. To pull off the magic, the guts of *FireFox* would have to be turned inside out. Instead of just responding to typed-in commands, the product would now have to wait for events—such as the mouse button being clicked or a key being pressed—and handle these as they occurred. But, before all that, **something** would need to be created to actually generate those events.

"…an Event Manager is the important piece, of course," Dave said. "Eric, maybe you and your roomie can come up with something there…."

On the Macintosh computer, there was a part of the operating system called the 'Event Manager'. This entity generated the events application programs, such as FoxBASE+/Mac, received and acted on. The DOS operating system had no such animal. Our first priority would be to write our own Event Manager for *FireFox*. Then we could implement code to respond to the events it generated.

That was only the beginning. Other parts of the Mac operating system would have to be aped as well. A 'Menu Manager' to handle the creation and operation of menus would need to be developed. Code to control dialogs, and the buttons that sat on them, would have to be written. Thanks to the 'SBT by Comdex' drive, we had code to create windows, but it was rudimentary compared to what we now needed. A new, more robust 'Window Manager' would have to be written. We would need a new text editor; a new tool to create mailing labels…the list seemed endless and there were only six of us to do the work. (Marty had his own fish to fry and Dave was rarely coding by this time).

Still, the whole thing was exciting. I was eager to help in some way. Maybe I could help Heindel with whatever he was working on. *Or help Bill or Eric….*

"Kerry will be working on the Report Writer," Dave said as part of his stream of consciousness.

*The what?* I knew Marty was working on something called a Report Writer for the Mac product, but it looked about as complicated as his Screen Painter. *I don't think I can...*

Dave went on to explain (briefly) that Fox had purchased a stand-alone tool for creating reports from an outside programmer. The intent was to release this product as a supplement to *FireFox*. Our consumers could design reports using this Report Writer with the data found in their *FireFox* databases.

However, when we finally got this product in our hands, it was found that—while the engine of the thing worked (you **could** create and run reports with it)—its interface and general usability was lacking. So, my job was to take all the soon-to-be-created managers, along with the inner workings of this outside product, and turn them into a fully integrated "Report Writer" with an interface consistent with the revamped, easy-to-use *FireFox*. In actuality, it was the biggest challenge of my life.

"Any further questions?" Dave said.

*Uh, yeah, about this Report Writer...I don't know anything about such things. Are you sure you want to just throw me on it?*

Dave checked our faces, paused a moment. "No?" he said to the silence. "OK gang, let's get started."

*       *       *

Following the FYP meeting, I struggled with the scope of my new assignment. The creative side of me was excited. I was finally given something wholly mine. A part of *FireFox* nobody knew a thing about. It was a chance to take a virtual lump of clay and mold it into a tool others could use and appreciate. It would also have my name on it. I could point at it and say, "Yeah, I did that."

On the other hand, the Report Writer was something **nobody knew a thing about**. Not really. All I knew about "Report Writers" was they were a tool for designing printed reports, much like Marty's Screen Painter was a tool for designing input screens. Only a few months before I'd watched Marty demo his Screen Painter and thought "I could never do that." A few months before that, I was happy when the code I wrote to sort a list of numbers worked out OK.

I had some large projects in college, of course—some that took me many months. But, in those instances, every other Computer Science student was struggling with essentially the same problem as I was *and there was always an instructor to fall back on....*

Now I had to work on something just as complicated as a Screen Painter, and I was entirely on my own. (Marty had just started work on a Report Writer for our Mac product, but because of differences between the two machines, no code could be shared). *I know nothing*, I thought as I made my way back to my office. *Can I do this?*

Still reeling, I stumbled into Heindel's domain. He sat staring at the floor, looking a little burdened himself. I undoubtedly looked worse.

"I knew you were going to get the Report Writer," he said when he noticed me.

"Oh?"

Heindel placed his hands over his midsection. "Yeah, I went to Bart's demo of the standalone product. His introduction was something like 'This isn't very good…but here you go.' I knew that wasn't going to fly with Dave. Pride in the product is an essential part of his character."

"Oh…," I said, and then paused. Time to come clean. "I have no idea where to even start on this."

Heindel nodded his head slowly. "Yeah, it's a pretty big deal," he said. "In my experience, with huge projects like that, you just start somewhere. Eventually you get it all done."

"Yeah?"

He nodded again. "Yeah."

"OK," I said slowly. "But where?"

Heindel looked down at the floor. Thought for a moment. "If it were me," he said, "I'd start with the global data."

"The global what?"

"The global data. Our product doesn't have a lot to spare. This standalone Report Writer probably uses a ton of it." Heindel gave a comforting smile. "I'd try to bring it all into a handle or something."

Heindel went on to explain that a program like *FireFox* made use of a computer's memory in a couple different ways. Global data— things with names that needed to be accessed by all parts of the product—took up space in a portion of the computer's memory that was very limited. A 'handle' was a convention used to refer to other portions of the computer's memory—portions not so limited. He was suggesting I change the code to move the Report Writer's global data from one chunk of memory to the other. It was a straightforward task, but it would require a ton of code changes.

I had that to look forward to no matter what, though. "OK…" I said. "I'll try that."

"Look," Heindel said. "Try not to get overwhelmed." He looked through me, toward Dave's office. "You saw all the work we have to do. This is going to be a **long** release cycle. Trust me." He turned his palms up. "Just start. You'll get there."

I said "OK", nodded my head once and left.

*Just start*, I told myself. *You'll get there.*

So, that's what I did. I plowed into the Report Writer code and by the end of December I was starting to make real progress. The family of foxes was on the run. I would not be left behind.

# Chapter 5
# Adjustments

By the start of 1989 everyone was coding up a storm. Heindel was busy adding commands to *FireFox* to ensure it was 100% language compatible with dBASE IV. Bill Ferguson was writing the first cut of the code to allow for the manipulation of controls and dialogs, later known as the Control Manager and Dialog Manager. Eric Christensen was working on the new text editor. Brian Tallman was pulling together code to create and manage windows and menus (the Window Manager and Menu Manager) and Amy Fulton was constructing a few of the dialogs Dave thought critical. One of these was a dialog to allow users to change the colors *FireFox* displayed itself in. I wasn't sure how this 'Color Picker' was essential exactly, but if nothing else, it made good use of the code Bill was still creating.

I, of course, was occupied with the Report Writer, and at weird hours.

The more I got into my new project, the more concerned I felt about getting it done in time. It was a lot like being given a 747 and asked to remove the parts for an essential system—like everything necessary for navigation—and then told to reconstruct that same system in another vehicle. In this case, though, the other vehicle wasn't another airplane—it was a cruise ship. And the additional changes I had to make to reign in the Report Writer's global data was like having to hit each airplane part once with a hammer to make it fit.

It wasn't that I thought I'd lose my job if I didn't succeed (though the thought crossed my mind occasionally); it was just I wanted to make a good showing for myself. If I was working on a team of superstars, I didn't want to be the only benchwarmer.

Multiplying my stress was the fact that, as far as I knew, the product was shipping in the spring. I began to have trouble sleeping at night, and at least one night a week I'd fail altogether and just go into work early—sometimes as early as 4 am. After a month of that I decided what I really needed was a future escape to look forward to.

"How do you get a vacation here," I asked Heindel one morning.

Heindel was engrossed with a DOS machine that sat on a rolling cart in the center of his office. His chin rested in his hand with his index finger aside his nose as he studied the screen closely. "Just a sec…" he said and squinted at the screen a few moments longer. Finally, he clicked a couple of keys and turned in my direction.

"How do you get a vacation?" he said. "Well, you talk to Dave."

"Oh," I said. I was hoping for something a lot less personal, like drawing a line on a calendar or something.

Heindel noticed my hesitation. "When do you want to take it?"

"Well, I was hoping for sometime in May."

"May, huh? Hard to tell how Dave'll take that."

"Well, it's my anniversary with this place…" A year seemed like enough time served to me.

Heindel leaned back in his chair slightly and thought a bit. He threw his hands up. "Ask him," he said, hunching forward again. "Listen, there are no good times for a vacation here. You end up just setting a date and taking it when you planned. Ask Dave. Everyone knows that spring's a pipe dream anyway."

I smiled, thanked him, and then turned to follow the outside edge of the inner cubicles to Dave's office. As was generally the case, I found Dave's door open when I arrived. I quietly stepped in and took a seat near the circular table. Dave was locked in conversation with a mustachioed man wearing a work-belt.

"You're maxing out the system," the man said. "You can either change the system or add another trunk." I assumed the man was talking about our phone system. There'd been a lot of strange phone behavior recently. Developers had been getting tech support calls. To protect himself, Marty had started to answer the phone as "Maintenance."

Dave leaned back in his chair and put his feet on his desk. "A new trunk? Well, how much would that cost?"

The phone guy looked tentative. "About a thousand dollars," he said.

Dave didn't even wink. "A grand…? No big deal then."

*No big deal?* I thought. *A few months ago I was happy if I had twenty bucks a week to spend.*

The phone guy shifted his stance slightly. "Yeah, no big deal."

"OK, get us a new trunk," Dave said finally. The phone guy nodded once and left. Then Dave turned to look at me. "Yes, my young friend," he said. "What can I do for you?"

"Hey Dave," I began, and paused. I really wished I could just draw a line on a calendar. "I was wondering if it'd be all right for me to take a week off in May? I'll have my first year in by then…."

Dave's face turned serious. "May? Oh no, May's no good. We'll be getting ready to ship by then."

"Oh…" I felt like I was just turned down for the prom. Still, Heindel had told me to get my vacation on the schedule. I quickly thought of a replacement date. "How about August, then?" My birthday was in August. It was the only date I could think of.

Dave leaned back and swept his palm over the top of his head. "August?" he said, staring at the ceiling. "August should be fine. We'll have long since shipped by then." He looked at me and nodded definitively. "Take it in August."

"OK," I said. I stood up and took a few steps toward the door. "Thanks, Dave."

That wasn't as hard as I thought it would be. I didn't get a vacation in May, but I was confident I'd take my first vacation in August. There was a schedule to contend with and Dave was being as reasonable as he could be.

*　　　*　　　*

During the winter months in my shared conference room office there was one subject that consistently came up.

"It's awful cold in here Marty," I said one day. My Mac still occupied my desk space so I had my DOS machine—a new 386s machine—on a rolling stand that faced the door. From my seat in front of it I could see Marty's coat-shrouded back.

"Awful cold in here, Kerry," Marty echoed back.

Both Marty and I still treasured our living space, so neither of us would complain about anything. But we'd come to find that the room's large windows came with a drawback. They leaked air so bad it felt like it was coming through the panes. It was beyond the ability of duct tape to fix.

Later in the day, the conversation was repeated.

"Awful cold in here, Marty."

"It's d*** cold in here, Kerry!" Marty exclaimed. He rolled away from his desk to look at me. "I bet they shut off that heat again."

That was another part of our problem. It was always the case that those who sat in the cubicles near the center of the building sweltered while those of us with offices around the exterior fought off the cold. It led to a constant war over the thermostat that usually resulted in neither group being entirely satisfied. The senior members of development survived by having small space heaters in their offices, but Marty and I didn't have one of those yet. It was all we could do to keep our hands warm enough to type.

I flexed my fingers, trying to revive them. The only alternative was to try and type with gloves on. And only Marty, who primarily coded using the Mac's Cut, Copy, and Paste functions (requiring only two working fingers), was able to manage that.

Marty pulled a screwdriver from his desk and stood up. "I'll fix 'em," he said. He walked past me and I heard the door open and swing shut, making a 'thump, thump' sound as it closed. Marty was on his way. The thermostat would soon be adjusted to our liking.

Until the support people found out, that is.

*My hands are numb, and I still have a ton of work to do*, I thought. *This is crazy. We'll never get all this done in time.*

*       *       *

I strolled in to ask Dave a question one January afternoon and found him in the middle of a conversation with a thirty-something man with straight, dark hair—parted neatly on one side. The man had the figure and presence of a young Santa Claus and his blue shirt was clearly monogrammed with the initials 'CLW'. Their conversation was about some part of the product's interface—a part I knew nothing about. So, I just backed up against the wall to wait. The CLW-man barely looked at me as I entered the room. Dave acted as if he hadn't seen me at all.

"I think you should build in as much leveragability as possible," Dave said. He was sitting with his feet on the desk again, a can of soda resting on his lap.

CLW nodded his head, glanced quickly at me, and then addressed Dave again. "That way, if Kerry here needs to use some of the components of MODI STRU (he pronounced it "mah-dee strew") in his Report Writer, he can."

I was amazed that this CLW guy knew my name and tried to include me in the conversation. *Seems like a cool guy*, I thought.

Dave looked at me and flipped a hand in CLW's direction. "Oh yes, Kerry," he said, "this is Chris Williams. He and his team will be joining us. They'll primarily be working on the UNIX port."

I smiled and stuck out a hand. Chris grabbed it and shook it heartily. *Personable in every way*, I thought. "Welcome to the team, Chris."

In lunch conversations I'd already heard about Chris and his people. Chris had owned his own local Perrysburg computer consulting business. Dave negotiated with him to buy his company—and as part of that deal—Chris, along with two other developers he employed— Sally Stuckey and Carol Garrison—joined our staff.

I didn't meet Sally and Carol until much later. Sally was also in her thirties and of smallish dimensions, similar to Amy Fulton. In demeanor she was Chris's exact opposite. If he was Santa, Sally was the dutiful and hardworking clf. Carol was closer to my age, newly-married and striking in appearance. She was also very new to programming, much more so than I.

The initial mission for Chris's team was to make *FireFox* work on the UNIX operating system as it was being completed for DOS. Ultimately this would allow Fox to provide a UNIX product without having to rely on an outside company to do the port. Years before, a company named SCO ported the FoxBASE+ product to UNIX, but they were so lax in correcting bugs in that product (FoxBASE+/Unix), they fell out of favor with Dave. With *FireFox*, Chris's group would take their place.

The work on the UNIX product only lasted about a month, though. By the end of February it was clear we had more pressing matters than a future UNIX product. *FireFox* was nowhere near ready for release in May, and the Mac product needed help as well. So, Chris's group was pulled in. Carol was put in charge of tracking bugs for the Mac product while Chris and Sally were drafted to help with *FireFox*. Chris immediately took on some of the larger dialogs that needed completing and Sally began working on a tool to create mailing labels

With eight of us on *FireFox* there was a renewed sense of optimism. The spring deadline almost seemed attainable. I was even able to sleep regularly again.

*        *        *

The first outside challenge to our schedule came in the form of a series of marketing meetings held in the first quarter of '89. Present at the meetings was a group of external advisers Dave gathered in order to show them *FireFox* for the first time. What specific criterion he used to select these advisers was beyond my knowledge. All I knew was the back corner office—the one that was perpetually kept unoccupied "for Dick LaValley"—was suddenly filled with people one day. They were there to offer opinions about the product's new look and suggestions for its final name.

One of the principal attendees was a fellow by the name of Glenn Hart. Glenn was a large, balding man whose appearance suggested "Mafioso" to me. Eric and Bill had a different—less complimentary—name for him though.

"So, guess what the *Emphysema Poster Child* suggested today," Eric said, a subtle smirk on his face. He took a bite of pizza and looked around the table at Bill, Heindel, Marty, and I. The five of us were at a Pizza Hut just across the parking lot from our building.

"What?" Heindel said. "Did they come up with a new name?"

Eric rolled his eyes. "Well, actually, yes…FoxPro."

"Hmm…," Marty said, nodding his head slowly. "FoxPro..."

"FoxPro?" Heindel said. "Why don't we just keep FireFox? I like FireFox. Fire, burning speed, that's our product. What's wrong with FireFox?"

"It's the codename," Eric said. "Dave wants something else."

"How about FoxFire?" I chimed in. I liked the Clint Eastwood movie of the same name. I had also just won the "name the company newsletter" competition with "FoxTrax." I figured I was on a roll.

Eric ignored me. "The name's not the big news, though."

"What's the big news?" Heindel asked.

"You don't want to know," Bill said.

Heindel looked quickly between the two. "What?"

Eric took a drink of water and smiled. "He wants a new command—SET INTERFACE OFF."

"SET INTERFACE OFF!?" Marty and Heindel said in stereo. Marty began to chuckle. "Whoa," he said, "That's a good one."

I was still new to the intricacies of the dBASE language. It had a litany of "SET" commands. I had no idea what they all did. "What's that mean?" I asked.

Eric frowned. "It means he wants the user to be able to change the interface back to the old style just by using a SET command."

My eyebrows rose instinctively. We'd spent several months working on the new interface and had grown quite fond of it. We certainly didn't want to give it up for the archaic Command Line interface FoxBASE+ had.

"That's great," Marty said, still laughing. "How'd that go over?"

"Can you say 'Lead Balloon'?" Bill said.

I smiled and took a bite of my Supreme pizza. Earlier I was told about Glenn's relationship with Dave; it was one of dedicated ambivalence. Glenn was well known in the dBASE community—and occasionally—had a good idea, so Dave tolerated his opinions. However, since Glenn was a 'marketer', he was viewed as more of a necessary evil than an asset. Marketing was a source of invariable derision at Fox.

However, in some respects, Glenn's reasoning about the interface was sound. Mouse-driven interfaces with pull-down menus and floating windows were virtually unknown in the IBM-PC/DOS world and usually only seen in applications written for the Macintosh. Most people that owned DOS machines didn't even have a mouse. We **would** be breaking new ground and Glenn was afraid we'd be breaking too much ground if we locked the product to it. He thought it would be better to give users the option.

Dave didn't see it that way, though. He knew enough about the internals of the product to know that switching interfaces on the fly just wasn't that easy. Nor, was it the right thing to do. By the time the meetings were over, "FoxPro" was the product's new name, but it would keep the interface we'd all come to know and love.

We'd survive the backlash if and when it came.

\*        \*        \*

Only marginally interested in the decisions of the marketing meeting, I remained hard at work on what I came to think of as **my** Report Writer. By March I had it to the place where it could create and print reports in much the same fashion it did when it was originally designed—except that it was now an integral part of FoxPro. It wasn't pretty to look at yet, but it was completely functional. I was happy with my progress, so one day I dragged Heindel to my office to show him.

"I think you should check it in," Heindel said after I finished my demonstration.

"Really?" I asked. Checking my changes in seemed like a big step. At Fox, as was the practice at most software companies, a developer would "check out" the source files that dealt with the part of the product he wanted to work on, and then toil away on them safely for a period of time on his own machine. During that time the rest of the team would generally only have a read-only copy of those files on their machines. They could view it, but not change it. When the developer deemed his code complete enough to expose to the rest of the team, he checked it back into the network. In my case, most of the files were new, but the process was the same. Once it was out on the network, the code would be fair game for everyone else to see and play with.

"I don't want to mess anyone up," I said, still feeling a little insecure.

"You're not going to mess anyone up," Heindel said. "No one else will probably even look at it. Everyone's too busy with their own stuff." He walked around my desk to stand near the room's swinging door. "Besides, if you get it out there you'll have it backed up."

"Good point," I said, shaking my head. I'd done a lot of work and was getting a little worried about losing it. I had a few copies on floppy disks in my desk, but there was still a danger of those getting erased or melted to a puddle in a fire. Checking my stuff in would ensure that there was a copy on everyone else's machine in addition to the main network machine—which was backed up regularly. "All right…if you think so."

"Check it in," Heindel said, and then raised a fist. "No fear."

I smiled and said "Okay." Heindel left and a few hours later everything I'd done was safely on the network.

*      *      *

My code wasn't out a day, though, before Dave swung open my door.

"Kerry, I've been looking at the Report Writer," he said, frowning, "and well—come on—I'll show you!" He turned and made a quick head motion. "I can't get **anything** to work!"

So I followed Dave to his office, and in an hour's time he'd completely redesigned the Report Writer's interface. It wasn't so much that he couldn't get anything to work, it was that he didn't like the way it appeared while it was doing it. He sent me back to my office with a one-page, hand-drawn mockup of the changes. I was overwhelmed again.

*This looks nothing like what was there before,* I thought. *How am I going to do this?*

Even though I'd done a substantial amount of work to get the Report Writer into the product, its inner workings were still foreign. Radical changes, like the ones I was just given, frightened me. I was also a little confused about Dave's management style.

Before the meeting I was feeling pretty good. In only a few short months I took this large standalone product with its own global data, its own way of interacting with users, its own way of putting out printable data, and successfully folded it into our product. And it worked! Wasn't that worth at least a quick "Good Job"? I had no idea whether what I did was a significant amount of work or not.

*Have I underachieved?* I wondered. Was the Fox team so good that what I just did was inconsequential in comparison? I quickened my pace back, eager to get started on Dave's new changes. I'd make an impact or die trying.

*      *      *

But, if I was hoping for a quiet place to complete the work, I was soon sorely disappointed. At the end of March, Carol moved into the conference room office with Marty and I. It was a graphic indication that, while all of us were busy coding, Fox Software was growing. The cozy little bank building of around 6,000 square feet was now trying to accommodate close to 70 people—and a production facility. The cubicle area where my first office had been located was now one big open corral filled with technical support personnel. They were packed in like cordwood. One lady's office was even in the entranceway to the men's restroom.

Thankfully, Dave Fulton and Dick LaValley started looking for a new den for the foxes to live in. Their search found part of the shopping center behind our bank building was available. At the time it housed a store, a number of business offices, and a radio station. It amounted to about 22,000 square feet of space—more than enough room for our busy little software company.

# Chapter 6
# Distractions

Sometime in March, Dave called the developers to his office.

"Now look," he said to the ten of us who now crowded around the table, "We need to get some people out of this building."

I backed away from the table to give myself more room.

*No kidding?*

"We gave some thought to which groups are most autonomous," Dave continued, "which ones can be easily separated from the rest of the company, and we decided it's the production facility and our group." He crossed his legs and placed one hand on the back of his head. "So, my friends, we will be the first to make the long trip across the parking lot. The builders are hard at work already and as soon as the bottom floor is complete the two groups will move over." He reached out to place a hand on the table. "Then, when the upper floor is finished, we will move upstairs and the rest of the company will move across." He panned our faces. "All right?"

Bill Ferguson deliberately hunched his shoulders together. "Great! When do we move?"

Many of us smiled. "In May," Dave said.

I glanced at Heindel. May had been our original release date. There wasn't much talk of that anymore. *A pipedream....*

Still, I was energized by the approaching change of venue. It indicated the company was doing well, despite the lawsuit. In addition, I hoped when the final move was made I'd have an office to myself. When I started at Fox, every developer, except Marty and I, had their own office with a door. Now that the Report Writer was functional, I felt like I'd finally accomplished something significant. An office of my own seemed an appropriate reward.

Moreover, the addition of Carol to the conference room significantly increased the noise level. Her task of verifying and tracking bugs for the Mac product brought in scores of chatty people. I needed my tranquility back.

The initial plan for the upstairs of the new building was available a few days later and in it, I was indeed allotted a window office. A week later though, when a revised plan was posted, everyone *except* Carol and I had offices. That fed my insecurities. I wondered what I did between one plan and the next to end up out in a cubicle again.

There was nothing I could do about it, though. I just shook it off and went on with my work. *I'll prove I deserve an office…somehow.*

\*      \*      \*

In little time at all, the day of the move arrived. On a Friday we boxed up our stuff and over the weekend the boxes were trekked across the parking lot for us, along with our computers.

When I arrived at the new building the following Monday, I found the layout for the offices downstairs was slightly different than the final upstairs layout would be. Instead of occupying one of the long walls of the structure, the developer offices hinged around one of the front corners.

There was one obvious similarity though. The machines for Carol and I were set up inside grey-walled cubicles. And my cubicle came with an additional bonus; it was right outside the office shared by Dave, Amy, and their infant son.

The littlest Fulton was part of an unprecedented baby boom at Fox. Almost everyone I worked with was having kids. Heindel and his wife just had a little girl. Chris William's wife gave birth to a boy. Bill's wife had twins. Eric Christensen's family had a new little boy and so did Dave and Amy. There were fourteen children born to Fox employees from the end of 1988 to the summer of 1989 and I was beginning to wonder if there was something strange in all that free pop. Whatever the cause, I knew I didn't want any. I had plenty of things to worry about already.

\*      \*      \*

The changes to the Report Writer interface were nearly complete. Dave and I haggled out every detail of the way it should appear ad nauseam, and in the process, it became a useful tool. Like the rest of the product, it could be driven by either a mouse or a keyboard. It allowed users to put text, boxes, and data fields from their databases in the report and change their location simply by selecting and moving them. And— in keeping with the company credo—it performed well. In fact, even though he didn't tell me directly, I knew Dave was pleased. I overheard him calling it "the best Report Writer in the world" to someone on the phone.

One aspect that was never quite right in Dave's eyes, though, was the colors of the Report Writer's display. I would be in the middle of chasing down some complicated bug in my code and Dave would storm over with a minor change to the colors to be put in ASAP. So, I was forced to drop whatever I was doing and tweak the two lines of coloring code to match what he wanted.

The rest of the team was experiencing a similar phenomenon. In fact, the only team meetings we had during the greatest part of the development of the first version of FoxPro were about colors. Anything that was a hot topic in Dave's mind was instantly important to us all, whether we liked it or not. In the end, these "color meetings" became such a distraction Amy finally told him to "go off and decide what you want and don't bother the rest of us until you're sure." Dave took her advice, and freed us—for a time—to continue with our work.

*        *        *

By the beginning of summer '89, FoxPro was turning into an impressive product. As an outgrowth of the new language added for compatibility with dBASE IV, and our new window-based interface, many items present in earlier Fox products were substantially transformed.

One of these was our text editor. Two commands in the language would present this to a user, MODIFY FILE and MODIFY COMMAND. In FoxBASE+, the editor was simplistic. It just filled the screen with whatever file was being edited. Only one file could be edited at a time, and there was a rigid limit to how big that file could be. It was functional for developing dBASE programs, but most hardcore users would buy an additional editing program to do real text editing work.

As coded by Eric, though, the FoxPro editor was an animal of a different color (no pun intended). It resided in a window and users could have as many text files open concurrently as they liked. They could easily copy and paste text between different files. There was no limit to the size of the file. (No attainable limit, anyway; the actual limit for a text file was larger than most modern disk drives.) It was also blindingly fast. It could open up hundreds of files in seconds and scroll text faster than could be read.

Another command, BROWSE, also got a face-lift. BROWSE presented an overall view of the data in a database, much like a spreadsheet. If my database contained mailing addresses, field names— things like "Name", "Address", and "Zip" —would make up the columns across the top and the values (data) would be the rows. In prior versions, it was also confined to a single window. But, in FoxPro, thanks to Brian and Eric, it resided in a window, data could be cut and pasted anywhere, and it even allowed for two panes (or views) of the data in that same window. It was really, really cool.

In addition, Sally's label creation tool was nearly finished. It would replace the simplistic tool from earlier versions in the same way my Report Writer would replace FoxBASE's earlier reporting tool. Sally was also working with Amy on a useful tool to manipulate any and every file on the hard disk (later known as "the Filer").

Bill was busy creating tools to help users debug their dBASE programs. Earlier versions of the DOS product provided little help with this, so anything he added was a vast improvement. Our Mac product already had two debugging tools; Bill emulated those in FoxPro. One, called the "Debug Window", gave them the ability to monitor the values of their "variables" (the portion of a program that could change over time). The other, called the "Trace Window", allowed our users to step slowly through their dBASE code to find problems as they happened.

For his part, Heindel continued to add dBASE IV syntax and work on expanding our printing capabilities. Both were mammoth and nearly thankless chores.

The most astounding product improvement, though, was its speed. It was fast—incredibly fast. FoxPro was clocked running code twice as fast as FoxBASE+ and up to seven times faster than dBASE IV.

When the product finally shipped, it would be a fully-loaded hot rod.

*      *      *

However, much was left to do. Not many of us were going in weekends yet, but I was. I still felt concerned—like the whole Report Writer was a facade that would tumble down around my ears at any time. Even though it appeared to be working, parts of the original code were still mysteries to me. I had to test it—I had to be certain it was right. In addition, the fact that it was considerably quieter on the weekends made them a much more desirable time to work

During normal working hours, the carpenters upstairs were a source of perpetual distraction. They were still hard at work trying to complete the top floor and we were well aware of it. An ordinary day's concentration might be shattered by a loud crash overhead or the sound of hammers pounding away.

Another source of distraction, for me, was the littlest Fulton. A short time after the move, Dave and Amy began bringing him in to work regularly. He was still very young and slept often so this shouldn't have been a problem. However, the Fulton's also brought in this "seat on a spring" thing which they kept connected to the doorjamb of their office. This meant I'd be sitting in my cubicle, attempting to solve a mystery, and have this "Boing, Boing, Boing" sound suddenly interrupt my thoughts. I'd turn around to find the boy jumping higher than any kid that small should be able and smiling from ear to ear.

Twenty minutes of that and I wished the carpenters would step up their hammering a little so I could get my concentration back.

*     *     *

Just around the corner from my cubicle, Marty was hard at work as well, trying to get the next version of the Mac product out. The testing cycle of that product was in full swing and soon produced another reason for my attention to be diverted.

I was seated at my desk one morning, staring hard at my computer screen, when I heard a familiar voice behind me.

"Kerry?" Dave asked, sounding serious.

*Ah man, not color changes again.* I turned to look at him. His face was equally serious. "Yeah, Dave," I said. *Uh, oh,* is what I thought.

"Follow me," he said with a wave. He led me to the right first past Chris's office, and then Sally's. As we went by Chris's, I noticed his door was closed. That was unusual. Chris was a sociable guy and preferred to leave his door open. The top half of his office was transparent, though, and in the split second it took me to pass by, I noticed someone in Chris's office with him, but I couldn't tell who.

We ended at Heindel's office. Marty and Heindel were already inside, waiting.

*What could this be about?* I wondered. The only thing Marty, Heindel, and I had any recent interaction about was some printing problems, but that shouldn't concern Dave much.

Dave motioned for me to shut the door, and then took a seat. "I just wanted to let you all know that we decided to let Carol go," he said, speaking softly.

*Whoa. Where did that come from?*

Carol was hired fresh out of college, and she fit into the low-key environment of Chris's firm really well. At Fox, though, she'd been judged "too untested" to have her hands in the FoxPro code initially. She was given her bug-tracking job for the Mac product as a first assignment. While that wasn't the sort of thing a developer normally did, I assumed she'd eventually pass the test and become one of us. *What did she do so wrong that she was now getting fired?*

"She just wasn't cutting it," Dave explained, shaking his head. "This is probably for the best. She was way over her head here." He looked first at Marty, and then at Heindel and I. His voice got more forceful. "She's personally responsible for the slippage in the Mac product's release date," he said. "It cost us weeks!"

Then his tone softened, sounding more apologetic. "I also wanted to assure you three that we're happy with your work. Nobody else's head is on the chopping block. Just Carol. She overlooked some critical bugs…" He shook his head. "Chris is firing her as we speak."

*Chris is firing her?* That was a little strange too. Dave was technically her boss. Stranger still, was the fact that she was the first developer to be let go. Not the kind of precedent I wanted to see started.

Dave dismissed us then. As I returned to my cubicle I saw Carol walking out of Chris's office. There were tears in her eyes. I looked away. *Was this really necessary?*

I found my seat and tried to return to work. Regardless of Dave's assurances, I couldn't say I was feeling any more secure in my job than before. If Carol was fired for losing a bug or two, what would keep them from firing me if I failed to fix one?

It was also clear from the office arrangements who was now the low man. Again.

I stopped in to see Marty later that same day. "So what was the deal with Carol?" I asked, closing the door.

Marty turned in his chair and rested his elbows on his lap. "Oh, somehow some bugs got misplaced," he whispered.

I wasn't sure why he was whispering. The door was still closed. "Misplaced?" I said in a normal tone.

"Yeah, you know how Carol had that bug tracking program she used?"

I nodded. Carol wrote a program using FoxBASE+/Mac to maintain a list of the bugs that were found. "Yeah, I remember."

"Well, somehow there were some bugs that didn't get entered into her list," Marty said, still whispering. "Consequently, I never heard about them and they didn't get fixed."

"No?"

Marty raised a hand to swat the air. "Well, not until I finally heard about them. It was no big deal though. The Mac product would've been delayed by something else." He shrugged, "I'm fixing more bugs now."

"Then why did Dave fire her?"

Marty shrugged again. "He just woke up one morning and decided Carol was the reason the Mac product slipped."

I shook my head.

"She got a raw deal," Marty added. "Especially since there were no clear guidelines given her."

"Unbelievable." I scratched the back of my head. "And he had Chris fire her."

Marty gave a short laugh. "Yeah, isn't that something. He had **Chris** fire her." He shook his head. "Poor Carol."

"Poor Carol for sure," I said and frowned. *My sleep patterns are going to be irregular again....*

Management randomness, it's a developer's nightmare.

*    *    *

In June I was given my second annual review and it was extremely positive—much better than I expected considering what just happened to Carol. Dave told me he appreciated my work and gave me a bonus that, to a recent college grad, seemed obscene. He also informed me that I would, in fact, be getting my own office when the developers moved upstairs. My quest for solitude was complete.

The final move occurred the following month. The developers moved upstairs and the rest of the company came over to fill a portion of the new building's empty space.

Finally, I sat in an office of my own. It had its own window and its own door. No loud conversations. No bouncing kids. No pounding hammers. It was everything I had hoped for.

Of course the view wasn't much. Through my window I could see the roof of the adjacent building and the dumpsters that sat behind it. The front side of my office only had a wall part way up. The top half was filled in with Plexiglas that creaked every time someone walked by. It felt a little like being in a fishbowl.

But, my office was also the last occupied office on "developer's row"—the exterior offices on the eastern side of the building. It was the furthest from the corner office—Dave's new home—and the way I figured it, if anything went wrong, I'd be the last developer he'd find. There would also be plenty of forewarning because of the creaking Plexiglas.

*Location, location, location....*

# Chapter 7
# Caves and Beaches

I was in on a Saturday afternoon in the middle of July. I wasn't there because I had to be, I was there because I wanted to be. The Report Writer was proving to be extremely solid. There were few bugs found in it at all, and finally I was feeling comfortable. Like the whole thing **wasn't** going to fall in on me. It seemed I accomplished what only months before seemed impossible.

A little more testing is always a good thing, though, so I was in to check a little more. I spent a few hours creating reports and watching them print. When I was satisfied, I turned off my machine. *It works. It's time to go home.*

I followed developer row toward Dave's office. There was a light on, so I assumed Dave was in as well. He was probably doing a little more testing himself.

As I drew near, I looked in and saw Dave at his desk. In his new office, the configuration had his wooden desk facing the door. To the right of the door as you entered was his round conference table and above it on that wall was a large whiteboard. Along the perpendicular wall to the left were two large bookshelves, filled with books.

I rounded the corner and moved by Dave's entrance a little more deliberately than I normally would. It's OK for the boss to know you're in on a Saturday, after all.

I was just passing by the adjacent conference room, when I heard Dave call my name.

I shrugged. *He must just want to say 'Hi'.* I back-stepped to his door.

"Hey Dave," I said. "How're you doing?"

His face was too serious for a Saturday. "Yes, Kerry. Come here. I need to talk to you about something."

I said "OK," and then walked in and sat down.

Dave had the Report Writer up on his computer screen with a typical report already constructed. Our Report Writer was what was commonly known as a "banded report writer." This meant its design surface was divided into a number of sections (bands) and each represented a particular portion of the final printed report. For instance, one band was labeled "Report Header." Anything (database fields, text, or rectangles) placed within that band would print only once, at the beginning (or head) of the report. Likewise, there was a band labeled "Page Footer." Anything placed within that band printed at the end of every page of the report. Another band labeled "Detail" was for information that filled the center (and usually the greatest) portion of every page. In the Detail band of Dave's report he had a handful of the fields from his database (a database of his laser disk collection) arrayed in a couple rows.

Dave made a motion toward the screen. "I can't create the kind of report I want," he said.

I squinted at his monitor. He had the text 'Title:' and next to that a rectangular area as a placeholder for the field named 'Title' from his database. In that area, the various values for that field would print in the final report. To the right of that he had a similar construct for the 'Description' field in his database. The 'Description' field was a little different, I knew. It was defined as type 'memo' in his database, so it could be really long. When it finally printed, the text for it could span over a number of different lines.

He had a third field in his report named 'Running Time'. This he had placed beneath the row with 'Title' and 'Description' on it. "That looks OK to me...?" I said finally.

"Yes, but watch when I preview it," Dave said. He selected the menu item that presented an onscreen mockup of how the report would look when it printed—'Print Preview.' The report design screen was obscured by the Preview window. I could see the three fields displaying as I expected they would. The titles of his laser disks ran down the left side of the screen. Beginning directly beside them was the descriptions for each one. Some of the descriptions only lasted a single line, others spanned on for a dozen. On the line immediately following the last line of each description, the value of 'Running Time' displayed. Its horizontal position was directly beneath 'Title,' but because the lengths of the descriptions varied, it could be many lines below.

That was exactly how the report should look. "Yeah, that's right," I said.

Dave frowned. "But I want 'Running Time' to always be on the line immediately following 'Title.' How do I do that?"

He couldn't. The report writer we purchased didn't allow for that, so neither did ours. "Well, you can't," I said. "That's how the Report Writer was designed."

Dave's frown deepened. He turned toward me. "I think we need to allow a field to be anchored, just like we do in the Mac's Report Writer."

The Report Writer that went out with the Mac product was built by Marty from the ground up. It allowed the text, boxes, and fields the user constructed to either 'float' or be 'anchored'. When placed on the design surface beneath a stretchable memo field the 'floatable' fields continued floating down the printed report until the memo field finished printing all its text. Then they would print. (This was essentially the way all items in my Report Writer behaved.) However, 'Anchored' fields remained fixed in place no matter what the stretchable fields above them did. That behavior was a part of Marty's design for his Report Writer since the beginning, though. I was just working with what I was given.

My mind went over the little I knew about the engine of my Report Writer. It was hardwired to work on only a single line of output at a time. "I don't think I can do that, Dave," I said. "The Report Writer doesn't work that way."

Dave got more serious. "I think we really need to do anchoring, though," he said, glancing at his screen. "This Report Writer is unusable without it."

*Well, it's been completely useable for the last few months.* I had no idea how to do what he was asking. "I don't think I can," I said. "Not by next month, anyway."

Dave sounded sympathetic. "I really think we need to do this, Kerry." He straightened in his chair. "Listen, you've done remarkably well so far. Our environment here...well, it isn't for just any programmer. You blended in much better than some." He nodded once quickly. "Carol Garrison for instance...," He paused before lifting a shoulder. "Or Sally even."

*Sally?! What's wrong with Sally?*

Dave didn't elaborate any further and I didn't ask. I stared at the floor instead. *He's really going to make me rip up the engine of the Report Writer only a few weeks before we're supposed to ship. But the thing is solid, so solid.* I looked at Dave again. "But, Dave...you said we were going to ship sometime next month."

"Well, how long do you think it will take?" he said. "It shouldn't take longer than a couple weeks should it?"

I looked at the floor again, shook my head slowly. "I have no idea. I don't even know where to begin."

Dave was silent for a few moments. "Well, I really think we need to do this," he said. "Maybe I can have Eric come down on Monday and give you some pointers."

I couldn't lift my eyes. The pain in my gut was too great.

"OK..." I said. "I'll try..." I stood up slowly.

"It needs to be done," Dave said as I turned.

I walked toward the door. "Alright, I'll see what I can do."

I went home, dreading the following week. The Report Writer hadn't fallen in on me. It was pushed over.

*     *     *

When I went into work on Monday I was still down. Defeated before I started. It was nice to know Dave thought more of me than he did others on the staff. It was a surprise really. I had the feeling the latest turn with the Report Writer was going to change that perception, though.

At my desk I brought up the three or four files that composed the Report Writer's engine and started paging through them. It took little time to realize my suspicions were correct. There was no easy way to do what Dave wanted.

As the outside author originally conceived it, the engine picked out the appropriate information from what the user saw on screen and transferred it to a separate chunk of memory, what he called a 'literal pool'. The next thing the engine did was build instructions (he called it 'pcode') that described the precise steps to take to print the report. Then, another part of the engine followed those instructions. He called that part an interpreter. The pcode instructions and the interpreter were black boxes to me.

One thing was clear, though. They were built to work on one line of the report at a time. There was no mechanism to go back and print something that didn't 'float'...or stay with something until it finished 'floating'. It just didn't work that way.

I noticed movement out of the corner of my eye. I looked up to see Eric standing outside my door. I waved him in.

"How's it going," he said softly.

I shook my head. "It's not." *You must understand. I've been given a task I cannot do.*

"Yeah, Dave told me to come and help. I'm not sure how much help I can be, though."

"Hmm," I said. "OK."

Eric took a seat. He grabbed a pen and a notepad from the top of my desk. "I looked at the Report Writer code a little. Some of that stuff is confusing...." He waved his hands in the air. "There's this literal pool stuff, and this pcode stuff, and this interpreter business." He frowned. "It's really not like Marty's at all is it?"

"Nope." *But we're going to try to make it act like it.*

Eric drew a few things on the paper. It looked like a bunch of rectangles in a circle connected by lines. "Like I said, I don't know if this helps you or not, but it seems like…well…maybe you can do something to make the Report Writer work on the pool until everything finishes printing, instead of what it's doing now."

I sat quietly. I knew Eric was smart, but he didn't really know much about the Report Writer engine. Nobody did. Not even me. What Eric was saying was about as much help as finding Scotland on a map and telling me to go there.

"Does that help?" he asked, looking hopeful.

"A little."

Eric shrugged and put the paper back on my desk. "Let me know if you need more." He gave a little apologetic smile. "Really, nobody knows this stuff better than you. It's up to you."

"Thanks," I said, forcing a little smile.

Eric opened the door and slid through. "I hope I helped a little."

I nodded. "A little…."

He gave a low, two-note chuckle. "OK," he said. "See ya."

It was really up to me.

*       *       *

I accomplished very little the rest of that day and the next. I made a few attempts to alter the part of the engine that interpreted the pcode. It was the only part that really made any sense to me. I thought maybe, if I altered the two places that specifically handled the literals—the elements that printed out—I might have a chance.

My attempts were floundering, though. They didn't work. Either the whole report printed on one line, or it didn't print at all. The only thing I accomplished was I learned a little more about the interpreter portion of the code. It was like holding a single match in a very windy cave.

There was another complication, though. In order to be able to calculate how much space to allow for the Detail (central) portion of the report, the size of the other bands had to remain constant. That meant the anchor/float mechanism could only occur in the Detail band. (The other bands of the report needed to behave just as before.)

However, the pcode really made no distinctions between the bands.

I was still lost.

*       *       *

Wednesday I floundered around a little more. I thought maybe if I changed the order of the pcode some—if I changed the description of the report the interpreter followed—maybe I could get something to work.

But I accomplished nothing. The Report Writer either froze my machine, or printed a partial report. The day was a total waste.

I finally decided outright prayer was the best option.

If it was really all "up to me," it was hopeless.

\*　　　\*　　　\*

Thursday I started to have a hint of something. Another match in my cave of despair.

I thought about adding my own pcode instructions to the mix. There would be no harm in that, I reasoned, because the way the pcode / interpreter mechanism worked, there was some room for additional instructions. I could add my own instructions, and try to get something that would work.

I would leave the old ones as they were—and that was good. It ensured the new anchoring behavior occurred only in the Detail band. The other bands should stay as they were. They should be safe.

Or so I hoped.

\*　　　\*　　　\*

Friday I wondered why I didn't start praying sooner.

*What I really need is a pcode looping structure,* I realized. *That way, I can have the stuff in the Detail band keep looping until everything has printed out.* The engine would no longer be tied to dealing with just one line at a time. It would deal with the whole band.

I could have specific pcode instructions for the literals in the Detail band. I would allow for the new 'anchored' behavior in those.

It might work.

\*　　　\*　　　\*

That Saturday and the beginning of the following week was spent earnestly pursuing the looping solution I came up with. It was clear that it would work, but it would take some time to clean up all the sundry details.

I was carrying a flashlight through the cave, and I had plenty of batteries.

\*      \*      \*

By the beginning of August I was out of the cave completely. Anchoring worked, floating worked—reports even printed on more than one line. In addition, I now knew everything there was to know about the Report Writer.

I could now call it completely my own.

\*      \*      \*

The month of my scheduled vacation arrived. As it turned out, it was convenient Dave agreed to let me take a vacation in August after he denied my original request for May. Over the course of the summer, a friend of mine got engaged and asked me to be the best man in his wedding. The date was in August and it was in California—thousands of miles away. I decided to use my promised vacation to attend.

I was greatly looking forward to a trip out west. I'd been working for Fox for well over a year and had only a couple days off during all that time. A week in the sun with friends was just what I needed.

The wedding was August 5$^{th}$. I already had my tickets purchased, but I still needed to remind Dave. Just in case he went looking for me while I was gone.

I found him hovering over a laptop computer at his desk. Both hands were at the keyboard and he was completely absorbed, but in a negative way. His expression spoke of stomach trouble.

"Yes," he said as he saw me approach. "What is it?"

I hesitated, contemplating coming back later. "Um…I just wanted to remind you of my vacation the first week of August."

Dave looked at me, but his hands clung to the keyboard. "In August? We're getting ready to ship…."

*Oh no*, I thought. *It's just like Heindel said. There's no good time to take vacation.* I looked out Dave's window, seeing the old building across the parking lot. *In fact, maybe the developers never leave.* "But, I asked in March," I said finally.

"Yes, yes, I remember." His eyes were back on the screen, "But take only as much time as you **have** to."

"It's for a friend's wedding," I said, "in California."

Dave's face softened a little. "A wedding? Well, that's not the sort of thing you should miss. It's an important life event."

"Yeah…."

"But take only as much time as you have to," Dave repeated.

*Since I already have my tickets, "as much time as I have to" is five days off of work.* "OK," I said, backing away.

I returned to my office and looked out my window. The dumpsters were being emptied below. *Sheesh*, I thought, shaking my head. *I'm going all the way to California for a wedding. A week is reasonable, isn't it?*

Still, Dave's reluctance made me feel a little guilty, and what happened when I returned didn't help.

*    *    *

As soon as I got back, Dave called a "five year plan" meeting to do the usual FYP stuff. After discussing the status of the product, Dave turned to look in my direction.

"And now that our vacationing developer has returned...." He paused and studied me for a few moments before jerking his head back. "You look tan!" he said.

The rest of the room laughed and I tried not to smile. "Well, I was in California, Dave." *And the beach was calling.*

"Hmm...," he said, looking unconvinced. He forced a subdued chuckle. "No, no, he was there for a good reason—a wedding. Those are important things, the things we shouldn't miss." Dave's eyes remained fixed on me.

*Why is he still looking at me?*

"Well, now that Kerry's back, nobody should take any **additional** vacation between now and the time we ship this sucker," he said, with a tad too much emphasis.

He finally looked away. "I'd also like to remind everyone of our eminent deadline. We expect this product to ship by the end of the month, the first of September at the very latest." He repositioned himself so his head rested in one hand and he wagged a finger with the other. "In fact, the product **must** ship by then because we'll be giving out copies at the Developer's Conference."

I checked the faces of the others in the room. On most of them I saw the same thing I was thinking. *The Developer's what?*

Dave must have noticed. "Oh yes, you probably aren't all aware. The Developer's Conference is a weeklong gathering we're throwing for our users from around the globe. It will be held downtown (Toledo) at the convention center. It will be their chance to see some of what we're doing..." Dave forced a little smile. "...and to ask for their favorite enhancement, of course."

Someone asked about the price.

Dave scratched his forehead. "The price is six hundred and ninety five dollars. That includes their meals, hotel accommodations, and of course, a copy of FoxPro version one point oh. We'll be handing it out on the last day of the conference."

*The last day of the conference?*

"But that should be no problem," Dave assured us. "The product will have long since shipped by then."

# Chapter 8
# Circus

It was noon on a Sunday and my parents and I had just returned back from the morning service at our church. Even though their house, the one I grew up in, was surrounded by fields, some things were close by. My high school was only three miles away and the church was less than two.

The town of Bowling Green and college was a bit further out. It was thirteen miles northwest. Perrysburg and work was further still—a little over twenty due north.

On this day I was glad church was close, though. Too much time spent traveling would've been an unwanted distraction. I was beat.

"What are you doing the rest of the day?" Mom asked as she busied herself with preparing lunch.

I dropped into my usual chair beside the slightly-lopsided dinner table. "Sleeping," I said.

"Is my poor boy tired?" she asked without a trace of sympathy.

Dad walked into the room on his way to their bedroom. He held his suit jacket in one hand. "Well, if you guys didn't stay out so late…" he said and smiled. "What time did you get in?"

I shrugged. "I don't know…three?"

"Three in the morning? What were you guys doing?"

As much as I loved my parents, there were certain disadvantages to still living at home. "Playing Balderdash," I said.

Dad paused and put a hand on the back of my chair. "In Bowling Green?"

I straightened up a little. Though most of my nights 'hanging with my friends' were fairly predictable (but entertaining nevertheless), this time had an added bonus. "Yeah, we actually met some girls on campus," I said, smiling. "Three of them. We all went back to their place and played Balderdash."

"Girls?" Dad said. "Really?"

I gave a half-hearted smile, and then reached back to give him a mild shove. Dad was the primary critic of my social life. He already predicted that my friends and I would be single our whole lives. He even put money on it.

Dad put up his "fighting dukes" and smiled. "So, no work today?"

I shook my head. "Nah, I was only in for a couple hours yesterday." The Report Writer was finished though, and had been for some time. I spent most of the day just testing the product. "Today, I sleep!" I said finally.

The phone rang. I stood up, and grabbed the phone on the wall near me. "Hello," I said, my voice cracking with fatigue.

"Hi Kerry, this is Janet."

*Janet? What is this about?*

Janet was Fox's product manager. She essentially played the part of product nursemaid. The list of things she did during the release cycle was long. Aside from managing the beta and verifying bugs, she was frequently a member of developer meetings with Dave. Her knowledge of the product and the dBASE community was extensive.
If Dave was the father of FoxPro, Janet was—quite respectfully—its mother.

"What's up?" I said.

"I need you to come in," she said.

*You've got to be kidding....*

"Is there something wrong with the Report Writer?"

"No," she said. "We just have a lot of bugs to fix before tomorrow."

"Whose bugs?"

"I don't know—just bugs."

"But, I didn't get much sleep last night...."

"We **really** need the help," Janet said. "Heindel and Chris were here most of last night."

*Was that my fault?* "All right," I said. "I'll be in."

I hung up the phone, and after a quick lunch, drove the long twenty miles to work. Heindel, Chris, and Brian Tallman were there, fixing whatever bugs were on Janet's list. Giving them my sob story about being out late got me no sympathy. So, I just worked on bugs and prayed the code I was writing in my sleep-deprived condition was halfway decent.

Because the next morning would be the opening day of DevCon and Dave's unveiling of our product.

\*       \*       \*

The following day saw us all draped in polyester, ready to attend the opening session. We slaved long and hard on the product and now had a good share of our individual egos invested in it. Everyone was curious to see how the conference attendees would view our new creation.

The only exception was Sally. When I stopped by her office, I noticed she was wearing the usual jeans and a cotton shirt.

"You're not going?" I said.

Sally shook her head. "Uh-uh. I can just see Dave when something goes wrong." She straightened in her chair. "There's something wrong with the blankity-blank Filer!" she exclaimed, bringing her hands up and flailing them in the air. "Sally! Where's Sally? Get her up here!" She returned her hands to her lap and shook her head again. "No way. No thanks. Enjoy yourself."

I smiled and gave a little wave as I stepped back into the hall. Though Sally worked like an ox, she sometimes had the temperament of a fawn. I went to join the others, who were gathering near Heindel's office. Soon we split into car-sized groups and were on our way.

When we arrived at Toledo's convention center, the conference attendees had already formed a large mob outside the room where the demo was being held.

*This is wild*, I thought. *People are lining up to see something I worked on!* As I watched the crowd press against the closed doors, I started to feel a little anxious. *This must be what parents feel like the first time their child goes onstage. You're excited and proud, but also not exactly sure what's going to happen.* I saw similar feelings reflected in the eyes of the other developers. Each of us was worried our part of the product might explode in Dave's face. The wait was intolerable.

The doors finally opened then, and we flowed in with the rest. Some of the more ambitious attendees raced to the front while the majority (numbering in the hundreds) silently filled the remaining seats. We developers chose to stand near the back of the room. "There are only enough seats for the paying customers," we were told, and that didn't bother us in the slightest. If anything went wrong, we were close to an exit.

The room (a converted ballroom) was decorated in deep shades of red. In front was a stage with a computer-bearing desk placed to one side. Behind this desk was a huge projection screen reflecting the image of what a user would see when they first started our product—a menu bar across the top and large letters that spelled out "FoxPro" on a blue background. During Dave's demo the screen allowed everyone present to view what he was seeing on his computer monitor.

Dick LaValley, the company's other co-owner, took the stage to begin the session. Dick was a large man with gray hair and the bearing of most farmers I knew. "I just want to welcome you all…," he began in a casual, drawn out manner. He meandered on for some time before making a quip about Fox being located in the heart of "Silicorn Valley."

Heindel stood near me. "That's my line!" he whispered excitedly. I glanced at him and smiled. I'd heard him use the phrase "Silicorn Valley" before and knew he was proud of it. Perrysburg was, after all, on the edge of farm country. I looked back to where Dick was now introducing Dave.

The suit-wrapped Dave mounted the stage, and after a brief greeting, seated himself at the computer. As the crowd quieted, he used the keyboard to navigate through the menus and open the "Command" window.

The FoxPro version of the Command window was maybe 2" x 3" square (resizable to any dimension) in which the FoxPro user could type commands for the product to execute. The window also kept a record of all previous commands executed; making it simple for the user to check everything they did since starting the product. When opened, it hovered above the blue background surface that displayed the product's name.

The first command Dave entered was "USE VIDEO," a command to open one of his databases. He quickly followed this with "DISPLAY STRUCTURE," a command that caused the layout of his database (VIDEO) to list out onto the blue background. As it appeared on the big screen, the results of the command (a long stream of text) were partially obscured by the Command window itself. The attendees were squinting to see what the command had done.

"Can you move the Command Window?" someone finally shouted out.

That was unexpected. I assumed most of the attendees were business people, usually a low-key, respectful lot. I was wrong.

Dave seemed unruffled by the request. "Oh, you want me to move the Command Window?" he muttered. "All right...."

He carefully waded through the menus to locate the proper item to move the Command Window. After finding it, he nudged the window over using the arrow keys on his keyboard. This brought a smattering of recognition from the audience. The output from the "DISPLAY STRUCTURE" command was now fully visible.

Dave clicked the window using the mouse pointer and moved it slightly. Following this—in an act worthy of a showman—he clicked the window again and shook it all over the screen. The crowd exploded with cheers and applause.

"Heh, heh, heh," Dave chortled. "Can I move the Command Window...."

From there the presentation took a turn into the surreal. Heindel later described what followed as an event somewhere between a rock concert and a pagan sacrifice ritual. He mentioned "rhythmic clapping, feet stomping, and the calling for a human sacrifice"—a description not far from the truth. Following the shaking of the Command Window, the show became a circus.

Dave proceeded to demonstrate nearly every facet of FoxPro. The minutest addition brought gasps and sighs from the crowd. Even a simple function we added to remove the spaces from both sides of a character string (called 'ALLTRIM()') brought a thunderous round of applause.

Through it all, the developers remained tense. Each of us, in turn, caught our breath as Dave demoed our part of the product, and then exhaled as he moved on—thankful our area of responsibility performed without incident, yet fearful the product would crash in the next section of code we'd written.

The worst, by any measure, was Chris. He seemed to be on the verge of a breakdown. And the things he was most concerned about didn't necessarily seem to be things he wrote.

"No, Dave!" Chris yelled as Amy and Sally's file management tool was brought forward. "Not the Filer! Don't bring up the Filer!" Chris had both hands on his face, nearly shielding his eyes. "Get out of there! Get out!" He turned and paced away from our group nervously. Over the months since I met him, I saw hints of melodrama in Chris before, but this time he reached a new level. I was glad the attendee commotion was loud enough to squelch him out. He turned back around, and after glancing toward the front, exclaimed, "He's bringing up the Report Writer!"

I checked the big screen and, sure enough, my child was on display. I felt confident, though. There hadn't been any problems reported with the Report Writer in quite some time. I watched as Dave put a few database fields on his report surface, and then selected the "Print Preview" menu item. The Preview window opened, giving him (and all the attendees) a glimpse of what the printed report would look like. Everything appeared to be working fine.

He tried a few other things. He drew out a rectangle, typed in some text—everything behaved as expected. Then he brought up the dialog for one of his database fields and changed its format, effectively altering how the field's data would display when it printed. When he finished with that, he previewed his changes again.

At that point, I saw something weird. Most of the display looked normal, but some output for the fields Dave changed looked a little garbled. *Oh crap*, I thought. I glanced at Chris and the others, who were all still staring at the screen. I checked the exit. *So near, so inviting*....

I looked at the stage again. Dave, who undoubtedly noticed the faux pas was closing up the Report Writer and continuing on with his demo. He only had a few things left to show.

"What was that?" Heindel leaned over to ask me.

I frowned and shrugged my shoulders. "I have no idea," I said, drawing the "no" out a bit, and I meant it. The behavior Dave saw almost didn't seem possible. The code that would exhibit the weirdness wasn't that complicated, and it got a lot of prior testing. Of course, it was possible by that point in Dave's demo the product was reaching of state of "unreliability." The Report Writer wasn't the only thing that exhibited some unusual behavior. There were some weird things with the Filer and debugging tools too.

But the crowd didn't seem to notice. When the demo finished, they rose to their feet for another rousing ovation. They loved our work and couldn't wait to get their hands on it. For a kid just out of college, it was an amazing feeling—something I wouldn't have felt if I was locked away with a mainframe somewhere.

Now, only one challenge remained—to actually get the product into the attendees' hands.

*     *     *

By Thursday we knew it wasn't going to happen. All along the plan was to give the attendees a copy of the final product, ready for release, but by the end of the week we knew that goal was unattainable.

Part of the Fox Software creed was "no product will ship with known bugs in it," and at the end of the day Thursday, everyone was still fixing bugs. So finally, Dave decided the version we gave the conference attendees would be a very, very late beta. It would be shrink-wrapped in a box like the final product—but it would really just be a beta.

Thursday night was a get together at the Toledo Art Museum for the conference attendees. The developers were allowed to go as soon as the last fixable bug was out of their section of code. I was one of the first to be released and over the span of a couple hours everyone made it to the party.

Back at the office, a version of the product was built and left with the production group. They would work through the night to spin out 600 copies.

*     *     *

The following morning was the closing session. Dave took the stage with a boxed copy of FoxPro in his hands. After some initial comments, he held up the nine-pound burden and looked at it. "For those of you who were disappointed you weren't a part of our beta program," he said, and then looked back out at the audience and chuckled softly, "well…you're about to get your chance."

He went on to explain the situation and apologize for any inconvenience it may cause. "We think the product is really close," he said finally. "We'll wait on you to make the final decision."

*      *      *

Not more than a week after the conference ended our phones were ringing off the hook. Evidently, everyone ran home with their "late beta" copy of the product and immediately tried to run their favorite piece of dBASE IV code. What many of them soon discovered was in places of the product where it was hard to emulate exactly what dBASE IV did—or if we found a better way to do something from how dBASE IV did it—we always ignored the exact dBASE IV syntax. Much of their straight dBASE IV code would not run without some minor changes. Our workalike was more of a work-it-might. The developers were summoned to the conference room again.

"These incompatibilities are intolerable," Dave said. "We lost our focus!" He pushed his head forward and looked sternly around the table. "We should have always allowed the dBASE IV syntax, even if it was in addition to what we had already."

Looks of consternation graced the faces of many in the room. Although Dave's assertion was true—we should have allowed the additional dBASE IV syntax—few of us agreed with the "**we**" part of his statement. Whenever any of us approached him with one of these dBASE IV dilemmas, he always said we should just "do what makes the most sense." Usually, what "made the most sense" was to ignore what dBASE did. We were just following orders.

While I listened to Dave scold us, I started to theorize about the possible explanation for him forgetting his prior instructions. It wasn't the first time I'd seen such behavior. On more than one occasion I encountered a situation where Dave would tell me to do something, I'd go off and do the very thing he told me to do, but when I finished with what he asked, he would turn around and ask me why I did it that way. *Maybe he has one of those pods from the "Invasion of the Body Snatchers" in his closet?* I thought, o*ne that switches with the real Dave every so often?* The meeting came to a close then, leaving me no further time for speculation.

Pod-person or no, we now had new marching orders. We trudged on into October fixing incompatibilities in what was starting to feel like the "product that wouldn't ship."

Fortunately, because the Report Writer was a new entity, I had few incompatibilities to deal with. So, I kept myself busy fixing the random bugs on Janet's list—a task that actually wasn't too bad. I got to find and fix problems and didn't have to feel responsible for putting them there in the first place.

*     *     *

Around this time Fox brought another developer on board—a fellow named Brian Crites. Brian was engaged to marry one of our most promising technical writers, and partially to encourage her loyalty, Dave offered Brian a job. (At least, that's the way I heard it.)

Brian was a clean-cut guy with an understated, frequently serious personality. He was about my age, and like everyone on the development team (except Marty and Sally), he graduated from BGSU. He was given an office one door down from mine, and his initial assignment was to add some commands to the FoxPro language for the next version of the product—a starting point with which I was all too familiar.

That wasn't Brian's only form of initiation, though. Less than a month later, Dave was sitting quietly in his corner office when his wife Amy walked in.

"Brian Crites checked in an mmm.h!" she said. "What is he doing checking in an mmm.h!?"

Mmm.h was a file nearly every C source file in our project utilized. Usually the changes one would make to it were harmless—things that wouldn't affect anyone else in the group. It did contain some vital information though. None of us—even the most experienced—would ever change that, and I know Brian didn't.

Dave leapt to his feet in response. "Brian changed mmm.h! Well, I'll see about that." He marched his way down the length of developer row, passing my office, to Brian's. He swung open the door and without a word, grabbed Brian by the wrist. Heindel and another employee were present in the room.

"What?" Brian said as he was led to the hall and past my office again.

Dave said nothing. He continued to lead Brian, past Sally's, past Chris's, past Heindel's, all the way up the food chain until he reached Eric's office.

"Yes?" Eric said as Dave and Brian marched in.

Dave looked at Brian. "Brian, this is your new Mom. Don't do anything without asking him." He then addressed Eric. "This is your new son. Watch him." He squinted for emphasis. "Carefully."

With that, Dave left the office and turned right toward his own. Ring leader of Fox Software's high-flying extravaganza.

# Chapter 9
# Fireworks

Around the beginning of October, in another FYP meeting, Dave asked which of us would like to attend Comdex. He was looking for two volunteers.

There was silence for a few moments. As a junior member of the team, I assumed two of the senior members (in my mind, Eric, Bill, and Heindel) would go again. Last year's event had certainly seemed climatic. This year we were going to have a new product to show. *It should be exciting shouldn't it?*

The senior members, apparently wiser for their past experience, stayed quiet (a few even groaned). Finally, after some time passed, Chris brought up a hand and nodded his head vigorously. That didn't surprise me much. What I'd heard of Vegas seemed to match his personality.

"Anyone else?" Dave asked.

I looked around. No one else seemed even remotely interested "I'll go," I said, shrugging. *Why not? It's a free trip to Vegas! Anything could happen.*

\*       \*       \*

The airline ticket I was given a month later said that I, Kerry Nietz, was flying out for Comdex on November 11th—a Saturday afternoon. That got me there two days before the fun started (on Monday) and I'd return the following Saturday after everything was finished.

The product still hadn't **quite** shipped, but on Wednesday the 8th we had a version built we thought could be the one. After weeks of infrequent bug fixes, the trickle of changes had nearly ceased. The intent was to sit on this build for a couple days, see if anything major came up, and, if nothing did, we would ship it on the final day of Comdex. This would allow us to announce FoxPro was "now shipping" while our booth at the event was still standing.

Wednesday afternoon I recognized the top of Norm Chapman's hairless head in the lower part of my Plexiglas. Then I heard a knock on my door.

"Hi, Kerry," Norm said, as he walked in. Norm was Amy Fulton's father. He started at the company a few months before as the Vice President of Administration, or as he liked to call it, "the Man in Charge of Everything." He was a diminutive older gentleman with glasses who usually dressed in polyester pants and a button-down shirt. Rumor had it he was the best person to take with you if you were going to buy a car.

I returned Norm's greeting and smiled. I didn't know him well yet, but I respected him. Even if I didn't, he was a member of the owner's family—I had to be nice.

"Yeah, Kerry, do you have that airline ticket we gave you?" he asked.

It was still in my desk drawer. "Yeah," I said, nodding my head.

"Good, give it to me. Janet is going to be you."

I raised an eyebrow. "Huh?"

"Yeah, she needs to stay here an extra day. We're going to switch your tickets."

I reached into my drawer and took out my ticket. My name was printed clearly on the front. "Are you going to call the airlines?" I asked as I handed it to him.

"No," he said, smiling. He handed me back another ticket. "There you go. You fly out Friday with the first group." He turned as if to leave.

I glanced down at the ticket. It had "Janet Walker" printed on it. *Is this legal?* I looked up to see Norm's back moving through the doorway. "Can I fly on Janet's ticket?" I asked.

Norm paused, turned slightly. "Sure," he assured me. "You could be a Janet."

My eyebrow rose higher. "OK...."

Norm made a calming motion. "It'll be fine. Don't worry about it." He left the room.

I sniffed. Early in my employment I realized the company was run like its owner was Scrooge McDuck. First aid supplies were under lock and key. Our office chairs were little better than sitting on rocks. Support technicians who brought me sample code illustrating bugs would wait until I copied the offending code to my machine so they could get their hi-density floppy disk back. It was almost comical.

As unbelievable as it may seem, though, under Norm's supervision the company actually got more parsimonious. He was a master at getting the better deal. Our suppliers were so squeezed they were afraid to talk to him. Norm opened all the mail that came to the upstairs offices; we suspected it was because he was looking for money.

And now I had witnessed his act first hand. I smiled and tucked Janet's ticket into my drawer. *Anything could happen....*

*     *     *

That night an organizational meeting was held regarding the upcoming event. Because both Chris and I were new to the experience, we stayed late to attend. We were the only developers in the building. The rest of the meeting's attendees were volunteers from other groups in the company—support technicians, writers, and salespeople. Everyone who would help man the booth at Comdex was present.

Dave Fulton was there too. It wasn't unusual to find him hanging around Fox Software late in the evening. Like a captain who is most at home on the bridge of his ship, Dave seemed most comfortable within the four walls of the company's building. The important things happened there daily. It was where the key decisions were made— where the product's course was charted. The livelihoods of over eighty employees were now dependent on Dave making the right decisions, on his following the best course. And on the week FoxPro was to finally release, Dave's captain-like feelings were undoubtedly magnified.

The Comdex meeting was relatively short and at the end of it, Janet Walker said she was going to give everyone a quick run-through of what they would be showing.

"I'm going to take them through the self-running demo," Janet said, looking at Chris and me. "You two probably don't need to come."

Chris and I looked at each other and shook our heads. We were quite familiar with the demo program because we'd been testing with it for weeks. It was a dBASE program Amy wrote to showcase many of FoxPro's new features. If left running unattended it could steer anyone who was watching through the product's important features. It could be directed to show only specific portions as well. Its primary interface was a checklist of features to view, and each item could be set on or off manually. The checklist itself was probably the most inventive part of the program. It made use of the language's powerful BROWSE command to present its list of items.

Janet led the rest of the group (about ten people) away to her office, and Chris and I returned to his. As I stood at Chris's door chatting, I could see the group gathering closely around Janet's computer. I also noticed Dave making his way back toward them through the central opening that ran between the floor's two banks of cubicles. Thinking nothing more of it, I walked in to take a seat beside Chris's desk.

A short time later there was the sound of a small commotion—and over the fray— Dave's voice declaring, "There's an Internal Consistency Error in BROWSE!" I looked at Chris, and then stood up to peek through the Plexiglas. Over half-a-building away, I could see Dave circling Janet's office like a shark. He was livid.

I turned toward Chris. His face paled and he reached for his keyboard.

I could only guess at what happened. An "Internal Consistency Error" was the severest form of error our product gave. It essentially meant FoxPro encountered something it didn't know how to deal with and it couldn't continue. Shortly after this error occurred, the product terminated and anything the user was working on was lost. End of story and good night.

If it happened in BROWSE, it was probably the BROWSE the self-running demo invoked. The product we thought "ready to ship" had a very serious and blatant problem.

Dave's mantra of "There's an Internal Consistency Error in BROWSE!" continued, growing louder with each iteration—until finally—he was shouting it at the top of his lungs. I saw him leave Janet's office and start marching in our direction; he wasn't losing any steam in the coming. Four-letter words became part of his ICE chorus. Things were not good.

I ran around the desk to stand next to Chris. To make the best use of our remaining time on earth, we tried to find out who was responsible for the change that created the crash. Since the problem was in BROWSE—one of the most frequently used features—the change would have been recent to not be noticed. We made a quick scan through the day's changes, and by the time Dave tramped through the door we were fairly certain Brian Tallman was the culprit. He changed the BROWSE code that very day.

"There's an Internal Consistency Error in BROWSE!" Dave said as he entered. "Who's responsible?!"

I moved away from the desk, shuffled a bit along the wall past Dave, and stood near the door.

"We think it's Tallman," Chris said, his voice hesitant, yet even— in the manner you'd use with a barking dog.

Dave then hit a new level of mad. Brian's name was added to the verbal inferno, along with threats to do things to Brian's body I didn't want to imagine.

I quietly slipped away to call Brian. I had a good idea he wouldn't be home, though. It was a church night and Brian would be at church. I waited for the phone to ring a sixth time before hanging it up. Things were definitely not good.

I returned to Chris's office and stood quietly by the door. Dave stopped kicking the side of Chris's desk to turn and glower at me. "Did you reach him?" he asked.

I shook my head. "He's not there. It's Wednesday night, he's probably...."

"Do you know where he lives?"

I'd been to Brian's house once, and I hadn't been driving. "Um...not...."

"Go to his house!" Dave said. "Find him!"

I ran down to my car to try to find Brian. I had no address. I had no map. There hadn't been time. I drove out into a town I barely knew, looking for a house I only went to once. My only plan was to head in the direction I thought Brian's neighborhood was in and hope for the best. I had to find him. Things were desperate. Time was short.

Finally, after many minutes spent circling, I found a neighborhood that seemed familiar. I began searching for his house. I vaguely remembered a curved roofline, so I looked for a house with that feature.

Eventually I found one. It was brown. The roof was curved. Things began to click. *Yeah, this is it,* I thought, *I know it is.*

I stopped the car and ran to the front door. I rang the doorbell, peered in the windows, and pounded on the door, but nobody answered. The windows were dark. As certain as I was that I found the right place—I was equally certain no one was home.

*Great,* I thought. *Now I have to go back and tell Dave I couldn't find Brian at all.* I returned to my car and contemplated just going home, just retreating to the farm. Things would get sorted out in the morning. If Dave got mad at me because I didn't return, no big deal. He was mad already.

*Still, why risk it?* I sighed, and reluctantly, turned my car for the office again.

When I arrived, Dave's secretary was busy trying to calm him down. "It'll be all right," I heard her say as I approached.

Dave only glared at the floor, shook his head, and grumbled. My news wasn't going to help at all. The floor squeaked and Dave looked up. "Did you find him?" he asked.

I shook my head. "He wasn't there."

Dave's face reddened. "That g** d*** Brian Tallman!" he said. "I'll burn his house down!"

Things were still not good. I didn't stay to chat. I went to check on Chris. *I hope he's still OK....*

He survived. During the time I spent circling Perrysburg, he made the effort—aside from ducking flying objects in his office—to call Eric and get a hint of what the problem might be. Together they backed out Brian's change and started another build. The resulting product would be as good as ever.

I thanked Chris profusely and headed for home, happy to be alive.

*     *     *

I stopped in to see Brian Tallman early the next morning.

"Howdy, howdy," he said as I entered his office. "What can I do you for?" Brian had a large supply of phrases he liked to use regularly. I just heard two of them.

I smiled and sat down. "So...Brian...is your house still standing?"

Brian cocked his head slightly. "Come again?" he asked.

I proceeded to describe the events of the night before. While he listened, Brian frowned, rolled his eyes, and occasionally shook his head. "That's sad," he said finally. "Just sad."

"Yeah..." I said and stood up. "Well, just so you know..."

Brian shook his head again. "There's no reason for that." He groaned and gave a little wave. "See ya."

Later in the day I stopped by to check on him again. Nothing was said. The storm had come and gone.

*     *     *

The next day, six of us met at the office to carpool to the airport. I rode with Norm, his wife and one of our tech guys—a Syrian native named Bassel. The other two—our marketer and a support technician named Bart—went ahead of us in another car.

"We'll take the luggage," the marketer said. "No problem."

Along with everyone else, I handed over my bags—a small suitcase, a garment bag, and my carryon.

After we arrived at Detroit's airport, Norm parked in the long-term parking lot and we began our trek to the terminal. Along the way we saw the other two. I was surprised to see they were empty handed.

"Where's the luggage?" I asked when they got in range.

The marketer—a balding man who wore his jacket with the collar turned up—looked at me and shrugged. "We checked it," he said.

"Checked it?!" I exclaimed. "One of those was my carryon."

He looked at Bart and gave a little chuckle. "Sorry. We checked them. That's what we do."

*Great*, I thought, shaking my head. Aside from reading material, my brand new Sony Discman was in my carryon. Like many in development, I had purchased one for my office. *Just great*.... Then I remembered something else.

"My ticket is in that bag," I said as we reached the terminal doors. I glanced at Norm. "Well, Janet's ticket, actually." I frowned. "But it's in that bag."

Norm glanced at the ticket counter, and then at the marketer. "Go see if they can get the bag back."

The answer to that question was "No". The clerk at the counter just shook her head sympathetically.

The marketing guy placed his credit card on the counter. "All right, we need to buy him another ticket," he said.

Norm came up behind me. "Give me that other ticket when you get your bag in Vegas," he said and smiled. "I'll come up with something. You had a doctor's appointment or something."

I gave a half-hearted smile. "OK...." The clerk handed me my new ticket. It had my name printed boldly on the front. *I may have lost a Discman, but at least now the flight attendant won't be calling me Janet....*

*     *     *

Vegas is a long way from Perrysburg, Ohio, in more ways than can be easily counted. As unusual as it was to have a database software company in a sleepy suburb of Toledo, it seemed more unusual that the world's largest computer conference was held in Sin City. The flashing lights and glitzy shows stood in harsh contrast to the warm glow of a computer screen and the hum of a hard drive. But, every November, those two worlds came together in the trade show called Comdex.

As a testimony to the size of the computer industry, the event maxes out Vegas every year to this day. Every hotel filled with the booths of one computer related company after another, each booth a shrine of company wares. Every niche represented, from video games and joysticks to mouse pads and pocket protectors. For one week only, the desert city becomes a geek boy's paradise.

In '89 the pavilion of the Las Vegas Hilton was reserved primarily for database products. On the central main floor, the colossal booths of Ashton-Tate, Nantucket, and WordTech dominated the landscape.

The Fox booth wasn't nearly so prominent, though. Down a side hallway—just a short walk from the main floor—was a 25' by 40' room designated for our use. Our display divided the room into two halves with cloth panels. Each side had a specific purpose. On one side were nine machines set up on square, carpeted pedestals. Booth attendants (of which I was one) used these machines to give personalized demonstrations to guests who straggled in. The other side was arranged like a small auditorium, with about thirty seats in five rows and a stage with a projection screen and a computer. Here, Chris and Janet presented a scripted run-through of the product, one show per hour.

It was a busy week for us. The side of the booth I was on—the personalized demo side—was constantly crowded. Pockets of humanity swarmed around each machine from early in the morning until late in the afternoon. It was exhausting work; we had very little free time, but it was great to see so many people had a genuine interest in our work.

And, every once and awhile, something interesting would happen.

\*          \*          \*

"Hey Kerry," Janet said to me one day, toward the middle of the week. "I'd like you to meet someone."

I turned to see her standing with a young Asian man. "Yeah," I said, painting on my exhibition smile. By that time my feet were aching. Nobody told me to buy comfortable dress shoes and the desert air had done something weird to my knees. They were sore too.

"Kerry, this gentleman worked on the Report Writer for dBASE IV. He doesn't work for Ashton-Tate now, but I thought you might like to show him the product."

"Sure!" I said, and stepped over to one of the machines. I took the former AT employee through the product, ending with a customized presentation of our Report Writer. "How many people did you work with?" I asked him finally.

"On the Report Writer?" he said. "Seven." His attention was primarily focused on the screen. He couldn't see my raised eyebrows.

He glanced at me. "How about you?" he asked.

"Just me," I said. "We had seven on the whole project."

He looked at me a little longer this time, and then back at the screen. "You guys did a good job," he said, and then nodded. "A good job."

\*          \*          \*

On Chris and Janet's side of the booth, things were hopping as well. By midweek the word was out on their flashy presentations, and people were starting to flock in to see them. During the busier hours, every seat was filled and standing onlookers spilled out into the hall. Excitement for the product filled the room.

Of the two presenters, Chris definitely had the most showmanship. His demos were great fun to watch and they regularly brought cheers and laughter from the audience. When I was in the room, he would often give me credit for the things I worked on. You didn't have to watch too many of Chris's presentations, however, to notice something else.

During one session, Chris filled his demonstration screen with a number of windows—each belonging to one of FoxPro's "Desk Accessories." In general, these accessories were useful tools that were added to the product as an afterthought. They included things like a calculator, a calendar, and an ASCII chart.

"All you see here," Chris declared, indicating the screen. "I did."

At times Chris had a hard time separating product-promotion from self-promotion. I was beginning to understand why most of his shirts were monogrammed.

*     *     *

The remainder of Comdex week went well for the company. The crowds continued to pour in and wherever you walked, you would overhear "Fox" or "FoxPro" being mentioned. The company had made it to the big time—and to solidify that fact—FoxPro was released on Friday as planned.

With bright smiles still carved into our demo-wearied faces, we announced to all that could hear: "FoxPro is now shipping!"

# Chapter 10
# Missing Pieces

Although FoxPro 1.0 was a very useful—and in many ways—revolutionary product, it still lacked some of the functionality of its largest rival, dBASE IV. One missing component was a built in Screen Painter, a tool to help our users construct an input screen for their applications. Our Mac product had this type of tool since the summer of 1988, but there just wasn't time (or able bodies) to get one into the first cut of FoxPro. So, we planned to fill that gap in the next version.

There are inherent similarities between a Report Writer and a Screen Painter. They are both tools with a design surface where 'things' are manipulated. Of course, the types of 'things' are a little different between the two tools. In a Report Writer they are database fields, boxes, and text. In a Screen Painter this list expands to include interface elements like radio buttons, check boxes, and push buttons (also called controls). Ultimately, the two tools are brothers. They both save information about the things (such as size, color, and position) to a file on a disk and restore information from that file. They both allow things to move around, have their sizes altered, and other properties changed.

It is only after the report or screen is designed that the paths diverge. A report is primarily intended for paper while a screen is primarily intended to be part of an application's interface. The things in a report turn into printed data, and the things in a screen interact with a user

The similarities were the reason I was chosen as the developer to add a Screen Painter to FoxPro. "Just leverage what you learned from the Report Writer," Dave said, and that was the only initial direction I got. That was enough, though. The parameters for FoxPro's Screen Painter were easy to discern. It needed to have the functionality of the one Marty made for the Mac, yet live within the confines of the DOS operating system. My experience with the Report Writer gave me enough knowledge about FoxPro and its interface to do a lot without needing further direction.

In fact, I'd come to realize that working with minimal instruction was a part of the job description. When it was a feature with a high margin of flexibility (like the Screen Painter) Dave would just give us an idea about what it was supposed to do, we came up with a design, and then started coding away. Usually, we ran the 'gist' of our design by Dave before we started coding, but sometimes not. We knew we could count on him to drop in to see how things were going as we progressed. That's when Dave was at his best—when he had something visual; something tangible he could see. The developers laid the foundation and started nailing up the boards, knowing full well the plans could change mid-construction. Rooms may be moved and walls torn down—but most of the time—the foundation stayed the same.

So, after Comdex '89, I began work on the first feature that was wholly mine. The land was clean and bare, and the plans were still mostly in my head.

I loved it!

*       *       *

By the end of 1989, Fox had grown to be a good-sized company in the sleepy town of Perrysburg. We employed over a hundred people. The bottom floor of the building was completely filled by the MIS, Accounting, and Production departments. The top floor was about one quarter full. It was occupied by Sales, Tech Support, Writing, and Development—each growing toward the center of the building from their own respective corners.

In that bustling crowd of people, though, I realized there was one face I hadn't seen in awhile.

"Hey, Heindel-man," I said one day when I was in his office. I'm not sure at what point I appended 'man' to Heindel's name. Somehow, it just felt right. "Where's Kevin?" I asked. I was referring to the Kevin I met my first day of employment. He and Heindel commuted from Bowling Green and knew each other from social circles.

Heindel shrugged. "I guess he got fired."

"Fired?! Really? What for?"

Heindel's shoulders rose again. "He took home some pop from the fridge. Dave heard about it and fired him."

*When I met Kevin he was a walking billboard for Fox and its products.* He was also a very hard worker. I couldn't believe he was terminated for taking home a few cans of pop. "Without a warning or anything?"

"Yeah, it probably wouldn't have been a big deal, but he took home Diet Coke."

I glanced skyward and smiled. That made a little more sense. Diet Coke was Dave's favorite in the old building, but since the move he became more of a diet Vernors man. "Unbelievable. Kevin was the most...."

Heindel flipped up a hand. "Yeah, I know. Dave fired him."

\*        \*        \*

By late December much of the Screen Painter was functional. Unfortunately, the only functional Screen Painter in the whole company was still on my machine. Our network source files were in a state of limbo.

This is how the source code of FoxPro was handled normally. On their office computers every developer had a copy of all the files needed to build the product. In addition, there was what we called a "canonical" copy of these files out on the network's file server. When a developer wanted to work on a particular part of the product, he would "check out" the files he needed and make changes to them on his computer. During that time, the files he checked out were marked as locked by him on the network, and everyone else was prevented from checking them out. When the developer deemed the changes complete enough for the rest of development to have (or at least their own work wouldn't be impeded), he would "check in" the files he changed. This process would place his new versions of the files on the network. The other developers (Dave included) could run a small "update" program to pull them down and build a copy of the product with the changes included.

In practice this worked as follows: I check out a source file for the Report Writer called Report.C and make a change to it. I "compile" the file on my machine—a process that takes the human-readable source file and turns it into a machine-readable form. Another process called "linking" joins the machine-readable form with the other compiled files of the product to produce a new product with the changes included. I verify the change works as I intended. When I'm certain it does, I check Report.C back into the network. Another developer, say Heindel, could "update" from the network and get my changed file. He would compile that file on his machine and build his own copy of the product with my changes included.

That was how everything worked during the longest part of the development cycle. Following the release of FoxPro 1.0, though, it was important that a version of the source code remained identical to what the product was like when it shipped. There were several reasons for this.

First, for localization. When we created the interface, we did so using English words, and it was thus usable by Americans and others (such as Canadians, UK, Australians) with English as their native language. However, in order to sell product to those who spoke other languages, we translated the interface to those languages, such as German and Spanish, and natives of those countries had a version of FoxPro in their native tongue. This process of translating the interface to another language is called localization, and we needed to translate from the master source code for the current shipping version.

The second reason was bug fixes. The company policy, from the beginning, was to address immediately the bugs users reported, and then mail them a special build of the product with the fix included. For obvious reasons, these fixes had to be made to the master code for the current shipping version. We wanted to give them a slightly newer version of 1.0 with the fix included, not a half-finished version of 2.0 with the fix—and a ton of additional bugs as a bonus.

So, after FoxPro 1.0 was released, the canonical sources for it were restricted; a file could only be checked in if it addressed one of those two issues.

However, as the weeks following 1.0's release went by, fewer and fewer of us were working on 1.0 issues anymore. Most of us were busy adding features for the next release of the product—FoxPro 2.0.

There were no official "canonical" sources for 2.0, though. The job of creating a new network source tree was a huge undertaking, and those that knew anything about it—Chris and Heindel—were otherwise occupied. So for months, those of us doing 2.0 work made whatever changes we needed to make **only** to the copy of the 1.0 sources that resided on our personal machines. This allowed us to proceed with our new development work, while keeping in step with any 1.0 bug fixes that came along.

There were dangers to this though. The developer who didn't keep a careful backup of his work ran the risk of losing it if his machine died. (A tragic circumstance, but also one you could only blame yourself for.) In addition, there were many instances where one might have a file checked out for new development work and another developer might suddenly need that same file for a 1.0 bug fix. In that case, the first developer would be obliged to undo his check-out for that file without checking in his changes. We called this process "going rogue" and the altered version on the first developer's machine became a "rogue" version. From then on, the rogue file didn't play very well with the whole updating process, and if you weren't careful, your changes may get inadvertently overwritten when the second guy checks his bug fix back in. That was a major pain.

Aside from all that, though, there was another reason the code's limbo state was starting to annoy me. Because the only functioning

Screen Painter was on my machine, Dave soon became a regular visitor to my office. This was fine initially, because I was normally in high spirits over my latest change and glad to show it to someone. But, by December Dave started bringing random people with him to see my work, many of whom were company visitors he was trying to impress. This created pressure for me to have something in a demonstrable condition—at all times, and that wasn't easy. It's difficult to guarantee you'll have a product to show when you're also making significant changes to it.

Other developers ran into the same situation, and solved the problem by setting aside a demonstrable version every day that could be whipped out at a moment's notice. I never thought of that. I was too busy trying to make forward progress.

I was frequently caught with my product's pants down, so to speak.

*     *     *

It usually went like this.

The door swings open and Dave's body frames the doorway. Behind him is…someone…

"Yeah, Dave, what's up?" I say. I just made a change and my version of the product just finished compiling. I was working on adding a new control to the Screen Painter. There are about five different parts to the process. Add code to internally create the control, add code to draw it, a dialog for the user to specify details on the control (like its color), code to save information about the control to the disk, and code to retrieve that information. I like to complete them one at a time. I just added the code to create the control. At least, I think I did.

"This is Leroy Davidson," Dave says. "I want you to show him the Screen Painter."

The person with Dave is someone I've never seen before, and will probably never see again. He looks excited about seeing something new. Something other people haven't seen. Something from the inside. He's probably someone Dave is trying to impress.

"Okay…." I reach for my keyboard and type "F-O-X-P-R-O."

The two of them move close to my chair. There's a hint of excitement in the room. Dave has his hands in his pockets. His pocket change jingles.

The product starts up. *That's a relief, at least.* In the command window I type "CREA SCRE". That's short for "Create Screen"—it's the command that brings up the Screen Painter.

"Ah yes," Dave says, "here comes the Screen Painter now…" Both he and the visitor lean in expectantly.

The window for the Screen Painter opens. Then, less than a nanosecond later, my machine is back at the DOS prompt. The product has quit. Abnormally. Apparently, I broke something. Bad. Maybe a few more pieces of the puzzle need to be in place.

Nobody says anything for a time. "Um…shoot," I say. "I was in the middle of adding something…"

"I see…" Dave says. His face is expressionless. The visitor's eyes move between Dave and the screen. Both faces say "Can't you fix it?", but only silence speaks.

"Sorry," I say. "Maybe if I…"

Dave starts to move around my desk slowly, reluctantly. I embarrassed him. The visitor follows him out. He looks back at me once, disappointed.

I'm grateful when the door closes. *I hate being the only one who has a Screen Painter!*

\*         \*         \*

In January, I was finally given the news I was waiting for.

"Chris and I are going to split the sources tonight," Heindel said with a smile.

"Yes!" I said, lifting both hands in the air.

That night, after everyone went home, the two of them "split the sources." This meant they took the 1.0 source files on the network and created an additional (duplicate) set of sources. This second set would be used as the 'work in progress' sources for 2.0, while the initial set would stay as a 'frozen' version that reflected the product's state when 1.0 shipped. When they finished, they performed the same operation on everyone else's machines and started them building. The entire process took them until two o'clock in the morning.

The next day the fresh 2.0 sources were open for check-ins.

\*         \*         \*

Two days later, after everyone else checked in the changes they were holding, I was ready to put my Screen Painter out. I came into the office early and looked over everything I'd done. After assuring myself all was good, I circled around to the developers' offices telling all who were present that I was about to put a big change out and to "not update unless you mean it."

This last step was important because I made changes that would cause every source file in the product to compile, a process that could take hours. A person who unknowingly updated and got such a change (what we called a "destructive" change) would sit for a long time waiting for their machine to finish. Since such changes routinely happened during the course of the day, many of us didn't update until we were ready to go home for the night. But, to be on the safe side, I warned everyone I could. I returned to my office and spent thirty minutes checking in my stuff.

An hour later, Dave stopped me in the hall outside of Chris's office.

"I saw you put out a change this morning that causes everything to be recompiled," Dave said, his face unreadable.

I made the turn toward my office. Two thin cubical walls now separated us. I was happy that my changes, some twenty or thirty files, were finally safe on the network. And now anyone could demo the Screen Painter. "Yeah, Dave, I put the Screen Painter changes out…"

Dave's face reddened. He stopped and hooked an elbow over the side of one cubicle. "You should've coordinated your check-in with what Chris and Heindel did."

I took a step back. *I can't believe he's mad about this…*

Dave was the one person who didn't update only before he went home. He would update and build constantly throughout the day in order to be right on top of changes as they were made. This method came with a couple drawbacks. One was that many times he would update while a developer was in the middle of putting out their changes. He'd compile only half of what he was supposed to and be mad because **something** didn't work right.

The other drawback I already mentioned. He'd get a change that caused all his files to compile, and for some reason (perhaps because he feared everyone else was waiting too) this last condition really ticked Dave off. Part of the reason he dragged a naïve Brian Crites to Eric's office and made Eric his new "Mom" was because his innocuous change caused a lot of files to compile. Brian walked a tight line with the network sources following that experience—and apparently—I should have too.

Still, Dave was anxious to get my changes before. *Maybe if I explain.* "That was two days ago, Dave," I said.

Dave backed away from the cubicle wall some. He now was this angry disembodied head. "That doesn't matter," he said. "You should've worked with them."

I turned slightly. I wanted to run. "But they were here until two in the morning."

He wasn't listening. "It should've been coordinated!"

I frowned. There were no rules or guidelines about coordinating check-ins. I probably could have worked something out with Chris and Heindel, if I wanted to complicate all our lives further. Dave was just hacked off because there was another large compile. He was being unreasonable.

"OK…," I said. "Sorry." I wasn't really, though. I was just confused. I took the remaining steps to my office, grateful to get away.

Nothing I could say would've mattered, anyway. Dave was mad, he found someone to blame, and just let them have it. This time, I was the guy.

Since the release of version 1.0, I saw a change in Dave's demeanor. He was more intense, more demanding. It was as if he was losing touch with how hard it was to write good solid code. Little by little, he was becoming more of a manager and less a developer. Less one of us. Others noticed a change too.

This first time, when I experienced Dave's new intensity up close, was the hardest. It marked the beginning of a new phase of my existence—one with a recurring cycle. Dave would chew me out for some inexplicable reason. I retreated to my office and tried to return to work. Instead of working, I would contemplate how nice it might be to work somewhere else. My contemplation would continue for some time, but before the end of the day, I would convince myself to stay. The cycle became more frequent as time went on.

Still, there were many reasons to stick with it. The work was interesting, and there weren't too many opportunities for similar work in northwest Ohio. The pay was decent, especially for the area of the country where I lived. I was close to my friends and family. Any other workplace would be missing one of those things.

But, most of all, I felt like Fox was the place I was supposed to be.

*       *       *

A few weeks later Chris swung open my door, tossed a couple sheets of paper on my desk, and then acted like he was going to leave again.

"What's this?" I asked. I reached out to pick up the paper.

"Just FYI," Chris said. "It's a resume for someone Dave's interviewing today." He stood in the doorway with a hand on the doorknob and the lower part of his body still in the hall.

"Really?" I glanced down at the front page. The name on the top was "Dave McClanahan". *Has the quota on Daves been raised?* We already had about a half-dozen in the company with that first name.

"What's he interviewing for?" I asked, stopping Chris before he could get away.

"Developer," he said. "Listen, I have to circulate the rest of these. I'll be back." He straightened back into the hall and closed the door.

I looked at the resume. It was two pages single-spaced. It brimmed with facts on the candidate's knowledge and experience. I also noticed a few spelling and grammar errors. The resume violated everything I was taught in my college technical writing course.

Chris returned. "Any more questions?"

"What's he going to work on?" I asked. Aside from the Screen Painter, some key features of dBASE IV still weren't a part of FoxPro. Most of those were spoken for already, though.

Chris paced into the room and circled around my desk a little. "SQL," he said.

That made sense. SQL, or Structured Query Language, is a set of commands that allow for the definition, control, and manipulation of data in tables. At the time of FoxPro 2.0's genesis, it was something of an industry standard. The perceived advantage was that no matter what product was used to manage a given database, the same SQL commands could be used to retrieve data from it.

I nodded my head and glanced down at the resume again. "It looks like he has a lot of experience… he has a PhD?"

Chris opened his eyes wide and nodded his head quickly. "Yes, that's the kind of person Dave wants. He decided not to hire any more kids fresh outta college for awhile."

*Huh?* I raised my eyebrows slightly.

Chris's tone changed. "Well, not that those haven't worked out before…it's just for SQL he feels we need an expert."

"Oh," I said, frowning slightly. Chris was not helping me feel secure. I was the only recent college grad who got in trouble recently. Was I the one to make Dave change his hiring standards?

Chris walked back toward the door. "I better go. See ya."

The interview must have gone well, because McClanahan was hired that same day. Short and timid, his appearance was similar to Willy Tanner, the befuddled father from the TV show "Alf." He had a strong theoretical view of programming, and as soon as he had an office, he was ensconced within, filling his whiteboard with hieroglyphic symbols, and typing away frantically.

I didn't understand any of it, but I was just one of those college kids. The kind we weren't going to hire anymore.

# Chapter 11
# Objects

Dave stopped me in the hall outside my office. "Just wanted to give you a head's up," he said. His hands were buried in his pants pockets again, his change jingling incessantly. "I've got Chris and Heindel working on a proposal for some changes to the language that will affect you."

"Oh?" I opened the door to my office and walked in.

Dave followed. "Yes, we're looking at adding some language extensions to FoxPro."

I nodded my head slowly and circled around to sit at my desk. It felt more comfortable to have my chest partially concealed by the bulk of my monitor. "What sort of extensions?" I asked.

"Some 'Object-Oriented' extensions."

I nodded my head again. The expression "Object-Oriented" had become the catch phrase of our industry. Every magazine was touting the benefits of some amazing new product with "Object-Orientation" built in. I had no idea what being "Object Oriented" really meant, though.

And from some of the articles I read, I wasn't sure the journalist knew either. *So, how does this affect me?* I wanted to say.

"We're also hoping to remove some of the redundancy in our code," Dave said. "Like in the Dialog Manager and READ, for instance."

That part of the problem I understood. There were portions of our product doing similar things, but making use of widely different sections of code. We had similar code to manage the interactions between controls in our Dialog Manager, and in the command called 'READ.'

Redundancy in code was undesirable for the same reasons two separate engines were undesirable in a car. It made the final product bigger, there were more parts that could fail (and therefore more to test), and there were no guarantees in the long run the two engines (or code) would work in harmony with each other.

I still wasn't sure how the language changes would affect me, though.

Dave, who stood just inside my office, glanced to his right and spotted the poster that hung on the wall there. It was of two bikini-clad women, but I wasn't the one to put it there.

"Eric and Heindel hung that up," I said quickly. "I guess they think it's funny." *Taking a shot at the single guy.*

Dave studied the poster for a moment. "Ah…Skippy, Skippy…," he said softly.

Skippy was the name we used for Eric during his impish moments. His usual trick was putting two fingers behind the heads of the unsuspecting. He branched out with the bikini poster. Heindel helped, of course.

Dave gave a little clucking sound. "Obviously virgins," he said to the poster. He turned to look at me again. "Anyway, you should keep abreast of what those two are doing."

Chris and Heindel. *Right.* "Okay," I said.

Dave sort of bounced his way through the doorway to the hall. "Yes. The Screen Painter will have to support whatever they come up with."

*Ah. Now I see.*

*     *     *

By February the Screen Painter was essentially complete. As Marty had done years earlier on the Mac product, I created a tool allowing users to visually construct an input screen. Functionally it would play the same role as his Mac version. Coupled with a yet-to-be-written "generator" program, it would make building database applications a snap.

In appearance, however, my Screen Painter was quite different from the Mac version. No cutesy palette of pictures ran down the left side nor were there any dotted grid lines to help with the placement of controls. Instead, my design surface was solid blue and it had a utilitarian status bar in the upper left corner that gave the position of the cursor (the spot where controls could be placed). As a part of our DOS product, my Screen Painter had to deal with the inherent restrictions of that character-based environment. It couldn't have as nice an interface, nor allow for the cool graphic elements (like pictures) common to the Mac. It was just as usable, though, and completely my own.

Meanwhile, Chris and Heindel toiled away on a document to describe the new "Object-Oriented FoxPro" (or "OOF"). Their work was important to me because I couldn't really call the Screen Painter finished until it supported whatever new language syntax they created. I **thought** it was done, but it was only with respect to the way FoxPro 1.0 defined interface elements like push buttons, radio buttons, boxes, and the like. Their new OOF document could change all that. I might even have to abandon everything I'd done and start over.

While I waited, though, there was nothing specific for me to do. Dave told me to spend my time mapping out the changes to the Screen Painter that would be necessary for Chris and Heindel's new syntax, but that was a hopeless cause because their syntax was changing by the day. As confident as Chris and Heindel were they'd have something great to show us eventually, even **they** thought it was a waste of time to try to design based on speculation. So, I continued to wait—almost to the point of distraction.

So, I started to tinker with things. I started rolling my own features for the Report Writer and Screen Painter and adding them without discussing them with anyone. I added a "marquee" that let the user select more than one object at a time. I made it easier to increase and decrease portions of the Report Writer's interface (the 'bands'). I added an auto-scroll feature that would scroll the screen if the user dragged an object beyond the boundaries of the screen—something even the Mac Screen Painter didn't do yet. I spent more than a month adding things I thought were useful and no one told me to stop. Everyone was so involved with their own projects, they never noticed. So, I stayed out of sight, and kept adding stuff.

*     *     *

The day finally arrived when Chris and Heindel were ready to unveil their "Object-Oriented FoxPro" document. The bulk of the development team was summoned to Dave's office and given a copy of the text. It was about twenty-five pages long and described in detail how everything in FoxPro (menus, windows, controls, and the like) would be defined and manipulated as an object. After we all gave it a quick read-through, we began to discuss it.

In my mind, the primary weakness with the new syntax was obvious. It was extremely wordy. In the current version of the language, the code to define a single push button took only one line. Like so:

```
@ 0, 0 GET ok FUNCTION '* \!OK'
```

Using the 'Object Oriented' syntax, a push button definition took at least five lines. It went something like this:

```
DEFINE PUSHBUTTON ok;
  FROM 0, 0;
  TO 0, 10;
  PROMPT 'OK'
  DEFAULT;
```

The problem magnified itself if you wanted to create a group of buttons (and buttons were commonly presented in groups). This was a group of two buttons in the current language:

```
@ 0, 0 GET okcancel FUNCTION '* \!OK;\?Cancel'
```

With the 'Object Oriented' syntax, a group of buttons looked like this:

```
DEFINE GROUP okcancel AT 0,0
  DEFINE PUSHBUTTON ok;
        FROM 0, 0;
        TO 0, 10;
        PROMPT 'OK'
        DEFAULT;
  DEFINE PUSHBUTTON cancel;
        FROM 2, 0;
        TO 2, 10;
        PROMPT 'CANCEL'
        ESCAPE;
```

That seemed like a big drawback to me. On the other hand, there was a certain descriptiveness to the OOF syntax that made it nice. It was easy to tell what it was you were defining. In addition, the new syntax for controls was very similar to the way menus were defined in our product already. (Of course, our users frequently complained our menu syntax was too wordy.)

The wordiness issue didn't get much talk at the meeting, though. Instead, someone (usually Dave) got hung up on an apparent trifle and we would discuss it to death. The worst instance, by far, was when we spent the better part of an hour debating whether the syntax for the command to initiate an object-oriented interface should be "Activate" or "Execute." *I should have stayed on the farm.*

Finally, after we frittered away most of the morning, Dave reached a decision. It wasn't about syntax, though.

"While I'm pleased with the work Chris and Heindel have done," he said, sounding sincere, "I think it needs Amy's touch to smooth out the rough edges."

Then the meeting adjourned. The discussion was over.

I followed Chris back to his office, and Heindel came too. Chris was clearly not happy. Whispered expletives escaped his lips.

"What's wrong?" I asked. "You just got out of work."

Chris eyes weren't blinking. He looked at Heindel and flipped his hands up. "I can't believe that."

Heindel took a seat and slid down slightly. "That's fine," he said, sounding ambivalent. "If Dave wants to give it to Amy, that's fine."

At least **he** seemed pleased. I couldn't get anything more from Chris, though. So, with a last look at Heindel, I shrugged and walked next door to Sally's office.

Sally always worked with her back to the door. When she heard me, she turned around and smiled. "That was great!" she said.

I returned the smile, not completely sure why we were smiling. "Well, Chris isn't happy."

"Of course not."

Sally was more of a student of human relations than I. "Why do you say that?" I asked, knowing I was going to gain some insight. She worked with Chris for a number of years before joining Fox and did a good job of being his barometer.

"Chris hates it when someone takes credit for his work," she said. "Hates it."

I nodded my head. Now, I was beginning to see. Though at times Chris might give someone the impression that he worked on something he hadn't, if someone took recognition for **his** work…

"And the fact that it was **Amy**," Sally continued, "makes it all the worse."

That part needed little clarification. If there was a hierarchy to the development staff, it flowed mostly along seniority lines, with Sally and I somewhere in the middle and Chris probably just ahead of us. But Amy held the top spot. As the spouse of the boss she had a place of unrivaled power, and we were all well aware of it. She was the only one who could cool Dave off when he was upset and the only one who could get him heated up over a seemingly trivial matter. Eric's forced adoption of Brian Crites was partly due to her incitement.

And because of her special position, Amy had a share of perks the rest of us didn't have. She took days off whenever she wanted—even when we were close to a product release. She was responsible for less of the product than most of us, and in general, the parts that were hers weren't as 'mission critical' as the rest.

Amy also had a certain aloofness to her personality that didn't help with her cohesion into the rest of the group. She hardly left her office during a normal workday—and when she did—it was rarely to speak with the rest of us.

Even if Amy was more sociable, though, her connection to Dave still complicated things. I liked her as an individual. She was always pleasant to me, and I found her more sympathetic and rational than her spouse. But I still limited my interaction with her for fear of gaining more of Dave's attention. I got an ample portion of **that** already.

Amy's detachment from the rest of development was evident in the work she did. The coding style she used in her areas of responsibility was different from the rest of the product and the way those areas behaved was different as well. It was almost as if she never bothered to see how anything else worked. She just did things the way she wanted to and left it at that.

Now she was in charge of a document that was supposed to change everything. A portion of Chris's concern was valid.

*             *             *

Amy's stint with the OOF document lasted for about two weeks. During that time I was **supposed** to be designing dialogs for the Screen Painter using Chris and Heindel's version of the new syntax. What it amounted to was a couple more weeks of coming up with things to do. The list of creative additions to the Report Writer and Screen Painter continued to grow.

The day finally came when Dave called us to the conference room to discuss Amy's revisions. It was a meeting I was greatly looking forward to. *At last I'll have some direction in my life*, I thought. We all took our seats around the large oval table, each with a copy of the current OOF document clutched tightly in our hands.

Dave glanced around the room. "OK, is everyone here?" he asked.

Heindel, Chris, Amy, Marty, Sally, and myself. Yep, everyone who cared was present.

Dave raised his copy of the OOF document slightly. "I've looked over this document, and let me tell you, I think it's a great bit of work. Once again, many thanks to Chris, Amy, and Heindel for their efforts—you've pulled off a virtuoso stunt." He placed the document on the table slowly. "However…after a little talk with Marty this morning, I made a decision." He paused and gave a nearly straight-line smile. "I decided we aren't going to do it."

My heart leapt in my chest. I looked around the room—all eyes mirrored my surprise. The dragster had turned.

Dave crossed his legs and put a hand on the back of his head, a posture he frequently took. "Marty had a lot of good points, but his best point was this—if it is so hard to spec this object stuff, how are we going to explain it to our customers?" He became more animated. "We spent what?—the better part of two months—trying to come up with this thing and we're still not sure how it is all going to work. I'd hate to be in Tech Support trying to explain it after we've finally figure it out!" He shook his head. "No. We just can't do that," he said. "I appreciate everyone's work, but we just can't do that." Dave frowned. "This product is complicated enough already."

*What a relief.* Somehow, Marty talked Dave out of the whole thing, making my life a lot easier. The Report Writer and Screen Painter were essentially done; all they needed was a little fine-tuning and a little more testing and they were ready to go out the door. *Wahoo!* I thought as the meeting adjourned. *Smooth sailing from here.*

Life at Fox was never that easy, though.

*    *    *

A few months earlier, while Chris and Heindel were still in the early stages of OOF, I started dating one of Fox's receptionists named Denise. When I needed a break from adding one of my "home rolled" features, I frequently called her at her desk.

On one morning, days after the final OOF meeting, I called Denise's desk and another receptionist answered the phone.

"Oh…sorry," I said, not giving my name. Sometimes the receptionists switched desks—I figured this was one of those times. I moved to place the phone back on its cradle.

"Is this Kerry?" the receptionist asked, now a little distance from my ear.

When I affirmed that it was, the girl proceeded to tell me that Denise was fired the day before.

"What?" I asked, feeling my stomach begin to turn. "Why?"

"I don't think it was about you," she said. "She had problems with our boss." There was a short pause. "I'm pretty sure it wasn't about you."

The pain in my stomach grew. Assurances aside, it very well **could** have been about me. Many of the non-development employees at Fox had the same uneasiness around developers as we had around Amy. Sally suspected this was an encouraged behavior, though certainly not by development. It seemed like management was telling the new hires to treat us like royalty.

I gleaned what more I could from the girl on the phone, and then hung up. No sooner did my hand leave the receiver than there was a knock on my office door. I looked up (through the Plexiglas) to see Amy standing just outside.

Amy **never** came to my office. *This is it,* I thought.

As my heart palpitated, Amy walked in and shut the door. "Kerry," she said softly, "I'm just here to tell you that Denise was fired yesterday."

"Oh?" I said, frowning. *I wonder what Carol Garrison is doing now...*

"I also wanted to assure you that it has nothing to do with you," Amy continued. "Denise had some tardiness issues." Amy smiled pleasantly. "Your job is as safe as ever. You're not next on the hanging list."

*Talk about your mixed blessings.* "Okay," I said. "Thanks." I was sure I heard that speech somewhere before, though.

Amy left and I felt my pulse begin to normalize. I tried to call Denise at home a few minutes later. What I heard shortly after Denise's "Hello" was the dial tone again.

I shrugged and turned back to my machine. My dating relationship had hit a snag, but at least I had a job. So much for dating girls from the office.

*      \*      \*      \**

As it turned out—in a separate meeting with Heindel—Dave made a decision that created some additional work for me. It was decided my Screen Painter would no longer create a special file to be used by a template generator (like the CodeGen program used previously in the Mac product) to generate code. Instead—Heindel proposed—the Screen Painter could simply create a database file and the FoxPro language itself would serve as the new "template" language. *Why did we need **two** languages in the product, really?*

It was an idea so straightforward and elegant we were amazed it wasn't thought of before. Everyone loved it, and Heindel and I soon got busy implementing it. My part was to switch my tools from writing out the tab-delimited files required for CodeGen to writing out database files instead.

*No problem*, I reasoned as I began the task. *This is the last change, and then I'm **finally** ready to ship.*

# Chapter 12
# Marketing Effects

In the spring of 1990, Dave conducted an interview in his office. Joining him around the table were some of the more senior members of the team—Amy, Eric, and Chris. The person to be interviewed was another graduate of Bowling Green, a master's student this time.

Her name was Gloria and she exuded competence and intelligence. Dave briefed his fellow interviewers ahead of time that they probably should hire her. The only problem was they weren't quite sure where she fit in. She took some programming courses, but that didn't seem to be her area of expertise or preference. She had some business experience…perhaps sales or technical support?

The interviewers peppered Gloria with questions for well over thirty minutes—and at times, she reciprocated. At last, she found a question that took everyone by surprise.

"So, tell me about your marketing department," she said.

Dave—who sat cross-legged with his coffee cup resting on one knee—glanced at the others, and then exploded into laughter. "Marketing department?!" he bubbled out. "You want to know about our **Marketing** department?" His laughter grew until his coffee finally shook itself from the cup, spilling down his shirt and pants. "Sh**!" Dave exclaimed. "Sh**!"

\*     \*     \*

Prior to May of 1990, the marketing department of Fox Software was virtually non-existent, but that didn't bother management in the slightest. The company sold its software entirely by word-of-mouth and the positive press received from magazine reviews. The prevailing view was our products were good enough to sell themselves—they were selling just fine—so why let marketing screw that up? Since my hiring, our in-house "Marketing Department" consisted of a single person—a thirty-something man named Richard.

Richard was a friend of the LaValley family, and Dave barely masked his dislike of him. There were multiple reasons for Dave's feelings, but Richard's profession as a "marketer" was at least one strike against him. Another strike may have been Richard's relationship with the LaValley family. Over time, I began to notice a strange, often-antagonistic rapport between the two ownership families. Every other week or so, I would see Dave and Mr. LaValley chatting amicably in Dave's office. Then, in lunch conversations, I'd hear Eric or Bill marionette that LaValley was a "bottom-feeder" or warn that "the company would soon be knee-deep in LaValley's" and I'd wonder.

I saw anti-LaValley behavior in Dave too. It was clear he didn't think much of our company payroll clerk (Dick LaValley's daughter). Dave once bounced three rigid juggling balls hard into his floor because she did something to anger him. Her office was located directly below his. It made me wonder how the partnership originally came to be.

Aside from all that, Richard had at least one character flaw of his own that was certain to get him into trouble. Dave had little time for people who didn't speak judiciously, but Richard was inflicted with a terminal case of "hoof in mouth disease." I witnessed the condition first hand.

After lunch one day, I went to the upper floor men's room. The facilities of the room were typical. Aside from a sink and a mirror, there were two stalls and two urinals, a sufficient quantity for the forty-plus men with offices upstairs.

The room had an additional bit of discomfort over most restrooms though. It was originally designed to have just one urinal. At some point, late in construction, the builders ripped out the one urinal and crammed two into the same spot. These remaining urinals were so close together that two people intending to use them would have to stand touching shoulders. It added a new dimension to an already uncomfortable situation. In general, I tried to avoid using the urinals upstairs.

In this instance, I had no need to. I was there to brush my teeth. While I stood at the sink, Heindel and "Marketing" Richard came in. Since both required a urinal, they went through the usual exercise of attending to their business—side by side and shoulder to shoulder.

Heindel finished first and turned to pry himself free. "Sorry Richard," he said. "I hope I didn't mess you up there."

Richard laughed. "No, no, I'm okay," he said. "But if you think **that's** funny, you should've seen the time Dave and Chris were in here. I thought those two would never get unstuck!"

Still brushing, all I could do was grin slightly at the joke. Both Chris and Dave were men of considerable girth. *That must have been tough*, I thought, struggling to keep the toothpaste in my mouth.

Richard and Heindel continued laughing as they washed and left the room.

I emptied my mouth and glanced up into the mirror. I could see the door of the stall behind me, and through the crack I noticed the shadowed edge of someone sitting within. *Who's that?* I wondered. Whoever it was, they hadn't said anything during Richard and Heindel's conversation. I bent forward to wash my hands and glanced back at the crack again. I could just make out the shine of a bald head.

There were scant few balding tops on the Fox staff. Norm Chapman had one, but his head was squat, angular, and slightly colored with age. This head was none of that. It was round and consistently white. It was one I saw nearly ever day of my development life.

*It's Dave Fulton! He's been here the entire time!*

I quickly collected my things and returned to my office, which was directly opposite the restroom on the far side of the building. From there I secretly watched for Dave to leave through my office Plexiglas. When he finally came out, he had a mischievous little grin on his face.

In that instant, I was glad I wasn't Richard. If his candor outside the restroom was the same as it was within, I could see why he (and Marketing) got little respect.

*     *     *

Marketing was a perpetual joke at Fox, but apparently some in management realized that state couldn't continue forever. The push to create an internal marketing team began, and the position of 'Director of In-house Marketing' was created to lead it. The biggest surprise came, though, when we heard who was chosen to fill that position.

"He'll be back," Sally said, shaking her head and smiling. "This is just like him."

"Why's that?" I asked. Dave had just informed us that Chris was going to take the new Director position. Even though I would never imagine it, it seemed like a good move for him.

"The grass is always greener with Chris. He'll be back, trust me."

I shrugged. "We'll see…."

For the first time, we were going to have a marketing department, and Chris was going to leave Development to lead it. I had no idea how any of it would effect the company as a whole, but mostly, I hoped it didn't affect me too much.

*     *     *

Chris's first marketing event—"the Fox Reunion"—occurred in late June. It took place over a long weekend and was an event to which only Fox "gurus" were invited. These "gurus" were a small contingent of people from the dBASE community who were recognized as its most outspoken leaders. During my two years of employment I had heard many of the names before—Tom Rettig, Adam Green, Pat Adams, and so on—but I had only met a few of them. All I knew was it was another chance for Fox to find out what users needed from our product.

It seemed strange to me, at the time, to ask what these people wanted from FoxPro 2.0 eight months after we started working on it. We already made significant additions—many of which derived straight from users' requests. *Shouldn't that be enough?* Theoretically, if we tied up everything we started and fully debugged the new code, we probably could get the product out by the end of the year. We'd then have a shipping product that offered everything dBASE IV did (which the 1.0 version of FoxPro didn't) and could worry about moving ahead from there.

Dave and the Marketing department didn't see it that way, though. As the Fox Reunion commenced, my singular wish was that the features it brought would either be trivial, or things that could be postponed for a later version of the product. I wasn't holding my breath.

The Monday following the Reunion, Dave bounded into work. The gurus requested numerous product additions and he was conspicuously gleeful.

"Ah, my young friend," he said to me as I sat in his office, "you are going to love what I have in store for you." He cackled—an almost sinister sound.

I frowned. The Screen Painter was finished and I had nothing specific left on my plate. I thought I might get a chance to help finish out other parts of the product.

"Read the list, Janet," Dave said, putting his feet up on his desk.

"They want an easy way to create menus."

Dave nodded. "Creating menus is egregiously complicated. Kerry will do that."

Janet glanced at me, and then wrote something down. "They want more control over the way information in groups in the Report Writer spans over page boundaries."

Dave nodded again. "Ah, yes, that's a good one. The Widow-Orphan effect. We need to do something about that. Kerry will take care of that."

*The Widow-Orphan what*? I frowned deeper. *What's that all about?*

Janet looked at Dave again. "They want to have multiple windows interacting in READ. That's probably a Heindel thing, though...."

"Multiple windows in a READ?" Dave put his hands behind his head. "That makes sense, I guess. Yes, I could see why they would want that." He smiled, looked at me, and then looked at Janet seriously. "Kerry will do that too."

*What the...? Was the sole purpose of this event to find work for me?* READ had always been Heindel's thing. I started to panic.

"I don't know anything about READ," I said.

Dave cackled some more. "I know, but Heindel's busy adding generator commands. It would be good for someone else to know what's going on with that READ code."

"Okay..." I said, but I wasn't really.

"That's all," Dave said, waving me away. "Let me know when I can test it."

I returned to my office, feeling ill.

*      *      *

Of these requests, the most burning issues for Dave were the Report Writer changes, so shortly after I recovered from my shock, he called Marty and I back to his office.

Put simply, the gurus' problem was that sometimes they didn't get all the information together on the same printed page as they liked. The problem specifically involved two special purpose bands called "Group" bands. Unlike other bands that printed continually throughout the life of the report (e.g. The "Page Header" printed at the top of each page and the "Page Footer" printed at the bottom) Group bands only printed if the value of a specific condition (specified by the user) changed.

A common grouping condition might be "State". The effect on a report with that condition would be every time the value of the database field "State" changed, the information in the Group Footer would print (closing out the information for the last State), a new Group Header would print (for the new State), and then the Detail information for that State would begin.

Now say a report prints the value of the State field (like "Ohio") in its Group Header and again in its Group Footer. In the Detail section, it just lists the employees that work in that State. What bugged the gurus is sometimes the size of the Detail section spanned out just long enough to push the Group Footer to the next page by itself—leaving it orphaned. Dave called this situation the "Widow-Orphan" effect and the gurus wanted some way to prevent it from happening. They wanted a way to keep the data that printed in the Group Headers and Footers of their report with the detail information it surrounded. It was a problem few report writers handled well, but Dave vowed ours would be the one to "do it right."

Dave, Marty, and I spent some time discussing the problem. Finally, we reached a point where Dave felt the need to offer up suggestions on how we should fix it, not from a designer's standpoint, but from a developer's.

"Well, I'll tell ya what you're gonna do," he said, stretching out the 'well' for a good three seconds. "You allocate some memory…"

Now, that suggestion really wasn't much help because almost **everything** we did involved allocating memory. It was a surprise though, because Dave had no idea how our Report Writers worked internally.

"Let's call it a buffer…," he continued.

I glanced at Marty who was nodding his head attentively. But I sort of knew what he was thinking behind that deer-like stare. *A buffer? Does it really matter what it's called?*

"Well, maybe two buffers…" Dave said, drawing out the 'well' again, "…two **big** buffers.…"

The rest of what he said isn't important. What *is* important is those first few lines became legendary among the developers from then on. If any of us had a question on how to do something, most likely the response would jokingly be, "Well, you allocate some memory…let's call it a buffer.…"

The "Widow-Orphan" problem was solved eventually, but in a way that didn't cause me to allocate a lot of memory (or buffers, for that matter). It marked the start of a long summer, and I had Chris's new marketing department to thank.

*        *        *

When the Report Writer dilemmas were solved, I moved on to the next burning issue on my plate, the menu design tool.

In the FoxPro language there were many ways to define a menu— to put it conservatively. This surplus of commands stemmed from the fact FoxBASE+ (in response to our user's requests) had a way of defining menus before dBASE IV (and its multitude of language additions) came along with another way. Then, after we added the dBASE IV syntax, we found there were problems with what Ashton-Tate did, so we were forced to add still more commands to compensate.

Altogether, it made it unclear what method of defining menus was preferable for what situations, or even which commands were intended to work together. Our users got confused, and rightfully so. To make matters worse, even after one knew precisely what commands and functions to use, there would still be a great amount of typing to do in order to finally get the exact menu system you wanted.

So, to correct all of that, we were going to add a new tool to the product. This tool—later called "the Menu Builder"—would allow our users to create menus with very little effort. It would also relieve them of the burden of knowing what specific commands to use. It had the potential to make their lives a lot better.

The first step in the development process was for me to investigate a little to see what other products did. If there were good ideas out there I could use, I'd use them, and if I saw something terrible, I'd know what to avoid. Like the tools I worked on before, I knew the final adjective to describe our Menu Builder should be "the best." I had to find what was "best."

I went to our company's small library and gathered up every competitive product I could find. I also raided the personal software collections of the other developers. I then started installing products on my machines. With the Report Writer and Screen Painter, I spent little time studying the competition until after the fact, and then only to make sure I didn't leave out anything useful. The Menu Builder was the first time my research was done before coding even started.

What that research showed though, was most products hadn't done anything at all. There were few examples of a 'menu builder' anywhere, especially among DOS products. The only examples I found were on the Macintosh, and they just weren't appropriate for our needs. They used cute interface tricks to bring a menu to life, but in the end the process took more time than creating a menu by hand.

So, the full design burden was on me. I had to come up with something that fit the way our menus worked, minus the tediousness and complexity. It was a tall order, but as I sat down to come up with something, I found I enjoyed the challenge.

The basic syntax for defining a simple menu system in our preferred method of definition went something like this:

```
DEFINE PAD _msm_file OF _MSYSMENU PROMPT "\<File" COLOR
SCHEME 3;
      KEY ALT+F, "";
      MESSAGE "Create, open, save, or quit"
DEFINE PAD _msm_edit OF _MSYSMENU PROMPT "\<Edit" COLOR
SCHEME 3;
      KEY ALT+E, "";
      MESSAGE "Edit text"

ON PAD _msm_file OF _MSYSMENU ACTIVATE POPUP _mfile
ON PAD _msm_edit OF _MSYSMENU ACTIVATE POPUP _medit
```

```
DEFINE POPUP _mfile MARGIN RELATIVE SHADOW COLOR SCHEME 4
DEFINE BAR _mfi_new OF _mfile PROMPT "\<New...";
       MESSAGE "Create a new file"
DEFINE BAR _mfi_open OF _mfile PROMPT "\<Open...";
       MESSAGE "Open an existing file"
DEFINE BAR _mfi_close OF _mfile PROMPT "\<Close";
       MESSAGE "Close the frontmost file"
DEFINE BAR _mfi_quit OF _mfile PROMPT "E\<xit";
       MESSAGE "Exit"

DEFINE POPUP _medit MARGIN RELATIVE SHADOW COLOR SCHEME 4
DEFINE BAR _med_cut OF _medit PROMPT "Cu\<t";
       KEY CTRL+X, "Ctrl+X" ;
       MESSAGE "Put selection on the clipboard and remove
it"
DEFINE BAR _med_copy OF _medit PROMPT "\<Copy";
       KEY CTRL+C, "Ctrl+C" ;
       MESSAGE "Copy selection to the clipboard"
DEFINE BAR _med_paste OF _medit PROMPT "\<Paste";
       KEY CTRL+V, "Ctrl+V" ;
       MESSAGE "Paste clipboard contents at the insertion
point"
```

*(Code generated using FoxPro's Menu Builder for illustration purposes.)*

This snippet of code would create a menu bar (the words across the top of the screen) that said "File" and "Edit." The "File" item would open (drop-down) a menu with the items "New," "Open," "Close," and "Exit." The "Edit" item would open a menu with the words "Cut," "Copy," and "Paste" on it. Each item had messages that would display along the bottom of the screen when it was selected, and some of them had special key combinations (like CTRL+X for the "Cut" item) to use in addition to using a mouse.

This syntax was straightforward in many respects, because each item in the menu system was defined one at a time. The syntax for defining the top level, the "menu bar" level, was a little different than the subordinate popup menus, but there were many similarities. Ultimately, the similarity that stuck out most to me was the tree-like structure of the menu system. A menu bar could have 1 to N menus attached to it, every menu could have 1 to N items attached to it, and those items could, in turn, attach to another menu, which itself could have items attached to it, ad nausea. Inherently it was like a tree, with the menu bar representing the first level of branches, the next set (top level) of menus representing shoots off those branches, and so on.

The other thing that struck me was the many properties of these items that had to be defined—names, numbers, prompts, etc—all that required a lot of text to be typed in by the user. This would be the case no matter what interface for the Menu Builder I eventually created. To me, it screamed out for some sort of list-like interface.

And from there the Menu Builder sort of created itself.

What I ended up with on my whiteboard was a window with a list in it that represented one branch of the menu system at a time. Also on that window was a control that gave the user an idea of where in the menu system he was currently. If he was working on _mfile popup for instance, "_mfile" appeared in that control and the information for the individual items of the _mfile popup appeared in the list.

I discussed this design with Dave a little, and since he had no major objections, I started coding it. The Menu Builder went from whiteboard to keyboard in only a few days, and from there to nearly functional in less than two weeks.

*       *       *

Aside from marketing, there was still one other team that, until mid-1990, was noticeably absent from our roster. Unbelievably, through the entire cycle of shipping FoxPro 1.0 and another Mac product, we had no in-house testing department. Regular employees and outside beta-testers continued to be our only testing source.

So, to correct that deficiency, Dave hired a former programmer from SCO (the company that provided our UNIX version of FoxBASE) to raise up a new testing department for us.

The programmer's name was Jim Simpkins and he was highly respected by all who knew him. In appearance he was around six feet tall, thin, and looked in his mid-twenties, although he was actually well into his thirties. His youthfulness carried over into his demeanor as well. Although usually sedate, he had a cocky confidence about him that was atypical for our group.

I liked Jim from the start—and that was a good thing, because I soon needed his help.

# Chapter 13
# Acting

Dave pushed the keyboard of his DOS machine forward so hard it slid into his coffee cup, disturbing the fluid within. "You're just asking me the same questions over and over," he said, his eyes wide.

I searched the faces of the others in the room…Marty, Jim, and Brian. They all looked as stunned as I was.

There had been a number of issues with the Menu Builder lately. Mostly with the code it generated. I thought our questions were legitimate, though.

"You're trying to make things difficult," Dave said, wagging a finger in the air. "But I won't put up with it. You four just go on…get out of here. Figure it out yourself!"

I moved to hide in front of the others as we made our way to the door.

*       *       *

The next day, there was a quick knock and my office door opened.

"Can I ask you a question?" the curly-haired young woman said. Though a relatively recent Polish immigrant, her voice had only the hint of an accent.

"Sure, Jadzia," I said with a smile. "What's up?"

Jadzia was one of the testers Jim Simpkins hired. During the course of the summer she was drafted to write much of the template code for the product. Similar to the templates I wrote years earlier on the Mac, her templates would take the information stored by our design tools and produce dBASE code. In August—while I was still finishing the Menu Builder—she was busy with its template. Jadzia was the nicest person I ever met who knew how to assemble a machine gun.

"Yes," she began politely, "I still can't get the Edit items in my menu to work right."

I frowned. By "Edit items" she meant the Cut, Copy, and Paste items in a menu she was trying to create using the Menu Builder and her template. Thus far, Jadzia had been very thorough in testing her template. So thorough, in fact, she turned up a half-dozen holes in our menu creation process. They weren't bugs in the design of the Menu

Builder, per se; they were problems with what happens after a user
designs a menu using the Menu Builder. How do we go from the
information in the design tool, to actual generated code? In addition,
when the code is generated, will that code actually work?

In Jadzia's latest scenario she was trying to create a duplicate of
FoxPro's Edit Menu. In FoxPro itself, when you select some text in an
editable area of any window, the "Cut" and "Copy" items are enabled.
After a user performed one of those two operations, "Paste" is enabled.
Jadzia wanted the same thing to happen in hers. It was a reasonable
request. Our users might want to do that.

Originally, this didn't happen, but I thought we had it fixed.
Recently, Brian Tallman added a new feature "System Menu Names"
to address it. This feature meant that every item in our menu system
had a name and our users could reference each item by that name. They
could even give their own menu items those names and have the
enabling and disabling done for them automatically. Jadzia should be
able to get her menus working fine now.

Even if she couldn't, though, it probably wasn't an issue with the
Menu Builder. It was probably a problem in our Menu Manager, with
the way the System Menu Names were implemented internally. *Still,
just to be sure...* "Show me," I said.

I followed Jadzia from my office and turned right. All of the
testers sat in a bank of cubicles just behind Dave's secretary and
across from the senior developers. Jadzia's spot was outside of
Tallman's office.

When we reached Jadzia's cubicle, she took a seat and ran the
program to create her menu. Her menu was defined so it would be
appended to the end of our System menu bar. She did this so she could
compare what her Edit menu did with what our Edit menu did. So,
while her program was running, it actually looked like FoxPro had two
Edit menus. It was kind of weird, but our users had a penchant for
doing weird things. It was a good test.

I saw her menu appear and it looked like it was working fine. She
took the steps necessary to end her program.

"Looks like it works to me," I said.

"Ah-ha!" she said, sounding like a detective who made an
important discovery. "But look at this!" She pulled down FoxPro's
own Edit menu.

Something about it seemed strange.

"No Cut, Copy or Paste items!" Jadzia said.

She was right. When her menu went away, it apparently took items
from our Edit menu with it. "Where'd they go?"

"I don't know!"

Dave was the one who came up with the "System Menu Names" to solve Jadzia's original problem. I didn't really like that solution though. It seemed like it opened up a lot of new functionality just to solve one little problem. That commonly happened at Fox.

There was only one person to talk to when it came to menu matters, though. I looked at Jadzia and tossed my head to one side. "Let's go talk to Brian."

*        *        *

By this time, Brian Tallman was master of everything window or menu related. Since the early days of FoxPro, he worked tirelessly on these two crucial, complicated, and often thankless areas. If there was an award given for "heart of a servant," Brian would be my choice.

His door was nearly always open. "Brian!" I said as we entered his office. "Jadzia has a problem."

Brian turned toward us and smiled softly. "OK," he said calmly. He reached out to grab his pants at the knees and straighten them slightly. "What is it?"

Alternately providing information, Jadzia and I described the offending scenario and what she was trying to accomplish. Through all of it, Brian sat with his arms crossed and nodded his head attentively.

"Yeah," he said finally. "That doesn't surprise me."

"Why not?" I said. "Those System Menu Names don't access our real menu items, do they?"

Brian gave a quick nod. "Sure do."

"What?" Now it looked like my original concern was well founded. It appeared that in trying to allow one small bit of functionality, we gave our users complete access to our menus. It was the kind of situation the more conservative of us called, "helping them shoot themselves in the foot."

"Is that what Dave wanted?" I asked.

Brian shrugged. "Don't know," he said. "It's the way it has to be, though." He chuckled. Brian had a boyish, full-of-joy laugh. The sound of it almost didn't seem right coming from a man whose house was nearly burnt down once.

"We could do something different," he said, "but…," he uncrossed his arms and turned his hands face up.

"What?" I asked.

He smiled. "You'll have to talk to Dave first."

I frowned and glanced at Jadzia. That wasn't the answer I wanted to hear. The last couple weeks had been an endless stream of Menu Builder complications. Only the day before Jim, Marty, and I so inundated Dave with questions that he got frustrated with us and sent us away. *If we bothered him again....*

"Oh, no," Jadzia said, giving voice to my fears.

Brian chuckled again.

I brought a hand to my chin, and then looked at Jadzia. "Why don't we talk to Jim first?"

\*      \*      \*

During his short time of employment, Jim Simpkins built a distinct rapport with Dave; one that none of the rest of us even approached. My suspicion was it had something to do with Jim's former employment at SCO, but even that reason didn't fit completely. Dave hired Chris and Sally originally because he decided to dump SCO, after all.

Perhaps it was just something about Jim's demeanor. SCO stood for Santa Cruz Organization and a lot of California came with Jim to Fox. Brash and confident, he wouldn't take flak from anyone—Dave included. Jim routinely told Dave to go off and do unmentionable things to himself and Dave would just laugh raucously. Dave not only tolerated Jim's behavior, he seemed to admire it.

And, as the head of the testing department, Jim was officially Jadzia's boss. I figured we needed him.

Jim's office was one of the exterior offices at the south end of the building, so Jadzia and I made our way there. When we arrived, we found Jim seated at his computer with his legs crossed in front of him like a yogi. The posture had nothing do with any religious dedication though. It was just Jim, being consistent in his Fox atypical-ness. His dress was atypical too. He wore a loose-fitting button-down shirt and pants a couple shades lighter than the shock of brown hair that lived on his head.

I asked Jim if he had a minute and he said "Sure." Noticing the concern on our faces, he laughed. "What's up?"

"Well, you know how Dave has been lately." I went on to explain Jadzia's problem. "I'm afraid Dave's idea about System Menu Names might not be a good one," I said, finishing the explanation. "In fact, we may need to talk him out of it completely. But considering what happened last time..."

Jim nodded his head slowly. "Yeah, he was pretty extreme."

*No kidding.* "So, what do we do?"

"Well, here's a thought," he said, uncurling his legs.

I held up a hand. "Wait, whatever it is—will you go with us to see Dave?"

Jim gave a short exhaling laugh. "Sure."

I nodded once. "OK. What's your thought?"

"What if we scripted out exactly what each of us will say when we're in with Dave." He put out his hands to mimic the movement of scales. "We'll try to weigh out ahead of time what Dave's response will be. Try to come up with the best way to avoid an explosion...like a play...or an opera."

I hesitated. *Last I checked most operas end in tragedy.* I glanced at Jadzia again. She didn't look convinced either. Still, we needed to do something. "It's worth a shot," I said, frowning.

\*       \*       \*

Trying to plan for a meeting with Dave seemed like a lesson in futility. Over the course of the year I'd traveled to his office dozens of times and witnessed some of the strangest behavior. It was literally all over the map.

When Dave was in a gentle mood, he had a number of mannerisms he performed while thinking I found distracting. Sometimes he removed his wedding band and twirled it slowly on his head. Other times he would hold a coffee cup or soda can on his head while tapping on the top with his free hand. Or, he might take his earlobes between his forefingers and thumbs and twist them repeatedly. In more reflective moments, he might simply stroke the back of his head with his hand or hold his head in his hands, right hand at the chin and left hand at the top.

There was also usually some food consumption going on. Dave's great loves were popcorn, coffee, Sen-Sens, and diet Vernors. Throughout the day, he could be found eating or spilling any one of them. His office floor was a graveyard of missed attempts at getting food into his mouth.

Other meetings were more combative in nature, though. Dave was very opinionated about the product and forceful with those opinions. If he didn't like something, he told you—and more often than not—he told you straight to your face and at high decibels.

As part of this, Dave had a library of catch phrases he loved to use. A statement that he didn't agree with might bring a "No, No, NO, NO, NO" with each "No" accompanied by a rap on his desk—the last "No" bringing the loudest rap of all. A bug he found could illicit a "You know what the problem is...I'll tell you what the problem is...," or it might just bring an order to "Heal it—quickly!" with a wave to get you on your way. Sometimes this statement was followed by "Today would be a good day. Now would be a good time." Or, if one of us didn't understand Dave's meaning we might hear "Do you want me to say it again...in Chinese?"

Personally, I found this later type of get-together difficult. Programming for me was almost an art form and harsh criticism was hard to take. It was like someone pushing over my sandcastle. Dave's style wasn't the sort of thing they tell you about in programming classes.

In this case, it was even worse, though. We needed a meeting and Dave didn't want one. I hoped Jim was a good acting coach.

\* \* \*

"I think you should start us off, Jim," I said.

Jim brought a leg close to his chest and wrapped his arms around it. "Alright, I'll go first," he said. "What if I say something like 'Dave...um, we have some questions about the Menu Builder....'"

"That's how we got in trouble the last time."

Jim's head moved up and down. "Right, right...OK, I'll say some issues have come up that we'd like to discuss."

"That's a little better," I said. "Now what?"

Jim looked at Jadzia. "Well, then I think Jadzia should talk. You know, use the feminine angle some..." Jim chuckled a little, and then got serious again. "No, I mean, Jadzia, just be factual. Tell him what you're trying to do."

"Just the facts," I said.

Jim glanced at me, smiled. "That's right, the facts. Then, Kerry, I think you should tell him why the problem exists. That it's because these menu names are tied to the actual items, and according to Brian that's the way it has to be. I wouldn't elaborate too much more than that. If Dave wants to pull the feature or whatever, we'll make that his decision. We'll try to lay it all out there. See what happens."

"OK," I said. "What if...."

The scripting and rehearsing lasted for close to half an hour. Finally, we thought we might have something that would work.

\* \* \*

One aspect of life at Fox I came to appreciate was the fact that there were rarely any scheduled meetings. When one of us needed some of Dave's time we simply walked to his office and talked to him. Anything other than a discussion-in-progress with another developer would be put on hold to answer our question.

On this occasion, the three of us arrived to find Dave alone. His desk faced the door, but his feet were up and he was absorbed in studying the screen at the right end of his desk. When he turned to look at us, he didn't appear pleased.

*Oh man*, I thought. *This was a bad idea.*

As we closed in on the chairs in front of Dave's desk, he just grunted.

*A really bad idea.*

"Dave…um…some issues have come up with the Menu Builder we'd like to discuss," Jim began.

Part of me was trying to remember who spoke next, the other part was amazed at how preposterous this all was.

Jadzia described the problem, how we discovered it, and Dave gave the predicted response—cautious acknowledgement.

"It's because the menu names are tied to the real items," I said. "I talked to Brian…" I continued with my lines.

In our earlier rehearsal, Jim thought it important we have a couple solutions to present. When I finished speaking, Jim listed these off. "So, Dave, now we're wondering what you think. We really need your decision to know how to proceed."

Dave sat quietly for a few moments, staring over our shoulders. I was a little nervous. *He's going to get mad again. I've seen that look before and I know.*

"Ah…" Dave said. More silence. Still not looking good.

We waited a few tense moments longer.

"Yes, yes," Dave said finally. "I can see the problem now."

*I can't believe it*, I thought. *I can't believe this actually worked.*

From there we discussed possible ways out and eventually ended up dragging Brian into the mix. In the end, the greatest part of the work was in Brian's code; many of the huge problems with the Menu Builder had the same result. The solution, in this case, was to add a new command to the language. A command that let our users restore the entire menu system to its original state, no matter how they screwed it up.

I returned to my office relieved. I guess everyone gets a chance to be an actor sometime.

# Chapter 14
# Wombats and Eggs

A few weeks later, the Menu Builder was finished, but then I had a new problem.

I entered Heindel's office, and after the usual "Hey Heindel-man" greeting, I got to the heart of the matter. "Dave wants me to add multiple windows to READ," I said. "I was hoping you could give me some advice." Heindel had his desk positioned so he faced the door. I walked left to stand near the end, next to his black guest chair.

Heindel's face tracked me as I moved. At the word "READ" his cordial expression suddenly turned sober. "Be very careful," he said. "And don't break anything."

I shook my head. "Thanks," I said flatly. At times, Heindel had the wit of a first-grader.

Heindel turned back to study his computer screen. "Don't mention it," he said. He then squinted at the screen as if the conversation was over.

There was a stuffed Cleveland Browns football placed prominently on Heindel's desk. I contemplated whether whacking another employee aside the head with it would be against company policy. *Probably not.*

Heindel turned back to look at me and chuckled. "I'll give you a walk through of the code for READ, but I warn you, it ain't pretty. And be prepared—every time I touch that code, I break something."

"Really?" I asked, easing myself into the guest chair. *Why can't it ever be easy?* The chair caught on the carpet. I fought to bring it closer to Heindel's desk.

"Really." Heindel cupped a hand and jerked it forward in the air as he talked; one jerk for each point. "Try as you might, no matter what, if you change anything, somewhere, somehow, someone's dBASE program won't work right anymore."

Not what I wanted to hear. "Well...I don't know if I want to...."

He tried to reassure me. "You're the creator of the Screen Painter, you can do it. Just be prepared to test. **A lot.**"

*Great. What have I been thrown into now...?*

\*          \*          \*

Though only a single command, READ was one of the most intricate
and convoluted commands in our product. The purpose of READ was
to animate an interface. A user, when creating an application's
interface, typically defined different elements of it using a list of
@SAY/GET commands. At the end of the list, they would issue a
single READ command to make the whole thing live. A simple
interface program written in the dBASE language might look like this:

```
USE dvds
@3, 13 SAY 'Title:' GET dvds.title COLOR gr+b, r/w
@4,13 SAY 'Description:' GET dvds.description COLOR gr+b,
r/w
READ
```

This program makes use of a database (dvds) created to hold an
inventory of the DVDs I own. When run in FoxPro, it would present a
blank screen with the string "Title:" on one line and next to it a
rectangle of text that displays the actual title of one of the DVDs in my
collection. The string "Title:" is the SAY portion of the command in
action and the title presented is the GET portion. The user of the
program could change the value presented in the GET portion. Directly
beneath the "Title:" line would be a similar line for "Description:" and
a corresponding changeable (GET) rectangle of text next to it.

That is an example of the interaction READ allowed. It also
allowed for more complex interface elements, like push buttons, radio
buttons, and checkboxes—the sort of things anyone who uses a
computer interacts with regularly.

My initial naive assumption was the code to implement the READ
command would be relatively straightforward. All it had to do was
handle the interaction of a few interface elements. We had code in our
Control and Dialog Managers doing similar things and it was all
accessible to me. Easy to read, easy to understand…it didn't take much
studying of the code to comprehend—at least in part—what was going
on. I could even make a change if necessary. I couldn't imagine READ
being that different. How bad could it be, really?

Heindel's initial walkthrough hinted at an answer and a short while
later—when I was sitting in my office with the code for READ printed
out—I knew for sure.

The answer was "really bad."

In my courses at college my instructors drilled into my head the
proper steps to follow in writing—what they called—"structured
code." At the time, some of the rules they gave me seemed a little
overzealous. A few of the important ones went like this:

1. A single subroutine (a small self-contained portion of code) should essentially have one purpose. This is the programmer's version of "A place for everything and everything in its place." Create a routine to do one thing, and use it for just that one thing. If you need it to do something slightly different, write another routine.

2. Every routine should have only one entry point and one exit point. This means as the computer makes its step-by-step way through the code it should have only one place to begin a routine and only one way to finish it. Just like reading a book...you start at the beginning and end at the end. No shortcuts. (Especially with this book!)

3. If you find yourself writing the same lines of code in a subroutine more than once, you should create another routine that consists of those lines of code and call it from the original routine. This is essentially like speed dial on your phone. If you dial a number regularly, you should probably put it on speed dial.

4. Document your code. This means put comments around any code you wrote to tell the next person what you were doing. Anyone who has put together a child's toy knows this one. The better the instructions, the easier it is to understand. For programmers, comments are the roadmap of another person's mind.

Unfortunately, the only thing READ had in common with this list of rules was it didn't follow any of them.

At an earlier time, Heindel gave me a way to maximize the amount of C code I could get printed on a single sheet of paper—using a very small font, it put out around seventy five lines of code per sheet. Even printed that way, READ spanned nearly twenty pages of text. And the code itself read like a horror novel.

It contained one huge decision structure (called a 'case' statement in C lingo) with multiple entry and exit points and several looping structures (constructs that tell the computer to do a section of code repeatedly) that spanned all twenty pages. Nearly everyone who was hired before me touched it (indicated by their initials near individual lines of code—with no additional comments), but none of them would ever claim responsibility.

The READ code was what my friend Rusty would call a "can of wombats." Now I was going to be right in the middle of it.

*          *          *

In the first version of FoxPro, a user could only define their interface
(@SAY/GET) elements in a single window. This behavior emulated
what FoxBASE+ and dBASE IV did, so there was no immediate
pressure for us to change it.

Neither of those products were really windowing environments,
though. dBASE IV allowed for the definition of windows, but the
primary interface of that product was still very much like its
predecessors. Each tool—their editor, their BROWSE command, their
Report Writer—were confined to a single screen and didn't interact
much with the rest of their product.

FoxPro wasn't like that. Our windows were sizable, they moved,
and they overlapped each other. Our tools lived inside windows of their
own. Having a READ command that didn't allow our users to provide
**their** users with a similar experience just didn't seem right. My mission
was to give them that ability.

Of course, feeling confident of my coding skills, I thought I could
clean up the READ code a little before I added the changes to make it
support multiple windows. In my first glimpse of the main READ
routine, I saw dozens of places where the exact same lines of code
were written. If I could break those places out into separate routines,
I'd not only get my feet wet in the ocean of code that made up READ,
but I'd help the code itself. Shrink it. Make it a little more structured.If
that worked out, I could press on to make it obey some of the other
rules of structural programming. When finished, READ would be a
concise, well documented—purely structural—routine. From there it
would be easy to plug in my multi-window changes.

So, that's what I did. I created a few new routines to replace the
duplicate code and made the appropriate changes in the READ code to
call them. I built a new version of the product and did some testing.

READ worked fine. I was confident it would, though. The changes
I made were about as innocuous a change as could be made. Usually, if
your product will build with them in, they work. After a little more
testing, I checked in the first round of my new and improved READ.

*          *          *

The next day Janet was at my door. "I'm seeing something weird," she
said. "Come take a look at this."

I followed her to her office. On her computer's screen was a
relatively simple READ in action. It had a couple of database

fields displaying their data in GET rectangles, some text, and a couple push buttons.

"Now watch this…" she said. She proceeded to hit the tab key a number of times. As she did this, the color of one GET at a time would change to show it was the currently selected one. When she reached a particular GET, instead of the entire rectangle changing color, a cursor appeared within.

"Yeah?" I said.

Janet looked at me. "Well, yesterday that GET would be completely selected. Today it is just showing a cursor. Heindel said you were working on READ now so…"

I hooked my fingers on my belt loops and looked out Janet's window. She was located in the back of the building. Beyond a small stretch of asphalt, she could actually see trees and houses. I looked back at the screen again. "And it didn't do this before?"

Janet shook her head. "Do you want the code to reproduce it with?"

*Not really.* "OK…."

I took a disk with me back to my office. After putting Janet's files on my machine, I brought up my version of FoxPro and ran her program. I saw the same behavior I saw in Janet's office.

I next took the steps necessary to "back out" temporarily the changes I made the day before, built a new product, and tried Janet's program again. Just like she said, it worked differently.

"Well for all the—" I shook my head. "How?"

I spent the better part of an hour figuring out "How."

Every GET element in a READ may have a number of "clauses" associated with it. In our manuals the description of the syntax for the form of GET Janet was using (and there were many others) went like this:

```
@ <row, column>
GET <memvar> | <field>
[FUNCTION <expC1>]
[PICTURE <expC2>]
[DEFAULT <expr1>]
[ENABLE | DISABLE]
[MESSAGE <expC5>]
[RANGE [<expr2>] [, <expr3>]]
[VALID <expL1> | <expn4> [ERROR <expC6>]]
[WHEN <expL2>]
```

Every line after the GET <memvar> line was what we considered a "clause" and every one of them in some way could affect the behavior of a particular GET, if they were included. With my changes I inadvertently altered the behavior of one of those clauses. Once the problem was known, though, the fix was relatively straightforward. One of my new subroutines needed to act slightly different when it was called from one place in READ than it did in all the other places it was called. It wasn't a big enough difference to elicit an entirely new routine, so I pulled another tool from the coder's toolbox. I made it so I could send a flag (a simple 'YES' or 'NO' value) into the routine. A 'YES' meant it was called from the place that needed to act differently, a 'NO' from all the others. I made that change to the READ code, tested it, and checked it in.

Later that same day, the writer named "Dave" (Venske) arrived at my office door. In his late thirties, he had full, slicked-back head of hair, and an easy smile.

"Janet says you're in charge of READ now," he said. "I have something that's acting weird for me today."

"Do you have the code?"

He handed me a disk and gave me a short explanation of the problem.

"Let's give it a shot," I said as I copied his dBASE code to my machine. "Maybe I've fixed it already." *Hopefully the changes I made this morning for Janet....* I ran his code and GETs filled my screen.

He chuckled. "Nope. Still there." He pointed a finger, indicating the problem.

I looked heavenward, frowning. "OK...I'll take a look at it."

An hour later, I figured out his problem. A different clause and a different side effect of the same trivial changes. I made another—more complicated—fix.

The next day, another person appeared at my office door. "I heard you're in charge of READ...."

"Yeah...?"

After about a week of similar occurrences, I finally had my initial changes to READ working. I also came to realize the code for READ was not just a "can of wombats," it was what the senior members of the team called "a tower of eggs." You can construct the tower once, but after it is up, it's best looked at, and never touched again.

I also decided not to press ahead with any more READ renovations. I'd just make the multi-window additions Dave wanted and get out. The odds that I could make those changes without breaking something were already incredibly slim—why push my luck?

*       *       *

I managed to finish the multi-window READ changes by the end of September, but by then, Dave had another list of enhancements he wanted added to READ. Those changes came with another level of complication.

"Look at this!" Dave said after he hauled me into his office. He brought up the Screen Painter and started pointing at his screen. "I can't seem to find the places in the Screen Painter where I can set a control's DISABLE attribute. Where are they?"

The answer to that question was easy. "They're not there yet," I said.

The corners of Dave's mouth turned down. "Why not?!"

My heart started to pound. For the last few weeks I not only had to add features to READ, I had to add a corresponding means for accessing those features to the Screen Painter as well. This round-robin approach was in direct opposition to the way I liked to work. I liked to code one part of a feature at a time and test it until I was confident it worked. Consequently, I liked to be responsible for one under-development portion of the product at a time and work on that until it was finished. Working on two large and complicated portions of the product, both undergoing frequent changes, with some interdependencies between them, but no code really being shared, was a lot to keep my arms around.

"Well…" I said. "I haven't had time, Dave. I've been working on adding it to READ first." I glanced at a set of juggling balls Dave kept within arms reach of his keyboard. Many in the development staff took up juggling as a hobby—Dave especially. I didn't know how to juggle and frankly, I didn't care to. One ball in the air alone was enough for me.

Dave studied me quietly for a few moments. Then, out of the corner of my eye, I saw Heindel pass by Dave's door.

"Oh, David!" Dave said to Heindel.

Heindel, who had just made the turn toward developers' row, quickly turned around and walked back to Dave's door. "Yeah, Dave?"

"How's your stuff coming?" Dave asked.

"Pretty well," Heindel said, shrugging. "Should be done soon."

"Good…good…" Dave said, drumming his fingers on his desk. "There are some READ changes that need made."

Heindel glanced at me. "Oh?" He thought he'd left READ behind.

"It **is** your bailiwick. Kerry has Screen Painter changes to make."

I remained silent and expressionless, but inside my emotions were mixed. Part of me felt like I failed for not being able to handle both areas concurrently, but the other part of me—the larger part—was feeling really good.

"OK," Heindel said hesitantly. "I'll work on READ...."

Dave waved us away and I followed Heindel back to his office.

"Dave wants me working on READ," Heindel said, mostly to himself.

"Sorry," I said. And I was. I hated others having to pick up my mess.

Heindel acquiesced, flipped up a hand. "Dave wants me working on READ. Fine...fine...."

Heindel was a proficient juggler. For that, I was grateful.

*     *     *

The following weekend I took our family friend, Marlene, in to see where I worked for the very first time. Few people were around that day, but in the middle of the tour, Dave strolled out of his office holding a bag of popcorn.

"Hey Dave," I said. "This is a friend of mine—Marlene."

Marlene smiled. "Yes, I sort of motivated Kerry into the computer field...into programming."

"Oh really?" Dave said as he stuck out his empty hand to clasp Marlene's. He bounced a little and cackled loudly. "Maybe I should hire you—to motivate him now!"

# Chapter 15
# Devotion

The first week of October found everyone scrambling around like mindless ants. Ironically, this flurry of activity—though predictable—went entirely against everything we were promised.

Weeks before, Dave called us to the upstairs conference room. "As you are all undoubtedly aware," he said, "the second Developer's Conference is fast approaching...."

Bill, who sat near the table with his elbows on it, covered his eyes and groaned. Eric snickered and most of the rest of us just smiled knowingly.

"Yes, yes, I share that sentiment whole-heartedly," Dave said, his face serious. He brought a hand up to scratch the back of his head. "Because of our experience last year, this year we decided to take steps to insure that our lives will be considerably easier."

*Now there's a switch,* I thought. Though DevCon the year before had its share of rewarding moments, the push to get a "final release" product done in time to hand out was borderline chaotic. Part of me suspected Dave loved that kind of chaos, though.

Eric was across the table from me. He sat with his legs crossed and his face partly buried in his hand. He nodded his head slowly as Dave spoke. It gave me the feeling Eric and Bill were involved in whatever it was we were about to hear.

"Two things will be different," Dave continued. "First, we will not give out product this year. This version of FoxPro is still a good six months away from shipping, with many features yet to be completed." Dave reached out to take his metallic "no-spill" coffee cup from the table and rest it on his knee. "I see no reason to risk our sanity by handing out a half-finished product. Undoubtedly, some of the attendees will be disappointed," Dave said, forcing a little smile, "but they will learn to live with it."

Dave moved closer to the table and rested his arms on it. "In addition," he said, "at some point, probably a week or so before the start of DevCon, we will freeze the product. This means after some predetermined time, no one will be allowed to check in any change that could interfere with my demo at the opening ceremony. Any development work completed after that point will just stay on your personal machines until the conference is over."

Dave panned the room. "It will be a stress-free, pain-free event this year," he said, his voice sounding sincere. "Any questions?"

There were a few moments of silence before Eric stuck up a hand. "Well, I have a question," he said. "Won't the code freeze interfere with your preparations for the demo?"

There was some murmured agreement from around the table. It was hard to imagine Dave restraining himself if he found a problem.

"Now look," Dave said, "a good presenter can demo a non-functioning product and make it seem wonderful. And, our product is more than functional." He wrapped a hand around his chin. "It will be just like I said—stress-free and pain-free."

\*       \*       \*

Immediately following the meeting, I stopped at Sally's office. She sat a little hunched over in her chair, with a leg crossed beneath her. She smiled as I entered.

"What'd ya think of that?" I asked, returning her smile.

She shook her head. "It'll never happen."

I shrugged. "Seemed like he meant it." I was trying to remain hopeful.

"Yeah, but you know how it'll be. The code will be frozen until Dave needs something *for the demo,* and then…"

Our frozen code would be liquid again. I was well aware of how it would work.

Sally brought a pen near her mouth. Many of her pens bore the evidence of nervous chewing. "Besides," she said, frowning. "The demo means Dave will be playing with the product."

An activity **known** to be dangerous—Dave's prolonged use of the product could lead to almost anything at anytime. I also knew more of my "children" would be in the spotlight this year than the year before. Not only would Dave be showing the Screen Painter, but he'd show off the enhancements to the Report Writer, the new Menu Builder, and the multi-window READ changes as well.

"We're doomed!" I said, quoting a line from Star Wars.

Sally laughed.

I smiled, and with a sigh, rolled around the corner to my office. "We'll see…."

\*       \*       \*

As planned, the code freeze happened the Monday before DevCon, and—as predicted—the freeze lasted about a day. Dave discovered some SQL issues needed to be addressed and since SQL was a crucial part of his demo....

I made it until Wednesday before I felt the trickle of the 'code thaw' run down my neck. That day I made two separate trips to his corner office. Both resulted in code changes that **had to** be in the product.

The first time was because Dave didn't like the way multi-window READ behaved. That was a minor issue and the changes to make it work the way he wanted were straightforward. I was able to get them in within an hour of leaving his office.

I wasn't so lucky the second time. That trip was for one of Dave's perennial hot topics—colors. In this case, there were some minor inconsistencies between the way the colors of certain controls were defined in the Screen Painter versus the way they were defined in READ. These differences were present for months and went unnoticed—but now they had to be fixed for the show. Heindel and I would have to make some significant code changes, and make them perfectly (for fear of breaking the demo).

After the scope of the changes were laid out, I returned to my office and contemplated what to do next. It was nearly three o'clock in the afternoon. At four-thirty I had an appointment with an allergist (I decided to confront **that** problem head on) so I would have to leave a little early. Following that, the rest of my evening was completely planned out. None of it included time spent at the office.

I briefly lamented the fact it was impossible to plan anything outside of work. Deadlines and ship dates were ever changing. One's workload might be multiplied tenfold in the course of a day, an hour or—in this case—a few minutes. A feature supposed to be put off until later might all of a sudden be given "show-stopper" status. My workplace was tense and volatile—difficult to schedule around.

Now I had these color changes to deal with. By conservative estimates, my portion of the changes was about two days of work. I had to change a handful of dialogs, tweak the code that drew the controls on the Screen Painter's design surface, and make sure the enhanced color information was saved to and read from the screen file correctly. It was a nice-sized little project.

The code for the Screen Painter, though, was like an old friend now; most times the work didn't take me as long as I initially thought and DevCon didn't start until the following Monday. I had the rest of the week and the weekend to write the code, test it, and get it out into the build. Dave hadn't said we needed to stay until the work was done that night. What would be wrong with leaving work at four as I planned? *I could come in real early tomorrow and work on this stuff.*

So, I decided to follow through with my evening. At four, I updated my machine, started it compiling and got up to leave. When I reached my door, I pondered briefly which way to leave the building. From my office there were three directions I could go, but only one of them would allow me to avoid Dave completely.

The first, and most bold exit, was to turn right, follow developer row to the corner (where Dave's office was), turn left, past his secretary, and cross the front of the building to the door located on the corner opposite Dave's office. From there, it was down the stairs to the front door.

The second was to follow the row past two offices (Sally's and another) and turn left. There was a large division between the cubicles there I could use to cross the building. I could turn right and—using the cubicle walls as partial cover—walk to the front and out the door. This had lower risk, but there was still a limited exposure area near the front of the building. If Dave left his office when I was still in the open, anything could happen.

The final route came with a downside, but the risk of detection was very low. From my office, I could turn left, pass Crites's office, McClanahan's office, and finally arrive at the rear of the building and the door at the leftmost (eastern) corner. This door led down the back stairwell—which in itself was the downside. The smokers in the building used this cold collection of cement steps as a break room, so I always felt like I was in a bowling alley when I went through it. However, once I made it to the bottom, I could pass through the ground floor offices to the front door and freedom.

*Option three*, I decided finally. *I don't have time for confrontations tonight.*

\*        \*        \*

The next morning I was in before six, and by nine, I accomplished quite a bit. I felt comfortable, in control, and confident I'd have everything done in time—well before the weekend.

Then came nine-thirty. I reached over to drop a CD into my newly-repaired (but still unreliable) Discman when I heard the distant sound of moving footfalls. Because of our building's less-than-adequate construction, the larger members of the company caused this booming sound when they walked the outer circle. I usually did my best to ignore it as I worked, but pounding footsteps shrunk the set of potential walkers to a small handful.

I continued to listen as the footsteps made their way closer. They were past Marty's office, and then Heindel's. They crossed over the dissecting hall and didn't make the turn. Closer, still closer...in front of Sally's office now...slowing....

My door swung open. Dave filled the doorway wearing a white FoxPro polo and beige pants. He looked mad.

*Oh, man...not again....*

"Why did you leave before the color changes were done last night?" he asked. His voice was controlled and steady, but it didn't mean anything. An explosion could be imminent.

*Because I want a life outside of work?* was my first thought, but I drove that thought away. I had to remain calm. "I had a doctor's appointment last night, Dave."

Dave paused. He wasn't expecting that. I hoped he thought I had a form of terminal illness and would go easy.

"Oh, a doctor's appointment, hmmm..." His voice quickened. "Well, why didn't you come back afterwards?"

No such luck. "I had plans last night," I said. That was the truth. I was busy until nightfall.

"What plans?"

I knew he was going to ask, but I was hoping he wouldn't. There were a number of us on the team who would consider ourselves Christians—"an inordinate amount for a group so small" according to Chris, our resident agnostic. None of us were just the church-on-Sunday types. We were the types most likely to attend a mid-week Bible study. That's where I was the night before. I was never in the position where my work conflicted with my faith before. That was about to change.

"I was at a Bible study," I said.

Dave paused again, for about a second. "Bible study? Well, sometimes we have to put our work in front of our personal engagements."

I knew that would be his response. Although many of us were believers, Dave wasn't one of them. From the little background I heard, Dave's father was some sort of setup man for a traveling evangelist and the whole experience left Dave bitter. It was like a scene out of Robert Duvall's film "the Apostle."

Dave's rant gained steam from there. He stayed late. Heindel stayed late. Janet stayed late. I acted irresponsibly and endangered the demo. I shouldn't have left before the changes were done and checked in (even if they took me a couple days).

Through it all, I stayed quiet and waited him out. He finally finished with a scowl, closed my door, and boom-stepped away.

As I heard the footsteps grow fainter, I fought with reverting to my typical response to one of his "ego-adjustment seminars." I contemplated other professions. Could I work on the farm again? How about life guarding? Maybe just random violence followed by resignation?

In the end, I knew I would stay. When the offer to work for Fox originally came along, it seemed like an answer to prayer. The job description was perfect and I had no other immediate options. I was just having a hard time finding the blessing in it now, but sometimes those take time to see.

If nothing else, my Fox experiences would make a great story someday.

*          *          *

By the weekend, Dave decided there were too many design issues involved with the color changes. We'd leave them out of the build for DevCon.

But my portion was within hours of being complete.

*          *          *

Monday came and the start of DevCon week. For a second time Fox users from around the world converged on Toledo, Ohio—anxious to see our latest and greatest. We would have plenty to show them.

Since the work Jadzia and I did with the templates and design tools were so interface intensive, they would compose a great part of Dave's demo. There would be other highlights, too. Thanks to the work of Heindel, Eric, and McClanahan a good working set of the syntax for SQL was in place. Amy Fulton also created a tool—called the Query Builder—that made generating SQL syntax easier. Though not yet complete, it was close enough to be demoed.

The most amazing addition was FoxPro's new "Rushmore Technology." Devised by Eric and McClanahan while laboring over SQL optimizations, Rushmore was—in essence—an internal mechanism to get information back from ad-hoc queries at blinding speeds. For example, a SQL query to retrieve a few dozen records out of a database of over a million took only a few seconds. Our favorite demo involved a table that contained every street in the U.S—over 2 ½ million records. The user could look for every instance of a street named "Abercrombie" and FoxPro would return the answer before the user had time to take their hands off the keyboard. Our closest competitor's product took about forty-five minutes to return results for the same query. It was incredible. FoxPro could retrieve information on a personal computer at speeds only ever attained before on a room-sized mainframe.

Altogether, we thought these new additions would make the attendees of Dave's session ecstatic. Remembering how fun the demo was the year before, everyone (including Sally) decided to attend.

When we arrived at DevCon that morning we found things were different from the prior year. The number of attendees—now close to a thousand—forced Dave's session into a much larger room, and though the additional space allowed everyone to have their own seat, the size of the room changed the atmosphere completely. As the demo progressed it became clear there would be little rhythmic clapping, no foot stomping, and definitely no calling for a human sacrifice. The attendee's reception was cool, almost business-like. It was a complete let down.

The only thing I personally worked on that received any applause at all was the "selection marquee" I wrote during my down time many months before. And I was really hoping for more, given all the abuse I took.

*     *     *

Two days later, the "FoxPro Feedback" session was held at DevCon. As Janet described it to me earlier, this gathering would be a chance for our users to tell what they liked (or disliked) about the product—and in most cases, to ask for their favorite enhancement.

Usually, being in front of a large crowd of people isn't my favorite place to be, but since the format was to be "question and answer," I figured I could handle it.

The session was held in a relatively large room with seating for three to four hundred people. The seating was divided into two equal sections with an aisle down the middle. In that aisle, near the front of the room, there was a microphone stand. Also in front was a table and chairs for the panel of developers. The members of the panel were Eric, Heindel, Amy, Brian Tallman, and me; all prepared to answer questions about our areas of expertise. Janet Walker sat with us as well. Her job would be to make introductions and field any questions the rest of us couldn't handle. Chris Williams hovered nearby, looking as if he regretted his decision to leave development. Marty and Brian Crites (now known as "the Mac Dweebs") were seated out in the audience.

When we first took our seats, the room was maybe one sixth full. *No big deal.* By the time the session was to start, though, the place was completely packed. I was really hoping nobody asked me anything.

Janet began the introductions.

"As you all probably know, I'm Janet Walker, the product manager. To my right here is Amy Fulton. She's responsible for the Filer, the Color Picker, and most recently, the Query Builder...."

I watched the audience. There was a polite round of applause.

"Next, is Brian Tallman. He's responsible for the BROWSE command, the menuing, and our windowing...."

The applause increased. There was some movement toward the back. A few people started to get to their feet.

"Next to him is Kerry Nietz. He worked on the Report Writer, and now the Screen Painter and the Menu Builder...."

Now everyone was standing. *Wow*, I thought, looking around. *This is different from the other day. OK, I can do this....*

Janet continued with the introductions and the audience remained on their feet throughout. People began to line up behind the microphone. One by one they asked questions or made suggestions, but in general, the feedback was positive. Then something surreal happened.

A female member of the audience reached the microphone after waiting the better part of an hour. She had short, light-colored hair and was casually dressed. She looked like someone's mom.

"I'd just like to say I listened to all that's gone on here," she began, "and I think it's all good stuff. There have been a lot of good answers and good suggestions." She smiled and her eyes scanned our faces. "But, I waited in line for a different reason." She paused, still smiling. "I'd just like to take this time to thank those of you on the panel. You and your product really changed my life. Before FoxPro, I was living in a tent on the street, unsure of where I'd get my next meal. But now I'm a highly skilled and well-paid consultant...and I have you guys to thank." She nodded once. "So thanks!"

*OK. That was a little weird.* I glanced at the other members of the panel. Their faces mirrored my thoughts.

Then it got stranger. The audience showed their agreement with another standing ovation.

I wasn't sure what to think. Here we thought we were busy creating a simple computer program, when in actuality, we were starting our own cult. I saw Marty and Crites applauding and laughing at the same time.

Still, it was difficult to leave the session without feeling appreciated. DevCon that year gave me a renewed sense of purpose.

Someone really cared about what I did—and from what we heard—made a good living using it.

Sometimes the blessings take time to see.

# Chapter 16
# Snippets

"What the Screen Painter needs, my young friend, is the ability to attach snippets of code to controls," Dave said. He had the product running on his computer with a Screen Painter design window open. He was almost mindlessly creating controls on the surface and clicking through their dialogs. It was an example of the activity we came to know as Dave's "dinking with the mouse."

"Snippets?" I was sitting in the chair at the end of his desk, the proverbial "hot seat." I leaned forward and squinted at his computer screen, trying to see what he was doing that brought about this new revelation. *But the Screen Painter is finished....*

Dave glanced over at me. "Yes, little snippets of code. For the GET clauses...WHEN, VALID, and the rest. Instead of putting in an expression, they'd be able to type in the actual code. The generator takes care of matching it all up at code generation time."

My stomach began to ache—and lunch was still a few hours away. Apparently, Dave was about to add more stuff to the Screen Painter the week after we showed it at DevCon. Now granted, the conference existed—in part—so we could gather information on what our users wanted from the product. Most software companies would use that information to design features for the next version of their product, though—not one they had already been working on for the better part of the year.

I didn't hear anyone at the conference ask for "snippets." This must be all Dave. "Did someone ask for code snippets?" I asked, trying to sound innocently curious.

Dave was staring at his screen again, mouse aflutter. "No...but they wouldn't know how to. Being able to attach snippets of code would give them the same functionality we were trying to achieve with that object-oriented stuff." Dave nodded his head slowly. "Snippets...we need snippets."

\*     \*     \*

Essentially, every control (push buttons, checkboxes, and so on) a user could place on the Screen Painter's design surface had a number of 'clauses' associated with it. This was because, when code for that control was generated, the GET command that resulted also had clauses as part of its definition. These clauses had a litany of names, such as VALID, WHEN, or MESSAGE and each had what was called "an expression" associated with it.

As part of the READ mechanism, these expressions would be evaluated (have their values checked) at different times in the life of a user's interface. For instance, the expression for the WHEN clause of a control was evaluated when someone first selected that control. We also called this evaluation process the time the clause 'fired'. So, if a dBASE program defined a push button control, the WHEN clause of that control 'fired' when a user first tried to push on it.

There were some rules for these expressions, but what they did was really in the hands of our users. In their most complicated form, an expression could actually be another chunk of dBASE code they wrote. This chunk of code was called a User Defined Function (or UDF, for short) and it was another instance of a place where we allowed our users to customize the performance of their program. With this power and flexibility, we also gave them the ability to "shoot themselves in the foot" if they wanted to.

In the current incarnation of the Screen Painter though, when our users wanted a clause to have an expression that was a UDF, they needed the actual code for that UDF defined elsewhere—in a separate code file outside of the Screen Painter. Then they just used the name of the UDF as their expression in the Screen Painter and the generated code would use that same name to call their UDF when the clause fired. It was up to them to make sure the separate file was available when their generated code was run.

Dave wanted to change that. He wanted the Screen Painter to hold and manage all the code for the UDFs itself, eliminating the need for a separate code file. Furthermore, Jadzia's templates would take care of naming the chunks of code.

In actuality, it meant the wombats broke free from their can and were now living under my desk.

*     *     *

Downtown Perrysburg is a quaint little historical area. Its principal dissecting street—Louisiana Avenue—ends at the foot of a statue of Captain Oliver Hazard Perry, the naval captain famous for his exploits in the War of 1812 and responsible for the phrase "We have met the enemy and they are ours." The Maumee River is just beyond the statue to the north. To the south, the street is lined with a handful of Victorian buildings that contain various shops and eateries.

Of the restaurants, a couple were on the "regular visit" list for the Fox developers. Principal of these was Kwongs, a small Chinese place we dubbed "the best lunch deal in the free world." On any day, you could purchase a full plate of food for less than five bucks, and lunch came with tea and an egg roll. Kwongs was the pick the day of Dave's snippet revelation. At lunch with me were Eric, Heindel, and McClanahan.

With a menu in his hand, Eric bent close to me. "What part of FoxPro do you like the best?" he asked using a distinct hillbilly twang. He used that phrase and dialect often. I'm not sure why. Tallman was the one who grew up in West Virginia. Eric was from Ohio.

I sniffed. "Not the Screen Painter," I said.

Eric looked at the others with mock astonishment and chuckled. "Do I sense a little animosity?"

I buried my head in my menu. I really didn't want to talk about it.

The waitress, an elderly Caucasian woman, interrupted the discussion. "What can I be getting you boys?" she asked. She gripped a small notepad in one hand and a pen in the other.

"Szechwan special," Eric said, handing her his menu.

McClanahan was next. "Um…yes, I'd like the Szechwan too," he said, pointing at the menu. "Vegetarian. No chicken, and um…no MSG." Aside from a first cousin, McClanahan was the only practicing vegetarian I knew. In the heart of farm country, he was determined "to not eat anything that ever had a face." Our lunch group just called him a 'picky eater'.

The waitress turned toward Heindel.

"I want the Szechwan too," he said, slapping his menu shut and passing it to her like it was a baton. "And I'd like a bucket of MSG on the side." He laughed and formed his hands into a large circle. "Yeah, a big bucket of MSG—just put it right here on the table."

The rest of us laughed. The waitress just stared at Heindel with a small smile on her face. "Are you serious?" she said finally.

Heindel, now almost to tears, gave a little wave. "No, I was just kidding."

McClanahan chuckled along softly and pointed a threatening finger at Heindel. The picky eater thing was an ongoing joke between them.

After the waitress left and the laughs subsided, Eric turned his attention to me again. "So, what is Dave adding this time?"

I looked skyward and shook my head. "Snippets."

Eric looked at Heindel. "Snippets? Que signife 'snippets'?" Occasionally, one of those two would drop into 'French mode'. It was a form of mental irregularity.

"Snippets," I explained. "He wants little code snippets for people's VALID clauses...well, all the clauses really." I shook my head. "It's a mess," I glanced at McClanahan, and then Heindel. "And I thought the Screen Painter was finally done." I turned to stare absently out the front window at the street beyond. "I wish I could talk him out of it...."

A pot of hot water was brought to our table. Eric picked it up and began filling our cups. "Well, good luck," he said.

Heindel put some sugar in his cup and stirred it. "Yeah, Dave has definitely reached the point where you can't talk him out of something because it's hard to do."

I took some ice out of my water and dropped it into my tea. I never was much of a hot drink person.

What Heindel said was true, but I didn't like to believe it. When I started with Fox in 1988, Dave was still occasionally coding on the product, so he still had a good idea of what was involved in adding a feature. Now, he was so far removed from the product's inner workings, and development pulled off so many seemingly miraculous things, he no longer cared about **how** something would be done. He just came up with features to add and we had to add them.

Heindel continued. "He just doesn't want to be bothered with implementation details anymore. The only way to talk him out of something is to convince him it is a bad idea."

That was hard, especially when it was **his** idea. There was something about snippets I didn't like, though. It seemed like a lot of work for little gain. *I have to get out of this*, I thought. The waitress arrived carrying plates for our table. *Somehow*.

*      *      *

I was never good at talking Dave out of things. I just couldn't come up with compelling reasons why something shouldn't be done. The only arguments that usually came to mind were: "This is really hard" or "There's something about this I don't like," and neither of those worked with him—at least, not anymore. They definitely wouldn't help with "snippets." Dave loved the idea.

What I was left with was a shot in the dark. I had to attempt to get snippets working and hope that when my boss finally saw what I did, and the inherent deficiency of his idea, he'd change his mind and drop it. That was my only chance.

Less than a week later, when I had the first cut of "snippets" added to the Screen Painter, I was still really hopeful.

Previously, every clause that the user could define would bring up a dialog we called "the Expression Builder" where they could construct an expression for it. With my new additions, though, there was now an intervening dialog where the user chose to either bring up the Expression Builder, or type their "snippet" of code into a small, six-line editable text area. The size of a "snippet" was limited to 64k of memory space—about the size of this chapter.

The new dialog wasn't very flashy though—in fact, I thought it was butt-ugly. There was also a certain amount of awkwardness to the whole process. Getting to the Expression Builder now always took an extra step, so those who liked to do things the old way would be slowed down some. For those who wanted to use snippets…well, trying to put code into a six-line editable area was a little awkward too. Our users were accustomed to using our text editor for editing dBASE code. They were spoiled.

My new dialog was fully functional and everything about it was just as it had to be. I was giving Dave the functionality he wanted in a dialog that was consistent with the rest of our interface. If the process was clunky, it was clunky because snippets were clunky. They were a bad idea. Dave should be able to see that.

*       *       *

Dave's hand was on his chin. "This dialog looks OK…" he said as he studied my changes for the first time. "But there needs to be a way for them to edit their snippet in our editor."

I shook my head quickly, as if to clear it. "Huh?"

"Yes, for small sections of code this dialog works fine. But their snippets could be any size."

I had looked up the definition of "snippet" in the dictionary. It meant "a small part". Our editor could edit a file nearly as big as a computer's hard disk could store. I had no idea what a "snippet" window that was an actual editor session would mean. All the sundry clauses were self-contained from the Screen Painter's perspective. They were carried around in memory as character strings and theoretically had the same size limit I gave the code snippets—64K.

I was still a little stunned. "An editor window?" I asked.

Dave shook his head. "Yeah, an editor window. In this dialog somewhere should be a button they can push to open an editor session."

"You want me to open an editor window on top of this dialog?" That was unheard of. No interface I ever saw allowed a floating, sizable window to come up on top of a fixed dialog.

Dave paused for a moment. "Well…maybe not on top. Maybe behind the dialog."

That seemed even weirder. "OK," I said as I stood up to leave. "I'll look into it."

I sounded calm, but inside I felt a blossom of good feeling grow in my chest. *I think I found my way out.*

*     *     *

My next stop was Marty's office. As the resident Mac whiz he was also sort of the resident interface whiz.

"Hey Marty," I said as I entered. "Got a question for you."

Marty hated the office chairs we were given, so he pilfered a straight, non-rolling chair to sit in. When I entered, he turned around, hooking an arm over the chair's square back. "What's that?" he asked.

"Have I told you about snippets?"

He shook his head. "No."

I filled him in on the genesis of snippets. "But that's not the best part," I said finally.

Marty was watching me attentively. For quite some time he had worked on the Mac code with little supervision, so he liked to hear about everything he was missing "in the spotlight." "Okay, Kerry," he said, "what's the best part?"

"Dave wants a snippet editing window to come up behind the dialog that opens it."

Marty moved in his chair slightly, causing it to thump on the floor. "What?! Behind the dialog that opens it? How are we going to do that on the Mac?"

That was the response I hoped for. "I don't even know how I'm going to do it in DOS," I said with a shrug. In general, our Window Manager was built to open a new window in front of other windows. I needed Brian Tallman's help to get around that one. I didn't even want to think about the editor issues yet.

Marty shook his head. "Snippets. What the heck is a snippet?" he asked as I moved toward the door.

*     *     *

Mentioning Marty's reservations to Dave did me no good. "The Mac?" he said, "Let's not worry about the Mac now." He frowned, scratched the side of his neck as he thought a bit. "I don't know what we'll do in FoxPro Mac." He paused a moment, slid his wristwatch up his arm a little. His watchband always seemed a size too big. "We'll do something else…something more Mac-like."

"OK…," I said. *Darn it! He's punting.*

Dave leaned back in his chair and laced his hands behind his head. "And I was thinking…we need snippets in the Menu Builder too…."

"In the Menu Builder?!"

"Yeah, they should be able to attach snippets of code to their menu items."

I felt my face begin to flush. "When do we need this stuff done by?" The last I knew our Beta cycle was going to start near the end of the year. Two and a half months might be enough time. But Dave had a knack for constructing deadlines. It seemed there was always something—some show or demonstration—we needed to prep for.

"Comdex. It must be done by Comdex."

Comdex was less than a month away, the second full week of November. *Oh, the pain, the pain.*

*     *     *

Lunch the following day was at the local Burger King, a place manned by automatons. "Hello, welcome to Burger King," the woman monotoned as each of us reached the front of the line. "May I take your order?"

A few minutes later we were seated in the greenhouse portion of the building, soaking up whatever sun we could on a chill October day.

"This snippet stuff is going to kill me," I said, venting. "Dave now wants snippets in an editor window…and I have to add them to the Menu Builder too." I scowled and pulled a fry from its cardboard container. "Oh yeah, and it all has to be done by Comdex."

Eric sat across from me, picking toppings off his sandwich. "Well, I'll tell you what you're going to do." He moved his hands so it appeared he was holding a small rectangular box between them. "You allocate some memory…."

I just glared back at him. Now was not the time for jokes.

He saw my look. "Call it a buffer?" he asked, still clutching the imaginary box.

I stayed silent. *No jokes.*

"No?" Eric watched me for a moment, and then took a bite of his sandwich. "You know," he began, his voice even. He was now in advice mode. "I used to get frustrated with some of the things Dave asked me for." He popped a fry in his mouth. "But I've learned to do what he wants even though I don't like it." He took a sip of soda and glanced over at Bill and Heindel before looking back at me. "He's usually right."

*Does that mean he's right now?* I wanted to say, but didn't. I knew my boss was a gifted man. You couldn't start a college Computer Science department **and** a successful software company without having a few things on the ball. There was undoubtedly a lot about running a company I didn't appreciate, many decisions and hidden pressures.

*But was it wise to add a feature just because you could?* Snippets? Why snippets!?

Still, if Eric was telling me to "shut up and do your work" it was probably time to do just that. End my complaining and work.

It was going to be hard, though. The snippet snowball was rolling downhill, and it felt like it was picking up steam.

*                *                *

The next week I succeeded in getting the editor windows to open up behind the snippet dialog (actually, behind the snippet dialog and whatever dialog brought up the snippet dialog) but there were many difficulties. It turned out the editor liked to be the "top dog."

Dave seemed happy with the change. Until....

"Look," he said after I arrived at his office. "When I edit this snippet...," and he went through the motions to open up a snippet editing window and paste a huge amount of text into it. Following this, he closed the window and went through the entire process to open up the editing window again. When he reached the place where the editor's window was open, he scrolled down to the end of his "snippet" of code.

"It's truncated!" he exclaimed. "Part of my code is missing!"

There was that 64K limit I mentioned. "Well, yeah Dave, those things are stored in handles. The limit is 64K."

Dave looked at me with both eyebrows raised. "What?!"

"You know, handle-size, Dave. The limit is 64K."

"A 64K limit? That's unacceptable."

*For a snippet of code?* "I thought these things were snippets." Now, granted, I took the path of least resistance, but time was short. *What does he expect?*

"Unacceptable! We will not have a 64K limit!"

He was really heating up. It was time to level with him. "Dave, here's how the Screen Painter works...." I proceeded to tell him about the Screen Painter internals. The gist of it was the Screen Painter didn't have anything to do with a file on the hard disk after the file was initially opened. Allowing for "snippets of any size" would change that. In fact, it would change a lot of things.

"And if I have to do this for the Menu Builder too, and before Comdex," I said, talking fast. "I can't get it done. No way. I just can't."

Dave thought for a minute. "What's Sally doing?"

The last I knew she was working on functions for the manipulation of arrays. "I don't know," I said.

"Well, maybe Sally can help. But a limit of 64K is unacceptable."

*     *     *

Sally was happy to get involved. "Alright," she said, throwing my office door open. "What did you get me into?"

"I'm sorry," I said. "Really."

We proceeded to divvy up the snippet tasks. She would create a "Snippet Manager" to handle the operation of snippets, their editor sessions, and the temporary files they needed. I'd handle everything specific to the Screen Painter and Menu Builder.

*     *     *

As our Comdex deadline approached, Sally, Jadzia (who was making changes to the generator code to stay in step with us), and I were getting real close to having snippets working as Dave intended. But at least a couple times a week, he'd heap on a new requirement.

"We need to store the snippet editing window's status with the screen file somehow," Dave said one day. "If my snippet window was open and minimized when I saved my screen file, the window should be opened and minimized when I open the screen again."

A few days later there was something else. "We need an option to open all the snippets with any code in them. Yes...maybe an 'Open all Snippets' item on the menu somewhere."

I could see where that was leading. "Do you want a 'Close All Snippets' item too?" I asked.

Dave thought for a moment, and then nodded. "That's a good idea...open all snippets and close all snippets...."

*     *     *

A short time later Marty looked into my office and opened the door. "What're you working on?" he asked.

I glanced up from my screen briefly. "Open All Snippets. Dave wants it in before Comdex." I motioned him closer and gave him a quick demo. His eyes got wide as snippet windows exploded onto the screen.

"Open all snippets," Marty said slowly. He shook his head. "Snippets provide no new functionality, you know. None. You can get everything you want the old way."

"Yeah…" Since their inception I tried numerous ways to talk Dave out of snippets—both subtly and blatantly. Their implementation code didn't fit into the product very well, but it worked. I lost the will to fight any further.

"It is just flashier this way," Marty continued. "Flashier to see hundreds of windows pop up on the screen rather than open up one solitary code window and put your procedure in there."

"I know," I said, glancing between Marty and my screen. "It's what Dave wants."

"And by Comdex," Marty continued. "What's that?" He pointed at me, but I had a feeling he was really pointing at the man in the corner office. "It's never enough to show the cool stuff that's already done. We have to have something 'for the show'. Have to show what's being done right this second." Marty smiled and swatted the air. "Bah." He moved back toward the door.

"We're doomed!" I said as he left.

He chuckled. "We're doomed!"

\*　　　\*　　　\*

Some time later Janet stopped by my office with a bag of candy in her hand. "Look, Kerry!" she said. "Snippets!" She took a couple pieces from the bag and handed them to me.

The candy looked a lot like a Tootsie Roll, but emblazoned across the wax-paper wrapper was the word "Snippits." The spelling was close enough. I gave a half-hearted grin and sniffed. "Thanks."

Janet beamed. "Snippets, Kerry, snippets!" Then she walked away, undoubtedly headed to Sally's office next door.

I pulled the candy from the wrapper and put it in my mouth. It tasted a lot like a Tootsie Roll too. I glanced at my monitor. On the top I stuck a small metal man my little brother (fourteen years my junior) gave me. It held a racket in its hand and bounced on a spring.

I pulled open my desk drawer and found a little metal twistee. Using it, I bound the candy wrapper to the metal man's neck.

Snippet-man was born.

# Chapter 17
# Holiday Happenings

By the time Fall Comdex rolled around we already had another
deadline. The deadline **this** time was the start of our Beta test cycle for
FoxPro 2.0, which would be near the end of December. Dave didn't
want the development team distracted from its work toward that
deadline, so none of us were allowed to go to Comdex.

Toward the end of Comdex week, the lunch crew gathered at Casa
Barrons—another of the restaurants downtown. Barrons was a dimly-lit
Mexican place known for its free supply of chips and salsa and the
paintings of half-naked women on the walls. Eric had the latest news
from the show and promised to fill us in.

"So, what's the word from Janet?" Heindel asked as he dipped a
chip. "Do the people like our stuff?"

Eric grabbed a chip of his own and waved it slightly as he spoke.
"Oh yeah, she says they're crazy about it. The booth is packed." He
munched for awhile, and then got a sly look. "Even Ed Esber stopped
by."

"Was he handing out resumes?" Heindel said, chuckling. Ed Esber
vacated his job a short time before. He was now the *former* CEO of
Ashton-Tate.

Eric smiled. "You're bad." He took a sip of water. "I guess he just
stopped by to tell us how much he liked our product. He told Janet that
it was **never** his intention for Ashton-Tate to sue us."

Bill stroked his facial hair. "Really?"

There was a glint of playfulness in Heindel's eye. More jokes were
on the way. "I can see how that could happen," he said. "The lawyers
probably just misunderstood. Ed probably said he wanted to 'see'
FoxPro and they thought he said 'sue'." Heindel tipped his head. "It
could happen."

Those three laughed. I just smiled and found a chip.

"So did Janet say anything else?" Heindel said, still smiling.

The food was brought to the table. It was a "twofer" day; two
tacos, two burritos, or two enchiladas for one low price. I was partial to
the enchiladas.

"Oh yeah, Chris is at it again," Eric said.

We all knew what that meant.

"So, what's he taking credit for now?" Bill asked.

Eric flipped his hands up. "Oh…the booth, the enhancements to the product…you name it."

I shook my head. Chris's overactive ego was never far from the surface. From childhood I was taught not to "toot my own horn" so it was hard for me to understand someone who not only tooted his horn, but frequently took credit for the rest of the band's performance as well. I didn't know if Chris saw his "all you see here" trait as a problem or not. I wondered if it would ever get him into trouble, or if it bothered anyone else.

*           *           *

Shortly thereafter we heard the news that Chris would be rejoining us in development. On his first day back, he went to lunch with the 11:30 crew. Afterward, I stopped in to see Sally.

"Sally," I said as I entered her office. "You're a prophet!"

Sally giggled. "Are you talking about Chris?"

"Yeah—how did you know he'd be back?"

Sally turned her seat in a back-and-forth swinging motion. "Things are always greener on the other side for Chris," she said, smiling. "He's just like that." She paused, raised a shoulder. "I knew he'd be back."

I slid over to take a seat on Sally's spare office chair. "Well, he told us at lunch he had a hard time accomplishing anything because the executive committee wouldn't give him enough money to work with." The executive committee was the ruling body at Fox. It was mostly composed of LaValley and Fulton family members, and given our locked first aid supplies and utilitarian surroundings, it was safe to say that group was conservative with company funds. Chris was a bit of a spendthrift, though. He was the only person I knew who had a big screen TV, an in-ground pool, and a second mortgage. A few clashes between the committee and him wouldn't surprise me.

But, Sally did. "That's what he told you, huh?" she said.

"Why…" I squinted. "What did you hear?"

Her seat started swinging again. "I heard Dave say Chris couldn't cut it in Marketing. It was either come back to development or he was gone."

I inhaled, breathing through my teeth. "Whoa…" I paused, shook my head. I didn't think Chris would have **that** much difficulty. All faults aside, Chris was a really hard worker in 'dev'. And he didn't even hint about a problem during lunch. "Dang!" I said finally.

Sally shrugged. "That's what I heard."

"Gosh. I thought maybe he just ran out of stuff to take credit for."

Sally laughed again and I got up to leave. Regardless of the reason, I was glad Chris was one of us again. He was a solid coder, an amiable guy, and—if nothing else—an interesting character. I missed him.

Soon after Chris's return to the top floor (the Marketing offices were now situated on the bottom floor, literally beneath our feet), he began work on something called the Project Manager. The purpose of the tool was to allow users to more easily manage the elements of their FoxPro application (code, screen, reports, and the like) by maintaining it in a project form.

It was a solution long overdue, and the perfect thing for Chris to use for redeeming himself.

*     *     *

In other matters, a company named LoadStone was making rumblings about wanting to sue us. Apparently, sometime during the period when *Rushmore* was in development, the people from LoadStone sent us a copy of their product to evaluate. They were hoping we would buy the source code and integrate it into FoxPro. The principle functionality of their product was adding information to the end of our index files that allowed some index-based operations to execute faster.

The fact their product added stuff to the index files made it undesirable for Fox, though. Our index file format hadn't changed since the early days of FoxBASE+ and there were literally millions of index files in existence. Any change to the format of that file would break nearly every application ever written for our product. We couldn't do that.

One thing the LoadStone product did *was* significant, however. The information they attached to the end of the index files was a 'bitmap'—a component integral to *Rushmore*, as well. Both products constructed a bitmap based on an index expression, and then made use of it to quickly retrieve samples of the data in a database (or databases). The principal advantage of *Rushmore*, however, was it built its bitmap in memory 'on the fly', and then disposed of it when it was through. The index file remained unchanged.

Not being directly involved, I never knew whether the LoadStone product was the catalyst for Eric and McClanahan thinking about index optimization, or if it was a mere coincidence that we received it around the same time *Rushmore* was under development. If I were to bet on it though, I'd bet on the later. Eric was **always** looking for ways to improve the product's performance, and usually he found them. It wasn't hard to imagine him dreaming up something like *Rushmore* while he was in the shower in the morning. He was just that good.

LoadStone didn't see it that way. They alleged we reverse-engineered their code and even had one prominent computer magazine articulate that theory.

Later patent searches proved they owned no rights to anything even close to *Rushmore* technology. After that, their legal challenges faded into the Ohio snow.

Now all that remained was the little disagreement with Ashton-Tate. One lawsuit down, one to go.

*　　　*　　　*

On the tenth and eleventh of December I had a role in a Christmas play at my church. My part in the play was trivial, but my attendance was key. Of the forty thespians, I was the only adult. Children were depending on me. I needed to set a good example.

I had no worries about the first performance. The tenth was a Sunday and though there was some weekend work at Fox, nobody was going in on Sunday yet. The Beta deadline was still a few weeks off.

It was the second performance that worried me. It was in the evening on a Monday so I'd have to leave for the play immediately after work. If something major came up during the day…well, I already knew what Dave thought about activities after work.

As I drove to work that morning, I knew there were no guarantees I'd successfully make it out that night. Virtually anything could happen. There were things I could do, though, to increase my chances. There **were** rules I could follow.

The rules were undocumented, but by now I had a good idea what they were. They were the things I had to do to avoid getting stuck; the things that avoided confrontation. The four from the top of the list were as follows:

1.  The network is sacred. Never check in anything you don't want Dave to play with, and **never** check in something that doesn't build completely.

2.  If your check in will result in a long (greater than twenty minute) build, let everyone know. Saving it until the end of the day is best.

3.  Never use the phrase "it works on my machine" to defend a bug. Dave's response to that will be, "Then I guess we'll ship **your machine**."

4.  Don't check anything into the network after about two in the afternoon if you want to avoid being dragged back in the evening and yelled at. Even the safest code could have problems—and Dave stays late.

If I adhered to the rules completely, I might have a shot, but no guarantees.

By the middle of the morning, I was certain I was home free. Dave was out most of the day, and I spent the time tweaking details in the information stored in the Screen Painter's file. In general, this was a low risk change. It was the least amount of work I could do and still be doing something productive.

After my change was made and tested, I checked in the code. It was just before two in the afternoon. I moved on to other projects I had on my list. Projects I wouldn't finish until the next day.

A little before five, I left for home. 'Home' was now in Perrysburg, because over the summer I purchased a small house on the outskirts of town. It took me less than seven minutes to get there. Upon arriving, I hurriedly ate and jumped in the shower. The play was at seven, and it would take me almost half an hour to get to the church. Time would be tight.

After my shower, I went into my room and located my lone dark suit. It was the only bit of polyester apparel I had for the last two years, and that was fine. Holding the waist up, I slid a leg in.

I heard the phone ring. I pushed my other foot through and went for the phone. *This can't be....*

It was. I recognized Janet's voice in my ear. "There's a bug in the Screen Painter," she said. In the background I could hear Dave fuming. "It's all f***ed up!" he said clear enough for me to understand.

I glanced at the clock. It read six o'clock sharp.

*I don't have time*, I thought, *I have to appeal to reason.* "I have a Christmas play tonight, Janet," I explained. "I **have** to be there. Can't I deal with this tomorrow morning?" Nothing important was happening the next day, and I usually got in two hours before Dave did. There probably **was** a problem in the Screen Painter, but I could fix it before he got in. *No big deal!*

"Well..." Janet hesitated, *wanting* to be reasonable.

"It's his responsibility!" Dave yelled. "Get him in here!"

So much for reason. "Never mind," I said. "I'll be in as soon as I can." I pulled on the rest of my suit and headed for the office.

When I arrived, Dave was standing at the front door. He was already wearing his coat and hat. *Hey,* I thought. *He's going home!*

"Ah, there you are," Dave said as I rushed past him. "Get that Screen Painter fixed!"

I clamped my mouth shut. Now I was **certain** I could've fixed the bug in the morning. Dave came in long enough to find a problem, had Janet call me in, and was now leaving without knowing if I fixed it or not. *I could just go upstairs and out the back door*, I thought, bounding four steps at a time. I reached the top floor and threw open the door. *My instincts have been wrong before, though.*

I found the problem almost immediately. It was the "trivial" changes I made that day. I quickly did what I had to do to undo them, and then sprinted from the building. I arrived at church just in time to go onstage. "Where were you?!" the kids said in unison. There was no easy way to explain it to them. They were twelve-year-olds.

The next morning Dave chewed me out for not testing my work better. Once again, I kept my mouth shut and let him rave at me for awhile. Once again, I returned to my office and contemplated being a lifeguard.

I didn't have to convince myself to stay this time, though. Apparently realizing he was a little hard on me, Dave later came to my office and apologized. *And just when I thought I had him completely figured out!*

The experience did give me another item for my list, though:

5. Always test your work thoroughly. Just running through the scenario you're working on is not enough. A problem that arises due to faulty testing will illicit a "Don't you test this sh\*\*!" from Dave.

*    *    *

Just as I was getting out of hot water, Chris was back in it. The January issue of the magazine *Data Base Advisor* arrived at the office a few days later. Dave was one of the first to read it, and the following sentence from a letter to the editor caught his attention:

"I never realized all the neat and wonderful things one can do with Chris Williams's Amazing Browse command."

Now, part of that statement was true. The current incarnation of the BROWSE command **was** an amazing piece of work. It allowed FoxPro users to view the data in their database tables in a plethora of different ways. In its simplest form it listed the table's field names across the top of the screen and the individual table records down the screen, providing a snapshot of the data in the table—but it was immensely configurable. It was one of the most powerful commands in the language.

Chris didn't write it, though. He hardly even touched it. That work was done exclusively by Eric Christensen and Brian Tallman.

When Dave saw the false declaration of ownership, he knew someone gave the writer that mistaken impression, and he had a good idea who that someone was. He decided a little "humility therapy" was in order.

After Chris went home that night, Dave made multiple copies of the suspect declaration. On each copy he increased the font size from the previous copy until finally the phrase "**Chris Williams' Amazing Browse Command**" screamed out in epic proportions. He posted these ascending copies on Chris's office window for everyone to see.

When Chris arrived the next morning, I walked over to see how he was doing. He was not so good.

"That guy is a freaking idiot," Chris said as I entered his office. I assumed he was talking about the misinformed magazine subscriber.

I tried not to smirk, but it was hopeless. "Well, why does he think you wrote BROWSE?" I asked. *Come on, Chris, fess up....*

"I don't know," he said. "I didn't tell him that." He directed his attention to his computer screen and began typing hurriedly. "He's a freaking idiot."

I watched him for a moment. "What're you doing?" I asked finally.

"I'm writing a retraction letter," he said. His eyes stayed fixed on the screen. There was no laughing this one off.

"Oh," I said. I watched him for a few moments longer, and, smiling larger, I left him to his writing. He was really into it.

Chris's letter was never sent, though. Dave squashed that plan when he arrived a short time later. "You'll not put our underwear out for the world to see!" he said.

So, left with no other option, Chris spent the rest of the day in his office alone. Sulking.

*       *       *

Meanwhile, the work on the product continued to be intense, mostly because Dave continued to be intense. He became so aggressive, in fact, most of us refused to fight with him over anything anymore. Our "agreeing not to disagree" gave rise to a new catch phrase among the developers: "LTWW."

LTWW stood for "Let The Wookiee Win," and any fan of the classic Star Wars trilogy is familiar with the reference. It comes from a scene where the robot (aka "droid"), R2D2, is playing a game of chess with an 8 foot tall hairy beast known as a Wookiee. In the middle of the game, the Wookiee gets upset over a move R2D2 made.

Another droid, C3PO, steps in to mediate. "He made a fair move," he says. "Screaming about it won't help you."

A knowledgeable spectator named Han Solo interrupts. "Let him have it," he says. "It's not wise to upset a Wookiee."

"But sir," C3PO says, "nobody worries about upsetting a droid."

"That's 'cause droids don't pull people's arms out of their socket when they lose," Han explains. "Wookies are known to do that."

"I see your point, sir," the now-sapient C3PO says. He leans close to his robot companion. "I suggest a new strategy, R2," he whispers. "Let the Wookiee Win."

To us, the similarities between Dave and the Wookiee increased as the days of development on FoxPro 2.0 went by. His temperament reached the point where it was just better to let him have his way. "L...T...W...W" was muttered more than once under someone's breath after Dave vehemently ordered a product change. Better to do the work rather than have your arms ripped off, after all.

To add to our amusement—and more solidify the analogy—one winter day Dave began sporting a full-length fur coat, along with a matching fur cap.

If he only knew.

*     *     *

Furry aliens aside, one thing that happened on December 11th, 1990 would make even a Wookiee cheer. With little fanfare, Dave called the development team and the various department heads to the upstairs conference room. He informed us the Ashton-Tate lawsuit was virtually over. Ironically, the copyrights Ashton-Tate claimed we infringed on were ruled "invalid."

In their original complaint, Ashton-Tate claimed the "organization, structure, and sequence" of their dBASE products reflected ideas completely their own. They alleged we illegally copied the "look and feel" of their programs, which included their menus, any text that appeared in their product, and their commands (i.e. the dBASE language, which incidentally, was now being called "the xBASE language" by many of the gurus).

The judge, though, issued an order invalidating Ashton-Tate's copyrights for their whole line of dBASE products because he found they lied to the US Copyright Office on their original copy registration (many, many years prior). They claimed the dBASE language was a language wholly their own, but it wasn't. It was derived from another language developed by NASA's Jet Propulsion Laboratory. The name of that program was JPLDIS, and JPLDIS was in the public domain. In other words, no one owned it, and no one could. Ashton-Tate's whole case was essentially kicked out of court on a technicality.

We realized, of course, Ashton-Tate would probably appeal the decision and force us to go to trial again. Nevertheless, the ruling was a big win for us. It may not solve anything from a legal precedents perspective, but it was like seeing the sun after a long, grey winter. Until told otherwise, we were free to do what we wanted to do all along—create the best database program ever!

It was a fitting finale to our year of hard labor.

# Chapter 18
# Small Rebellions

Another lunch, another discussion about our fearless leader.

We were at another local place called Charley's. It featured Greek cuisine and walls painted—quite convincingly—to look like marble. I always admired the walls. I found it fascinating that something that looked so real, so much like something carved from the earth, was really the product of an artist's imagination. The painter's work really isn't that much different from coding. A program, like FoxPro, is essentially just a mirage.

"Boy Dave's sure…um…**intense** lately," Heindel said, giving a little uncomfortable laugh.

"No kidding!" Bill said in response to Heindel. He took a bite of his gyro, beginning the war between gyro sauce and facial hair. The sauce took an early lead.

Eric rolled his eyes and simultaneously dipped a fry in ketchup. "Oh yeah, he's really got a bug up the butt." He pushed his head forward emphatically. "And I don't know why. There's nothing different this week than last week."

"Well, I think he's just worked up about the bugs," Heindel said, "and the beta…"

Eric shook his head. "There will **always** be bugs," he said, staring Heindel hard in the face. "There'll always be betas." He shook his head again. "Getting upset doesn't solve anything. He needs to just lighten up." Eric looked up, studied the walls. "Maybe Amy's been holding out on him," he said finally.

I smiled and Heindel and Bill chuckled. It was nice to see I wasn't the only one feeling the heat. *Finally, they're beginning to understand…*

*        *        *

Since my office was near the end of the row, the job of collecting people for lunch sort of fell to me. A few days after the trip to Charley's, I was in the process of fulfilling that duty. I already gathered Crites, Heindel, and Bill. Tallman and Sally never went. McClanahan was entrenched in his work and waved me off. Marty was "watching his figure." Chris didn't want to go. Next up was Eric.

I entered his office. He sat with his legs crossed and his fist pressed firmly against his lips.

"Lunch?" I said.

Eric turned to acknowledge me. He looked a little distant, a little mentally involved. "Just a second," he said. He walked past me and turned in the direction of Dave's office. I tagged along.

Dave was up and mobile. Pacing his office.

"I'm going to lunch now," Eric said.

"Well, don't go until you have those bugs fixed," Dave said. It was clear he was agitated. I decided not to venture any further into his domain. I waited by the door.

"Dave, there will always be bugs," Eric said.

*Uh, oh.* I heard the phrase before, but couldn't believe I was hearing it again. Eric was usually the compliant one.

Dave's body began to shake as he moved around the room. "We're going to release a new beta, Eric."

Eric shook his head. "There'll always be betas…."

Dave swore repeatedly. "This is important, Eric! It's crucial. We have to get this stuff out…."

*Don't make me angry. You won't like me when I'm angry.*

Eric dropped his head slightly and walked past me again. "I won't be going," he breathed.

*     *     *

Throughout January and February things were tense. As far as Dave was concerned the product could ship at any moment. Yet, in direct opposition to that goal was the fact we continued to add features to the product—features that came directly from the new "bane of our existence"—the CompuServe traffic.

Since the start of our Beta program, near the beginning of '91, our Beta-testers were able to log onto a forum, via CompuServe, where they reported any bugs they found. These external bug reports were extremely helpful because the product was now so complicated our burgeoning testing team couldn't test it fully.

The reporting process was the problem. In addition to the useful bug reports, the Beta-testers commonly sent along their favorite enhancement requests as well.

Now, in theory, that shouldn't be so bad. A simple request from a single user was never enough to get the feature in question added to the product. However, because the area where the reports were filed was a 'forum' the other Beta-testers could easily read each other's reports and append comments of their own. That's where the trouble began.

It usually happened this way. A Beta-tester would find something in the product they wished acted differently and would casually mention it on the forum. Other testers would read this comment and start a discussion among themselves about a possible enhancement. In forum lingo this discussion was called a "thread." The thread would eventually escalate into a thunderous rallying-cry. The Beta-testers simply "had to have this enhancement or the product will be completely unusable." Then Dave—who now read the traffic every morning—would get caught up in the hullabaloo. He'd call a meeting to see what could be done and by the end of it we would be adding another feature to the product. The next thread would start the process all over again.

Before long, this continual "feature creep" and Dave's growing intensity level began to impact the development staff. Our morale was soon at an all-time low.

*       *       *

Since his hiring, McClanahan furiously toiled away on his SQL implementation, completely on his own and with little supervision. He virtually barricaded himself in his office for months, coding tirelessly—yet his work remained shrouded in mystery.

His whiteboard was filled with scores and scores of formulas. "All necessary for my work," he assured us—and we had to believe him— because no one understood what his cryptic gobbledygook meant. He had some SQL queries working in time for the last DevCon, so we knew he was making progress, but no one was real sure what he was working on exactly or how close his code was to being finished.

In addition, McClanahan tended to be reclusive. He worked in his office alone and rarely asked any questions. That could mean one of two things. Either he was so ahead of the game he didn't need anyone's help, or he was hopelessly lost and afraid to admit it.

Not one to like a lot of mystery, Dave started to get anxious. He decided it was time someone knew what McClanahan was up to. He assigned Eric to "take a look around" and help out, if need be.

Eric's investigation returned mixed results. McClanahan **did** have a good share of work done, he found. He also noticed McClanahan duplicated in his own work, code previously written elsewhere in the product—code readily available for him to use. All he had to do was ask. To top it off, there was still plenty of SQL work left to be done.

That news failed to encourage the good doctor. After hearing Eric's report, Dave turned up the heat on McClanahan. He hoped the added pressure would motivate the diminutive vegetarian. What it did instead, was make McClanahan more frustrated than ever.

Fox's *unstructured* work environment was taking a toll on McClanahan. When I stopped in to greet him, it was clear he wasn't having much fun. "This is ridiculous," he'd say, shaking his head furiously, "Ridiculous!" He didn't enjoy being directly under Dave's spotlight. It was unlike anything he experienced before. He was even forced to postpone his family vacation until after his work was complete—a goal line that grew increasingly further and further out. He was stressed, frustrated, and had few places to turn.

\*          \*          \*

The rest of us shared some of those same feelings, we just dealt with them in a different way. As an outlet for a number of us, a regular morning gripe session developed in Sally's office. These meetings started out innocently enough. Sally and I both got in early, and our offices were adjacent, so I dropped by in the morning to say hello and shoot the bull about whatever was on our minds.

As the days progressed and the pressure grew, our morning get-togethers turned into a forum for all the latest news and complaints—many of which centered on Dave and the unreasonable thing he'd done lately. Over time, the numbers in attendance at our gripe sessions grew as well.

One of the newest attendees was Marty Sedluk, and he had plenty to complain about. His job, since the summer of 1989, when FoxBASE+/Mac version 2.01 shipped, was to work on the Macintosh version of FoxPro, FoxPro/Mac. This meant for all that time—nearly eighteen months—he was dutifully moving code from the FoxPro/DOS code base to the FoxPro/Mac code base, making whatever changes he deemed necessary to make it work consistently on the Mac. Nobody asked how he was doing. Dave never bothered him. Essentially, no one cared.

"I could sit and code in my office buck-naked," Marty joked one day, "and nobody would ever notice!"

On the rare occasion Dave did give Marty attention, it was usually to harass him. I witnessed this first hand while in a meeting with Dave and Janet.

The three of us were discussing the way certain windows behaved in our product. Dave felt if a user clicked a window in the background (behind another window) it should not only come forward, but whatever was within the window—in the area where the user clicked—should also be selected. Our text editor behaved that way. It would bring the window forward and select the word under the mouse cursor. Every other tool—Screen Painter, Menu Builder, Label Writer, etc—just brought the window forward. It took another click to select something.

To justify my position, I told Dave the tools were behaving according to the interface rules of the Macintosh computer. The Mac was our erstwhile guide for FoxPro's interface, so it seemed like a reasonable argument.

Dave scowled at the reference. "The Mac!!" he exclaimed. "I don't care about the Mac! Apple never did anything for us!" He picked up his phone and started dialing.

I heard Marty's polite "Hello" through the receiver.

"Marty?" Dave asked.

"Yes?" Still polite, compliant.

"Marty!" Dave continued, now more animated. "Apple never did anything for us!" Then, ker-slam! He hung up without waiting for a response.

Marty had good reasons to grumble. He was a welcome addition to our early morning group.

*     *     *

Beyond the membership of our gripe session, the frustration was apparent in others as well. In a separate meeting with Dave—this time with Heindel, Chris, and Jadzia in attendance—I got to see the effect it was having on Heindel.

In the middle of the discussion—as frequently happened—Dave broke into an unadulterated tirade. The issue this time was "scrollable lists." While playing with the product the night before, he noticed these interface elements looked slightly different in the Screen Painter than they did in the READ command. He preferred the way they looked in the Screen Painter.

Dave pointed at his computer screen. "Look at this!" he said. "The lists look like this in the Screen Painter and like this in READ. READ is wrong! It's ugly! It's a wart! It's a melanoma!" He punctuated each sentence with a firm slap on his desk. "It's like a pimple on the product! It's obvious it doesn't work! It never worked! No one ever tested it!"

As always, the rest of us sat in stunned silence.

Heindel spoke up. "Listen Dave," he began with mild agitation. "It does work. I did test it. It worked when I put it out!"

Now Chris, Jadzia, and I were stunned and staring at Heindel. Dave acted as if he was going to speak again, but he wasn't quick enough.

"Dave, you're getting all excited about a few little bugs," Heindel said. "When you get excited, I get excited, and then I can't think. It's just a bug!" His hands were cupped and he was slapping one in the other as he talked. "Now we know about it and we'll fix it. You don't need to yell!"

Dave joined the rest of us sitting stunned and speechless—one of the few times I saw that happen.

Normally easygoing and fun-loving, Heindel reached the point where he back-talked Dave—and he lived through the experience. My esteem for Heindel rose to a new level that day. I was amazed.

It inspired me to try a little revolt of my own. I could never be as overt as Heindel, but I had an idea....

\*     \*     \*

One of the things Dave was famous for was his random use of large, often-obscure words. In the course of normal conversation, he would fling out a word that only a regular reader of the dictionary could understand. If you wanted to know, you'd have to halt the discussion to get the definition. If you didn't want to know, you were left trying to figure it out from the context, and that could be difficult.

It wasn't clear why Dave chose the words he did. Maybe he was trying to expand his vocabulary, maybe he was trying to educate us, or maybe he was just trying to keep us slightly off kilter—but, whatever the reason, he did so constantly.

In my covert rebellion, I hoped to hit him where he lived. I would find a word—**any** word—that he didn't know and use it seamlessly in conversation.

It became my mission to find the perfect word. I searched word lists and kept my eyes and ears open. My word had to be so close to the periphery of our language that some of the smaller dictionaries wouldn't have it. It didn't have to be complicated, or even technical, but it had to be right.

Then one day the perfect word dropped into my lap. While perusing a trade journal, I found the word "agnosia." It meant, "lacking the ability to understand." *This is it*, I thought. *I've never heard it before, it's easy to say, and I can even use it in a conversation*. I only had to find the right time to use it.

A few short days later, Dave called me to his office to discuss a Screen Painter detail. As often happened, the discussion arrived at the proposal of a new feature.

"I think that would be a good addition," Dave said, nodding his head once.

"Well Dave," I said nonchalantly, "I don't want to sound like I'm suffering from *agnosia* or something, but...."

Of course, in the back of my mind, I knew Dave might already know my perfect word, and its definition. *But, if that's the case,* I reassured myself, *it's no harm done—we're just making conversation. He may even think better of me for using a word on his level.*

Dave interrupted me. "Agnosia?" he said, sounding mystified. "I don't know that word. Is that a word—agnosia?"

I answered as calmly as I could. "Agnosia? Yeah, it's a word. It means *lacking the ability to understand.*"

Dave jerked his head back. "Really? Agnosia, agnosia…" He brought a hand to his chin. "That's a word I don't know." A pause. "I'll give you a bonus for knowing a word I don't know."

"It's a word," I said. "I can get a dictionary…"

Dave pulled his glasses off and rubbed his eyes. "No, no, I believe you," he said. "It makes sense. Agnosia, that's a good one. OK, where were we…."

I fought off a smile. *I doubt if I ever see that bonus,* I thought. *But, I already got my reward.*

I had a great story to share with the rest of the team, and as soon as the meeting was over, that's precisely what I did.

*　　*　　*

While the Ashton-Tate lawsuit against us was on appeal with the 9th Circuit court, the original judge (Judge Terry Hatter) received an affidavit from the Register of Copyrights. In that affidavit, the Register—Ralph Oman—claimed Judge Hatter was too harsh when he invalidated Ashton-Tate's copyrights. "The copyrights should have been amended, not invalidated", was essentially what Oman said.

The judge agreed, and in April of 1991, he reversed his December decision. Following that, the 9th Circuit court sent the case back to Hatter for further proceedings.

After a short respite, Fox was officially a rebel in a legal war again.

# Chapter 19
# Attitude

I was passing through the front portion of the building one Saturday afternoon, en route to my office, when I noticed something peculiar. I stopped dead in my tracks.

*What happened this time?* I wondered, staring at the closed door of Dave's office. The door being shut wasn't abnormal. Most of 'dev' shut their doors when they left. The peculiar part was the knob to Dave's door. It was completely missing. In its place was only a half circle of emptiness, the rough wooden edges a clear indication that something violent took place.

*Oh, there **has** to be a story behind this...*

While I stood admiring the destruction, Matt Pohle—one of our new testers—came walking out of a nearby cube. Matt was a stringy fellow about my height who only a few months before was promoted from Tech Support to Testing. Although I'd just met him, it was clear he liked to have fun. I heard his laugh a lot during the day. When he saw me, he grinned big.

"What happened to Dave's door?" I said.

Matt covered his grin with one hand and bent forward slightly. "Dave kicked it open!" he whispered.

I shook my head slowly. "Do I want to know why?"

Matt's grin got larger. "Well, you know his little boy?"

*The boy who used to bounce in the seat-spring? How could I forget?* I nodded. "Yeah, I know him."

"Yeah...well, this morning Dave came in, put his keys in his office, and he walked back out here," he said, motioning toward the open area normally occupied by Dave's receptionist. "And the little boy followed him. But on the kid's way out, he pulled the door shut—Ker-slam!"

I smiled and shook my head again.

"He locked Dave's keys inside."

I sniffed. "I bet Dave was happy," I said.

Matt waved his hands over his head. "Oh, he was storming around...there was a lot of swearing." Matt pointed a thumb at the door. "And then he just kicked the door open!"

I looked at the door again. It was a clean hole. "Couldn't he have just called a locksmith or something?"

Matt shrugged. "Probably, but he didn't. He turned around and just mule-kicked it open!" Matt's eyebrows went high. "Can you believe it?"

I studied Matt a moment. Things were rough in the department he came from, I knew. Fox offered free phone support to anyone who used the product, and some of our users not only took advantage of it, they exploited it. Some called nearly every day.

To make matters worse, the call list for Tech Support was maintained on a huge stack of pink 'While You Were Out' notes. It was insane. Apparently, no one thought to use our perfectly good database product for the task, or if they had, they were overridden. *Isn't that what a database is for, after all?*

In addition, the Tech Support people had mandatory overtime. 'Mandatory' in that if they left, they didn't need to bother coming back the next day. When Matt was promoted, his colleagues cheered his success. He was finally getting a better life, they thought.

They had no idea.

I placed a hand on Matt's shoulder and gripped it firmly. "Welcome to Fox Software, Matt," I said. "The **real** Fox Software."

*...the place where crazy stuff happens nearly every day. I hope you enjoy your stay, 'cause most of the time, I sort of hate it. Keep your head low, Matt.*

*   *   *

A few weeks later, Heindel called my name as I walked by his office. "I need to talk to you about something," he said. He looked serious, an uncommon disposition for him.

"Sure," I said and walked in.

Heindel stood up over his desk and shut the door. He *was* serious.

Of any, Heindel's office probably looked the most occupied. He had two white shelves, haphazardly filled with books and old software. He had a bulletin board with notes, phone numbers, and a low golf score tacked up on it. He also had a brass and white burlap chair he brought in from home. In contrast, Eric still sat on a broken-down black chair and hadn't unpacked his moving boxes yet.

"I need to talk to you about your attitude," Heindel said.

I didn't see that coming. "My attitude?"

"Yeah. It sucks."

Wounds from a friend. I couldn't help but feel a little defensive. Heindel obviously didn't understand all I went through. It was now

April 1991 and the development cycle for 2.0 had stretched out for a long time. Way too long, in my opinion. I started work on the Screen Painter in the fall of '89—and almost a year and a half later—I was still working on the Screen Painter. If my attitude was bad, it seemed justified.

"You fight everything Dave wants. I don't want you to get a bad reputation."

I picked up the stuffed Cleveland Browns football that he kept on his desk. It was my favorite thing to fool with when I was there. It was getting ratty looking, its stitches starting to break. I squeezed it as I thought.

Heindel was probably right. I did resist change a lot. I was sort of at the end of my rope. All my gung-ho-ness was wrung out. Replaced by what? Anxiety. Stress. A little fear? Dave told me recently I "fought too much" but a few days later, when Janet persuaded me to make a Screen Painter change, he said I didn't fight enough. I wasn't sure how to behave anymore.

I thought we were all in the same place, though. We'd been on a death march for so long we were starting to look like zombies.

"I don't think you understand…" I said. I tried to explain my situation.

Heindel was undaunted. "Just my impressions," he said finally. "What you do with it is up to you."

"OK," I said and got up to leave. If Heindel thought I was fighting too much, I'd try to ease up a little. It'd be hard. Work wasn't much fun anymore. All I really wanted was for the product to ship. I needed a break.

\*     \*     \*

Any given morning was much the same as the last. Overnight, or over the weekend, Dave would have an opportunity to play with the product. While doing so he would find some problems that fell into one of two categories: 1) bugs to be fixed immediately; 2) things he didn't like about the product (*melanomas* in Dave-speak) he wanted "fixed" before the end of the day. These problems were cataloged on a list he made and beside each item would be the initials of the developer(s) he thought responsible. The culprits were notified of their guilt in a variety of ways.

The most likely method of notification would be via phone from Dave's secretary, Melody. Passing by her desk, Dave would say something like "Mel-ooo-dee! Get Kerry, Chris, and Heindel in here!" She then set about calling everyone he mentioned and told them "Dave wants to see you in his office. Right away!" The summoned would drop what they were doing and trudge to Dave's office, usually with downcast heads, the fear of impending doom evident in their gait.

Sometimes, though, the call came from Dave himself. When that happened he was usually calling from his car phone (he was the only person I knew that had one) as he was on his way in. If he resorted to this tactic, it meant he was demonstrating the product to someone that very morning. His problem would need to be fixed ASAP—preferably before he arrived.

The final method of summoning was the most intrusive. Dave would arrive at the office, drop whatever he was holding, turn on his computers, and set off to get the people he wanted individually. This was the method with the built in early warning (boom-step) system. It was like a scene from "Jurassic Park". All of us knew Dave was coming, and hoped he wasn't coming for us.

When Dave finally arrived at the unlucky soul's office, instead of just walking in and asking them to follow, he would peer through the Plexiglas (usually with a stern look on his face), knock on it with a forefinger, and motion for them to come out. It was like being summoned for that last long walk to the electric chair; I expected a member of the clergy to be walking just behind me.

The scenes that followed in the corner office were rarely pleasant. Chris called the experience "getting a rebuttal"or "getting a new orifice carved out for oneself." In morning meetings Dave was seldom diplomatic. He was normally agitated and unreasonable, and almost always loud. He had his list of problems laid on his desk and blasted through them one at a time, careful to state how awful and unusable the product was now, and how quickly the change had to be made. "Egregious infelicity!" he'd say. "Heal it! Quickly!" This was not the time for discussion. The naïve developer might try to argue a point, but that was a good way to get your arms ripped off, so to speak. Never argue, and definitely never say something was hard. Dave didn't want to hear it. He didn't care. Morning meetings were for addressing Dave's concerns and the concerns gleaned from the CompuServe traffic. Implementation details were best left for later in the day.

Afternoon meetings, though, came with their own set of difficulties. Dave was more introspective. He liked to ponder how problems might be solved. Consequently, his mannerisms would be on full display. Rings would be spinning, ears would be flipping, and popcorn would be spilling. At times we bit our tongues to keep from laughing, but we did what we had to do to get our problems solved.

Unfortunately, the problems just kept on coming.

\*         \*         \*

Even into May the CompuServe Traffic continued to feed the feature mill. We never knew what changes would need to be made next. We all lived in constant fear of a change coming in that was beyond our abilities. That somewhere, out there—swimming in the CompuServe Sea—was one feature that would finally cause us to go running from our office and screaming out into the night. I essentially held my breath every day, and was grateful the majority of my last minute changes were minor. Not everyone was so lucky.

One fateful day, after reading a particularly long and protracted discussion thread on the forum, Dave realized the way the READ command was currently working would never be acceptable.

READ. The can of wombats. The tower of eggs. The command that energized an interface. The command that was often the pivot an entire dBASE application turned around. It reared its malformed and unstructured head again in a terrible way.

What the CompuServe traffic hinted at (*screamed*, really) was the fact that there were serious problems with the way READ interacted with other areas of the product—areas a dBASE programmer might normally have in an application—like the BROWSE command, or menus, or any other non-READ window, for that matter.

Specifically, the problem was that READ was never designed to work with other windows. In the days of FoxBASE+, there weren't other windows to deal with, so READ filled the entire screen and handled every key that was pressed. In the initial version of FoxPro, our principal goal was to have READ function just like the one in dBASE IV. dBASE IV maintained the same functionality for READ as Ashton-Tate's earlier products did—and so had we. There wasn't enough time or able bodies to do anything more exhaustive.

However, in 2.0 we inadvertently pried the lid open. Heindel and I tweaked the READ code to allow for multiple windows. It was a nice addition, but it gave our users the expectation that those windows were fully able to interact with the rest of the product. Such was not the case. READ was still designed to have one of its windows—no matter how many there were—be the one on top. If one of them wasn't, the READ would terminate and the user's program would continue on.

Most of the time.

Sort of.

Or not.

So, when the problems became obvious, Dave called a meeting to address them. The final result was a list of extremely difficult READ enhancements. These enhancements were collectively lumped under one primary feature—called a "Foundation READ"—that could handle interactions from the multiple windows involved in the READ, and everything on the FoxPro desktop at the time. Because of its all-inclusive nature, and the recent ending of the first Gulf War (that Saddam Hussein promised would be the "Mother of All Wars") we called the Foundation Read, The "Mother of All Reads"—or MOAR for short.

*     *     *

Because my name was on Dave's list for a totally unrelated problem, I was present when he piled the MOAR enhancements on Heindel. It was not pretty. My friend's face was ashen and his responses slow, deflated. I thought he might need his heart restarted.

"Dave," Heindel began, "I don't know about this." He hesitated, shook his head. "I mean I don't even know where to—"

"We have to do this," Dave said. He was serious, but sympathetic. His eyes were fixed on his computer screen, presumably to avoid having to watch Heindel's reaction. On the screen was a READ window and a companion BROWSE window—each failing to behave well with the other. "READ is unusable without these changes," Dave said.

Heindel glanced at the screen, and then shook his head again. "Yeah, I can understand that," he said, "but READ…well, every time I go into that code, I break something."

I fully understood how Heindel felt. Until that instant, I was certain **I** was going to be the one to have something major dumped on him at the last minute. With as many trips as I made to the corner office it certainly seemed likely. Now it looked like it was going to be Heindel. I felt for him, but to be honest, I was also a little relieved.

I briefly tried to communicate non-verbal empathy, but Heindel was too busy staring at the floor. I glanced across the room. Dave recently had a clock hung on his wall that looked like a map. It followed the path of the sun across the earth. There were plenty of hours of daylight still left.

Dave looked at Heindel. "Yes, yes…READ is bad," he said, still sounding sympathetic. He looked at me.

*Why is he looking at me?*

"Kerry will help you," he said.

The world seemed to grow dark. *Me? How did I get involved?*

Then, with little further discussion, Dave waved us away. I followed Heindel back to his office.

He threw the door shut. "I can't believe this!" he said. "It's me again! Every time we get to the end of a project, I'm on the critical path!" He rounded his desk and dropped into his burlap seat, causing it to make a clanking sound. "I thought I was home free this time, but it's me! Again!" He glanced at me, his eyes wide. "I have no idea how to make these changes!" He paused, shook his head. "I can't believe it's me again!"

I remained silent. Heindel was right. In every project he worked on since I'd known him, he ended up held over the fire at the end. In FoxBASE+ 2.10 there was the CodeGen stuff, and then the integration of CodeGen again in FoxBASE+/Mac. On the FoxPro 1.0 effort he had some printing work that went the distance and now READ with 2.0. It almost didn't seem fair.

I really wasn't sure how to help, though. I hated READ. It was chaotic.

Then a few ideas started to come to mind. I thought about some of the things we had to do for snippet windows. Sally and I wrote a number of routines to loop through windows looking for the appropriate type. Then I remembered the places I had to change for multi-window READ. What if READ sort of *hibernated* when another window came up, another window that didn't belong to READ?

I felt a burst of confidence. "Wait, Heindel-man," I said. "I think we can do what Dave wants."

He looked at me as if I'd finally lost it. "Huh?" he said.

I raised a shoulder. "I think I've got an idea where to start, anyway."

Before long I moved a machine into Heindel's office and we were coding in tandem. We worked for days, from early in the morning until late at night, and eventually good things began to happen.

*     *     *

Here's an example of the sort of behavior we were trying to fix. A dBASE developer has some code he's written that has a READ with two windows involved (a typical multi-window READ scenario). The users of the application could click on either window, type in any editable areas, perform any normal interface behavior, and READ would work just fine.

However, if the dBASE developer's code opened a BROWSE window **before** the READ, so when the READ executed there were three windows in play—a BROWSE window and the two that belonged to the READ—a weird thing would happen. If the users just interacted with the READ windows, everything would be fine.

However, if they happened to click in the BROWSE window, the READ itself would terminate. After that, the users could no longer interact with the two READ windows anymore. They were completely dead. Only the BROWSE window was available.

Now to avoid that, the dBASE developer puts a button on one of his READ windows that brings up a BROWSE. In that case, when the button was pushed, usually a BROWSE window would open and come forward, but the READ window that contained the button would still think it was in control—it wouldn't realize a window was brought up on top of it. So, it would still be trying to take every keystroke and mouse click for itself. This would leave the BROWSE window in a state where it **looked** like it could be interacted with, but it really couldn't. It was sort of a zombie BROWSE. It looked alive, but for all practical purposes, it was dead.

The whole thing was confusing for us, and we weren't trying to make our livelihood by using it. Unfortunately, what really needed to be done to READ was the same thing that happened to most of the product for the first version of FoxPro. It needed to be turned inside out so it was truly event-driven.

There was no time for that, though, and no way to test it all when we were through.

So the hope was to move wraith-like through the READ code, being as judicious as possible, yet still make it behave the way it should. It was a tricky endeavor.

That's where hibernating the READ came in. The idea was to detect the specific places in the READ code where window-switching could happen, test to see if such switching occurred (like that the BROWSE window opening on top), and then put the READ to sleep temporarily. Then, when the BROWSE (or whatever other window went away), we needed to wake the READ back up again.

It was tricky, but it turned out I knew enough about the event-driven parts of our product and Heindel knew enough about READ it actually started to work.

*     *     *

"Computers will never work, you know," Heindel said.

I smiled. It was less than a week after we started the MOAR changes, and they were nearly complete. Heindel's spirits definitely improved, and surprisingly, so did mine. I heard wise men and scholars say that the quickest way to make yourself feel better is to help someone else out who's in need. I think there's a lot of truth in that. It worked for me.

Ironically, the person I helped was the one person who told me my attitude was poor in the first place. Things just happen that way sometimes, I guess.

"OK," I said, biting on the line that Heindel tossed out. "Why will computers never work?"

"Well, you've got all that electricity flying around through silicone and stuff," he said circling his fingers over his keyboard. "It shouldn't work. It can't work. It's just way too complicated."

I laughed. I crossed my legs, rested an elbow on one knee, and put my chin in that hand; my most relaxed posture. "Why are we doing this then," I asked.

Heindel checked his screen. "I don't know about you," he said, trying to sound serious, "but I'm just doing it to feed my family." He looked back at me. "But I'm going to have to do something else before long. Because someday everyone is going to figure it out...."

I nodded my head. "Yeah, and then we'll be in trouble."

"That's right!" Heindel said, now starting to laugh. He cupped his hands and slapped the back of one into the other to emphasis each word. "Computers will **never** work!"

I laughed and stood up. I had one of those non-working computers to return to my office. "All right, Mr. Heindel. Whatever you say. Let's hope they don't find out too soon." I unplugged the chords from the back of my machine and wrapped my arms around the monitor.

"Never work," Heindel said as I left. "Never."

*　　　*　　　*

A few days later Melody brought me a memo. It said—beginning with the next weekend—we would be working every Saturday until the product finally shipped. The actual release date was still unknown, but Dave thought it would be sometime in the month of June.

Unfortunately, the flow of wishs, gotta-haves, and "this product is unusable without" threads was still as steady as ever. And now we'd be losing our weekends because of it.

It wasn't fair—but somehow we survived it.

At least, **most** of us did.

# Chapter 20
# Desertion

*This is like something from the back of a comic book.*
It was my first trip to California, when I was only a college freshman. I traveled with my friend Rusty to visit a couple friends there (one who was the groom in the wedding I attended years later). Rusty and I were catching rays on the beach while our California friend was on the boardwalk buying shirts. The name of the beach was Venice and suddenly I felt sand hit me in the face.

"You two were looking at us weren't ya?"

I turned to my right, in the direction of the voice. Standing over Rusty were two shadows. Shadows, because the sun was almost directly behind them. What I could make out was a thick shadow and a thinner shadow. Their hair was straggly and matted. They were unshaven, and—on a hot, summer day—they were wearing flannel and blue jeans.

*What brought this on?* I looked at Rusty. My pale-haired and sunburnt friend was staring forward, doing his best to ignore our nameless tormentors. The thicker shadow pulled back his foot and kicked again. Another wave of sand hit Rusty, and then indirectly hit me.

"Answer me. Were you looking at us or not?"

Rusty continued to stare forward. "No," he said.

"You weren't looking at us?" The foot came back. More sand and the thin one laughed.

"I think you were looking at us," the thick one said. "I think you **like** looking at us."

*Man, I never saw you before two seconds ago.* I looked at Rusty again. He was still staring forward. *How are we going to get out of this?* I searched the beach in front of me. Not a lifeguard or policeman anywhere, and even if I were big enough, I wouldn't take these guys on. They could be hiding anything in their clothes.

Another kick. Rusty's right side was now partially buried in sand. I decided to join him in staring straight ahead.

The sand flew a couple more times, and then there were some swear words and finally—after a few more taunts—the shadows just moved away. Undoubtedly to harass someone else.

"What was that about?" I said after they moved out of range.

Rusty still looked a little scared. "I don't know," he said.

"Were you looking at them?"

He shook his head. "I never saw them until they were standing here."

I looked out at the ocean and thought for a moment. "I guess it's time to start pumping some iron," I joked.

Rusty frowned, repositioned himself on his beach towel. "I think it's time to buy a gun."

I laughed, but when we returned to Ohio, I did start lifting weights. Over my remaining years in college I gained over thirty pounds from what I weighed in high school. It wasn't enough to make me look like "Ah-nold", but it was enough to keep me from being bullied physically again.

There are other ways to be bullied, though. My work on FoxPro 2.0 proved that.

*        *        *

The Friday before Memorial Day 1991, Dave called a development meeting. The purpose of the meeting boiled down to two sentences: "There's a three day weekend coming up. I expect everyone to work two."

*That's good*, I thought. *My life was way too relaxed.*

We were past the breaking point already. The enhancements were still coming, the code had to be kept in perfect shape, and we already lost months of Saturdays to work. Even our time away from the office didn't seem like time away anymore.

*        *        *

"I'm afraid of the phone," Sally said one day when I was in her office.

"Why's that?" I asked. It seemed like a strange admission.

Sally again had a pre-chewed pen near her mouth and a leg crossed beneath her. "I'm afraid it will be Dave trying to call me in. Every time I hear the phone ring I tense up."

I didn't realize Sally was called in that much. I remembered a time when Janet had her come in because a single pixel was the wrong color on a dialog. I didn't think that Dave ever specifically called Sally in, though.

Still, children don't have to actually be dropped to be afraid of the experience. Sally may just have felt some 'sympathy anxiety' from listening to me. I worked on the visual tools—the things Dave liked to play with. Consequently, I was called in more than most. At least, that's how it seemed to me.

But I wasn't afraid of the phone ringing. Since I moved to Perrysburg, I got a lot of calls at home after work. Most of the people I knew were twenty minutes away now. The sound of the phone ringing usually meant the voice of a friend on the other end. I couldn't imagine that changing any time soon.

*       *       *

Because of the routine I started in college, at least three evenings a week I tried to make it to the gym. This brought me no small amount of grief from my fitness-challenged workmates, but I didn't care. Besides keeping me in shape, it gave me a positive way to keep my attitude in check—which improved following the MOAR solution, but at times was still a struggle to maintain.

Around the time Dave cancelled our Memorial Day, I stopped by the gym after work. My current workout place was located in Perrysburg. It was called Holiday Fitness and a few weeks earlier Fox employees were given the option to join. It wasn't a free membership, mind you. We just got a reduced rate.

The gym was located on the east side of town, on a street called Holiday Lane. It was right next door to an earlier Fox home, a small white office building that served the company in the years before I joined it. I never saw the inside of that building, but I always wondered what it was like. The only story I heard from Heindel was about how his partitioned office space steadily shrunk as the building's occupancy grew.

The fitness center itself was not crowded. In fact, it was better than most gyms I frequented. It had an indoor track, a pool, and a good selection of free weights and aerobic machines.

Since the California incident, my preference was always weightlifting. So, as I did every visit, I changed into my gym clothes and went about my normal routine, working my way slowly through their assortment of equipment. At about the halfway point of the workout—just as I picked up a set of dumbbells—I heard someone call my name. I looked up to see one of the gym attendants clutching the wall phone's receiver.

"Are you Kerry?" the gym attendant asked.

"Yeah…"

He held out the receiver. "This is for you."

"Who would call me at the gym?" I wondered aloud. "I don't even know the number." I shook my head and returned the weights to the rack. "Who would call me here?" I crossed the running track to where the attendant stood and took the phone.

"Hello?"

"Yeah…Hi Kerry! It's Melody." It was Dave's secretary; the tulip that grew outside the lion's den.

"Hi Melody," I said, feeling my stomach muscles beginning to tighten. "What's up?"

"Well Dave has this problem." She paused. I heard activity in the background. "Just a minute."

Melody's voice disappeared and I expected to hear Dave's next. I could hardly wait.

Bill Ferguson's low timbre suddenly filled my ear. "Kerry?" he said. "Never mind. We figured it out. It was something Chris did."

"What?" I was still hearing a lot of commotion.

Another slight pause, "Never mind," Bill said.

Melody was back. "Hi, Melody again. Dave had a problem and he wanted me to call you in. I tried your home, but you weren't there, so I figured you were at the gym." She talked quickly but it sounded like she was smiling. "Anyway, Bill figured it out. It was something Chris did. So, never mind. Bye!" Then she was gone.

I held the receiver in my hand for a moment—dumbfounded. I was almost called in—from the gym! I replaced the receiver and brought my hands to my sides. I was now on call no matter where I was, at a moment's notice, and at Dave's every whim.

I had plenty of energy for the rest of my workout.

Still, the endorphin rush couldn't dampen the feeling that I was becoming a slave. Little of my time was my own anymore, and the time that was supposed to be mine, was slowly being encroached upon. *This product really needs to ship*, I thought. I needed a break.

*     *     *

Dave McClanahan wasn't enjoying the Fox Software experience either. He was struggling to get all the bugs out of his SQL implementation and there were still whole parts of it that weren't finished—even with Eric's help.

When I asked McClanahan what was left to do, I'd get one of two responses. Either he'd smile and point to the infinity sign I placed—months earlier—in the midst of his whiteboard's display of symbols, or he started talking about things like "join conditions" and "tuples" until my eyes glazed over. Whatever it was that needed doing, only he—and maybe Eric—really knew.

It must have concerned him, because one day McClanahan saw no alternative but to walk into Dave's office and level with him. He told Dave how stressed he was, brought him up to date on the status of SQL, and said he needed at least two more weeks to complete it.

Dave wasn't very sympathetic. He demanded the SQL code be finished on time and McClanahan do "whatever it takes" to make it happen.

*        *        *

On June 28th—a Friday afternoon—Dave called the developers to his office. It was awhile since we heard a "ship this sucker" speech, so I assumed it was that time again.

As I entered the room and found a seat, I noticed Dave's demeanor. In such meetings he was usually quite animated, eating popcorn or juggling something in the air. This time he slumped in his chair. His movements were slow, nearly despondent. Something major was up.

He wasted little time. "I called you all here to tell you McClanahan resigned today, taking his wife with him…."

*McClanahan quit!* I couldn't believe it. No developer ever quit before and Dave prided himself in that fact. He mentioned it frequently in interviews. (We **did** lose Carol, of course, but I don't think she counted toward the record.)

*And McClanahan's wife left too!* She was in Marketing. She was a sweet lady who laughed when we called her husband a "picky eater."

Dave looked at Eric. "Unfortunately, this means the product will be delayed for a week or so, in order to give Eric enough time to complete the remaining SQL work."

The office grew very still. Aside from the shock of McClanahan's departure, none of us wanted the release to drag out any longer. Equally unsettling was Dave's apparent emotion over the whole thing. It wasn't easy for him to finally *lose* a developer.

Dave perked up a little. "Listen, McClanahan's health wasn't very good," he said. "He had problems…."

That justification wasn't very good. We weren't in army boot camp, after all.

Dave looked at Eric again. "…and there is some indication the Emperor had no clothes. Some of the things McClanahan was doing…duplicating code…well, he just wasn't much of a coder."

I didn't know whether that was true or not. I heard about the duplicating code issue, but that was ancient history. Dave was sort of hurling stones at the guy's back after he left. McClanahan deserved

better than that, especially given the conditions we all toiled under.
Apparently, he was now our black sheep son.

His departure **did** leave us one developer short with a product left
to finish, though. Two more weeks meant at least twelve days of
CompuServe traffic and the risk of additional enhancements.

\*     \*     \*

"We're going to lose another summer," Sally said, shaking her head.
"Three years!! I can't believe we're going to lose another summer."
She hunched down, turning her office chair slightly. "I hate this place."

June dwindled away, and we were now into July. Unless Eric
finished SQL soon, we had only the winter chill to look forward to. I
sighed and dropped my head. I shared in Sally's frustration.

Ohio has strongly marked seasons. The spring and fall months are
usually pleasant with an occasional thunderstorm or tornado thrown in.
The summers are nice and warm—sometimes too warm, but in general,
they are perfect weather for doing anything outside, especially any kind
of water sport. The winters, on the other hand, are about as close to
Hell as anyone would like to come. The months of December through
February are filled with near continual snow, wind, and
ice—not great conditions for a day at the lake, or anything else for
that matter.

Thanks to a roughly one-year product cycle, Fox was in the habit
of shipping a product in the fall. Shipping a product in the fall meant
the bulk of the work was done in the spring and summer. This meant
we essentially missed the best months of the year for close to three
years. That can really get on your nerves. Any joy you get from
releasing a product quickly dissipates when you stick your foot into a
pile of ice cold slush. Now, all that stood between us and another lost
summer was Eric's efforts with the SQL code.

*Time to start praying...*

\*     \*     \*

Thankfully, he was up to the task. Eric completed the SQL work in
roughly two weeks—the same two weeks McClanahan asked for
originally. Dave called a meeting to announce the completion. He
was gleeful.

"Dave," Janet said as we began to filter into his office, "Pat Adams
called and she has a problem she wants to talk to you about." Pat was
one of the dBASE gurus. She had suggested changes steadily since the
Fox Reunion, now almost a year ago.

Dave rested both arms on his desk, and then rested his chin in one hand. "Pat called, did she?" He thought for moment. "Pat called...Pat..." He hopped forward in his seat, grabbing a pack of sen-sens as he did so. "Well, so what!" He laughed and straightened himself. "I wish they'd all shut the f*** up and give us their money!" He chortled louder and some of us joined him. When silence returned, he got more serious.

"As you may or may not know, Eric finished SQL, which means we can finally ship this sucker." He looked at Eric, and then played the crowd. "Eric has done an amazing thing. He's done what nobody else could do." He scratched the side of his face. "What McClanahan had was not good, my friends. The Emperor just had no clothes." Dave panned the room again slowly, making sure to catch everyone's eye. "Eric essentially rewrote SQL in two weeks. Nobody else could've done that," he said. "Nobody."

*Nobody?* I started to feel ambivalent. Part of me wanted to be glad our misery was finally over. The other part felt a little hurt by the way Dave kept repeating that Eric did something "nobody else could do." I didn't see a lot of joy on the faces of the other developers either.

Most thought Eric was the brightest among us. It was impossible to take away from the work he did over the years or some of the miracles he pulled off. He sped up the product in numerous different ways. He wrote substantial portions of our text editor and BROWSE. He did tricks with code swapping so our bulky product could run in an extremely small memory space. He came up with Rushmore (or, as he called it, "the amazing bit-stacking algorithm"). All of it amazing, amazing stuff.

There were many talented people in the room, though, each working extremely hard for Dave, and all pulled off a miracle or two in their past. Yet, when you got right down to it, we were all expendable. Eric was the only developer Dave wouldn't fire (aside from Amy). We knew it and we learned to accept it. The "SQL's finished" meeting felt like Dave trying to rub it in.

To Eric's credit, he never held his "most favored" status over us. From comments he made to me earlier, I knew he appreciated the work the rest of us did, even when Dave didn't.

No matter the presentation, the SQL implementation was done and Dave promised to put blinders on long enough for the product to ship. The official release date was to be July 12th, early enough for us to enjoy part of the summer.

After nearly two years of coding, we would soon be free.

\*     \*     \*

Of course, there is always one final trial.

On the twelfth, I stood in the central cubical division talking with Amy and Janet. Everyone was starting to relax a little. The final build was made and the testing department was making one last verification pass through it; just one last sanity check, and then it was out the door. Amy commented about how much hair she lost during the development cycle.

I squinted. "It doesn't look that much different to me," I said, smiling.

"Well, no," she said. "But I can tell. More hair falls out in the shower."

Janet nodded. "Stress can do that."

*I'm surprised I have any hair left,* I thought.

John Beaver, one of our younger testers, walked up and stood just behind me. He was one of the two college grads recently made testers—the other being Matt Pohle. Both were CS students. Dave decided to use testing as a training ground for potential developers.

Personality-wise, the two were about as different as night and day. Matt was an extravert and a frantic hockey player. John was quiet, polite, and probably enjoyed a good book even more than I did. He waited patiently for us to notice him.

"Yeah, John," Janet said finally. "What's up?"

John brought a hand up to straighten his glasses, and then pushed his bangs back. "Uh, yeah, I got a crash in one of my verification suites," he said. The testers were pushing to automate some of their testing and the suites were part of that effort. Essentially, they were programs they wrote to run against our product to severely exercise various features. An example might be a program that created, opened, moved, and then destroyed a thousand windows using the appropriate FoxPro commands to do that. The suites were still an unproven science though.

"Really?" Janet said. She crossed her arms and started to rock side to side. "What in?"

I took a few steps back. Janet and John had work issues to discuss. The last thing I wanted to think about was more debugging.

"Um...the Report Writer," John said.

Time stopped for a moment and everyone turned to look at me. I felt my life begin to drain out through my shoes. I looked down to watch it go. *This can't be happening,* I thought. *Just when I thought it was over, a bug springs out to get me. This product will **never** ship.* I couldn't take anymore. I wanted to run...or strike out at something. I looked at John. *You, tester, you....* I pulled my eyes over to look at Janet.

She looked skeptical. "The Report Writer?" she said. "That's been stable for months."

"I know," I said softly. My chest tightened so much I could hardly speak. "I haven't changed *anything*."

Janet continued to rock. She looked at John. "Show us."

We followed John to his cubicle where he quickly reproduced the problem. It occurred only under extremely low memory conditions.

"I don't think we'll hold the build for this," Janet said.

I felt my life start to return.

"Just try to reproduce it," she said to me. "See what you find."

"OK," I said. I still didn't really want to deal with it. I dreamed of being able to grip them both Vulcan-style and say "Forget…," and then I pinched myself.

John gave me the necessary files to reproduce his "low memory" problem. I crept back to my office to take a look.

For FoxPro version 2.0 we were actually shipping two separate products in the same box. There was "the standard product," the one that started if a user typed "FOXPRO" at the DOS prompt. This one was built (compiled and linked) in a manner similar to what version 1.0 of FoxPro used. The advantage of this version was it ran on essentially every computer the 1st version of FoxPro ran on. The disadvantage was it was confined to using roughly 640K of memory (maybe a couple hundred more depending on how the machine was configured) so there was a limit to the complexity of user applications that could run on it.

The other version of the product was our extended version ("FOXPROX" from the DOS prompt). It was primarily geared toward higher end—more expensive—machines, but its principal advantage was it could make use of "extended" memory. This allowed a lot more wiggle room for the applications our users wrote, because the extended memory on a machine could be configured as high as 8000K.

It had another advantage for the Fox developers, though. We could debug on it using "source level debugging." This meant we could use another program—a debugger—to see the human readable code we wrote on the screen and step through it a line at a time to find a problem.

That wasn't the case with the standard product. Because of the 640K memory constraint, any debugger we used for it couldn't use much memory (i.e. it had to be a 'light' debugger). That meant no source code. All we'd be able to see was the machine-readable form of our code—strings of letters and numbers most people would think is gobbledygook. We didn't much like the look of it either. Most of us hated having to debug the standard version.

So, my initial hope was that the problem was reproducible in the extended version. I also had another complication. Because John's bug only happened under low-memory situations, I had to run another program—a memory eating program—to swallow up enough of my extended memory so I could reproduce the problem, but not so much that I could no longer make use of my source code debugger. It was a high wire act. One I succeeded in performing, but with disappointing results. After getting the memory set up the way I needed it, bringing up the product, and getting John's program running, I couldn't reproduce his problem at all. The Report Writer worked fine for hundreds of iterations of John's code.

That left me with only one option. I'd have to try it in the standard product. So, after restarting my machine (to clear out the memory eating program I loaded) I fired up my 'light' debugger, the product, and then ran John's program. All I had to do was wait for the product to crash (the behavior John reported). When a "crash" occurred, the debugger would pop up and show me where in the product it happened. Of course, all I'd see was machine code, but I would have a few small human readable clues to go by. Just enough to tell me which subroutine (a small part of the product's code) the problem was in out of the litany (thousands) of subroutines that composed the product. Then I could eyeball the source code for that subroutine and see if I could figure out the problem.

That's precisely how I found it. After John's program ran for only a short time, the product crashed and I saw where the problem was. It wasn't in the Report Writer code, per se. It was in another part (subroutine) of the product the Report Writer used. I brought up a code editor to examine the source code for that routine and I saw the problem. It was an unlocked handle over a subroutine call.

A "handle" was a thing we used in our code to reference chunks of the computer's memory. We had a rule about handles. If your subroutine calls another subroutine, you need to make sure that the handles you are using get "locked." This keeps the memory you are accessing from moving around on you because of something the called subroutine does (in fact, sometimes the act of calling the routine itself could move your memory on you). Having your memory move on you when you didn't know it was going to is like coming home from work and finding your house missing. Not good.

The fix to it was simple, though. Lock the handle down. I made that change. Compiled it. Tested it. Found that it worked. I had my fix.

I went to tell Janet.

"So…" she said when she saw me. She looked a little tense.

"Found it. Fixed it. What do you want me to do?" I gave a brief explanation of my detective work.

"Save it," she said finally. "We'll probably have a maintenance release later anyway."

"OK." I returned to my office and stared out the window. The summer sun was still shining bright and boxed copies of FoxPro would soon go out to meet it.

*Over. I think it's finally over.*

# Chapter 21
# Spit and Polish

At the height of development of 2.0, Dave gave me a jazz CD entitled "Walking on the Moon." I wasn't really much of a fan of jazz. I was more of a Classical or Pop person—at least for music to listen to while I coded, but I took the CD anyway. It wasn't the music style that made it interesting, it was the performer. A musician named Phillip Kahn.

Phillip was a saxophone player, but that wasn't why he was known in the software industry. A French native, Mr. Kahn started his own American software company in a garage the year before I graduated high school (1983). The company's name was Borland and its first products were programming language packages, one of the more popular being a Pascal program named "Turbo Pascal."

Led by this self-proclaimed "barbarian," Borland grew to be a recognizable force in the software industry. By 1991 their popular spreadsheet program, Quattro Pro wrestled away substantial market share from the once-dominate Lotus, and their non-dBASE-compatible database program, Paradox, cut a significant slice from the database pie. Ashton-Tate accounted for 39% percent of database sales, Borland's Paradox was at 35% and the remainder was divided among other database companies.

Fox Software was a part of that remainder, and at the time of 2.0's release we were still somewhat a niche player. We had a great product, and it was out there, but there were still a lot of unknowns. The lawsuit against us was just reinstated; so our legal woes continued. We were a small company, and our fight was now primarily against large opponents. Our marketing team was still floundering.

For a few months in the summer and fall of '91 though, I actually kind of liked jazz.

*     *     *

Following the shipment of 2.0, our next official work item was to create a version of FoxPro for Microsoft's new operating system, Windows.

During my first few years of development, Microsoft's Windows got little respect in the industry. Originally released in '85, it attempted to splice a graphical interface, similar to the one found on the Macintosh, on top of the prevailing—but aging—DOS operating system.

The first two versions of Windows were novelty items really. Their usefulness was limited by the fact they had to share the 640K of memory most machines came with, with whatever application someone tried to run on them. With both Windows and a word processor running, little memory was left for creating a document. Few software companies—beyond Microsoft—produced anything that ran on Windows 1.0 or 2.0.

The third version, released in '90, removed the memory limitation, improved the interface, and was actually somewhat useful. More independent software products were developed for it, and eventually more than 10 million copies of Windows were sold.

It wasn't until the next version, version 3.1, that Fox finally got onboard. Scheduled for release in '92, it was hailed by the trade journals as the 'next big thing', so every company was scrambling to make their software work on it. Dave decided we'd be one of them.

Because Windows ran on DOS and was functionally similar to the Macintosh, it seemed a natural progression to take with FoxPro. The general feeling was we could create a 2.0-equivalent Windows version with a minimal amount of time and effort.

There wasn't a strong immediate push to get started on it, though. "Doing a Windows product is about as interesting as a bucket of spit," Dave said during an interview—and he believed it. He felt the upcoming version of the pseudo-operating system would "do about as well in the market as the previous version" and that just wasn't enough to excite him. Privately, he told the developers that we were doing a Windows product solely for its token value. "It's a checkbox item for magazine reviews," he said, "no more and no less."

Still, after working on the DOS product for nearly two years, most of us were looking forward to a change of scenery. Windows would bring us that.

We had our own reason for not wanting to get started right away, though. None of us had a vacation in well over a year, so there was a lot to catch up on. Chris—who already missed one week of his annual family reunion—left immediately after 2.0 was in the box. And, knowing the best time to take off was just after a product shipped, the rest of us escaped in turn, hoping to enjoy as much of the summer as was left. While the weather was fair, Windows could wait.

\*         \*         \*

As an additional distraction, a major event occurred in another part of the dBASE community. In a move that was no surprise for many industry pundits, Borland International bought our long time rival, Ashton-Tate. The purchase was made through a stock swap of nearly $439 million in Borland stock—a pricy investment at the time.

Regardless of whether it surprised anyone in July of '91, a few years earlier no one would have even dreamed it. In 1989 Ashton-Tate was the top producer of database software for the PC. They had a 60% share of the market and over 300 million dollars in sales. (Our sales were probably a twentieth of that.) They were one of a trinity of dominating PC software companies, along with Microsoft and Lotus.

But due to the release of a bug ridden product (dBASE IV), better than adequate competition (FoxPro 1.0, and others), and the bad public relations they gained from suing us, Ashton-Tate went into a tailspin they wouldn't pull out of before someone was able to buy the whole plane. It doesn't take many mistakes to lose it all.

The buyout (which was finalized in the fall) also had a pleasant side effect for Fox. Concerned that the new Borland company—which would own two popular database products—might stifle competition, the U.S. Department of Justice required the case against Fox be dropped before they would allow the takeover bid.

So, after living under the shadow of the lawsuit for nearly three years, we were free to innovate again, unhindered by any legal entanglements.

\*      \*      \*

One day, while waiting for my machine to compile, I studied a photocopy I was given. Any time Fox was mentioned in an article in a publication I'd find a Xeroxed copy of it on my desk. Early on I wondered what to do with these things (aside from reading them) and Heindel told me he kept a file in his desk. So I did the same thing. Three years later, my "photocopy file" was over two hundred pages thick.

This newest item for my collection was interesting. It was an article from our local newspaper, the Toledo Blade, and it discussed the ending of the lawsuit. Following the specifics of the case and the Borland buyout, the writer's source began to speculate about the eventual fate of our company.

"It increases the pressure on Dave Fulton and Fox to be able to compete," the source said. "He makes great products, but he just doesn't have a big enough company behind him."

The article went on to outline two possible scenarios. The first was we'd "stay private" and "gamble" that we'd stay ahead of our larger competition. The other was we'd be purchased by one of the two remaining software powerhouses—Microsoft or Lotus.

I wasn't sure what to think about the article's conclusions. I couldn't see Dave selling something he obviously felt so strongly about and the other option seemed to suggest stagnancy. "Staying private" sounded like something hermits do. But we were a fast, highly-driven software house. It didn't make sense that we'd stay stuck in the mud when the rest of the industry was moving ahead.

Hinted at in those statements though, was actually a third option, one that wasn't nearly so static. It was called "going public" and I knew the term because I heard it around the office. It had something to do with the stock market, but that was all a mystery to me. The closest I ever was to 'the market' was helping my father take corn to the local grain elevator.

I needed more information. I needed to understand.

I checked my monitor. The machine was still compiling. *Alright.* I pushed away from the desk. *Time to get some answers.*

I left my office and walked the thirty-something feet to Heindel's. After the normal greetings, I got right to it. "Did you read that article about what's going to happen to us?"

Heindel was facing his machine, but at the question, he turned his head to look at me. Everyone found it easier to socialize after the product shipped. "You mean the one in the Blade?" he asked. He paused to straighten his hair with his hand. "Yep. I read it."

"So what do you think? Do you think Dave would sell the company?"

He turned over his hands. "Dunno. But I doubt it."

*That's what I thought.* "One thing's for sure," I said, "Dave doesn't need the money." I reached out to grab the stuffed Cleveland ball and started spinning it in the air.

Heindel watched the ball. "Nope," he said.

Our boss was one of the first people to buy a ZR-1 Corvette (the initials alone cost $27000 over the price of a regular Corvette) only to have the engine give up on him in the first month. Dave's new toys were a constant source of discussion. Since I started at the company, his purchases included luxury cars, telescopes, and things made by Stradivarius.

Heindel turned his seat toward me, anticipating what I was going to do next. "And any company we were sold to would want us to move somewhere," he said. "Nobody would go."

That's sort of what I thought too. Part of Dave's plan from the beginning was to hire people with strong ties to the area. Most of us had something in Ohio more important than work. We were living in the Midwest because we wanted to.

"So you think **nobody** would move?" I bombed the ball hard at Heindel's chest.

He caught it. "My kids' school is here. My family...we're really involved in our church. I can't leave." Heindel thought for a moment. "I don't think Eric would leave either, for the same reasons."

I nodded. There was another reason I couldn't see Dave selling, though.

I threw the ball back hard again and chuckled as Heindel gritted his teeth. "Dave couldn't take orders from someone else anyway," I said. It just wouldn't happen. Not in my wildest dreams. Never.

"True enough." Heindel caught, returned the ball. "It's funny," he said, "Eric and I were talking about this the other day on the way into work." He and Eric both lived in Bowling Green and carpooled whenever Heindel's car was wrecked—which was actually quite often.

Heindel continued. "Eric said the only way he could see Dave selling was if he got bored."

We saw no sign of that, though. Frequently I **wished** the good doctor was a little more bored. "What about this 'going public' thing?" I asked, throwing the ball back. "What's that all about?"

Heindel shrugged and started juggling the ball between his hands. "Well, it means there would be a Fox stock, I know that. It would have a ticker symbol like IBM and Microsoft do." The ball came my way again. "Actually, ask Chris. He knows all about it."

The passing went on a little longer, and then I left Heindel to his work. I went to check on my build again. It was still going strong. Next up, Chris's place.

Chris was one of the few people who actually had artwork hung in his office. Marty was the other. Marty's paintings I understood. Boats sailing on a pond. The focal point of Chris's pictures—both of them—was a large red dot.

"Hey Chris," I said as I entered. "Heindel says you can tell me about a company going public. So, what's it mean?"

Chris leaned back in his chair. He recently taught a course at one of the local colleges and obviously still liked the position of instructor. An elbow was on his desk and he grabbed the air with his hands as he spoke. "Well, it means there would be a public offering of stock in Fox. Most companies use it for an influx of capital."

I knew the definition of 'capital'. It meant money. Our company really didn't need any. Sales had been good for quite some time.

Dave's toys proved it. And we still had little overhead, beyond salary. We were sitting on chairs like rocks, after all.

"Why would we do that?" I asked. "Dave doesn't need the money."

Chris shook his head a few times quickly. "No, but the company needs the clout. When I was in marketing, I ran into that a lot. Some companies won't buy from us just because we're privately owned."

*Why would someone be that concerned about the company they bought software from? You buy it, you use it. As long as someone answers the phone when you call....* "Really?" I asked.

Chris widened his eyes and jiggled his head. "Oh yeah. Some of them have policies against it. They're afraid the company will fold when the owner dies, or something."

That seemed silly. Especially when mismanaged publicly-owned companies could be just as instable. Hadn't we just witnessed Ashton-Tate's melt down? "OK," I said. "It seems dumb...but OK." I took a few steps toward the door, contemplated checking my build again.

Chris's eyes tracked my movement. He fluttered an eyebrow. "If I were you, I'd **hope** the company goes public."

"Why?" The 'influx of capital' wouldn't be coming to me, after all.

Chris's voice sped up. He was on a favorite subject. "Well, in other companies, like Microsoft, the key developers have gone from being poor smucks like us to millionaires overnight."

I took a step closer. "How?"

"Because commonly the developers are given low-priced shares at the initial offering. The price shoots up...," he threw his arms up. "Woohoo!"

"OK," I said. "Give me that again."

Chris slowed himself a little. "OK, say you are given ten thousand shares of the Fox stock at its IPO price—say a buck."

"I-P-O?" I asked.

"Initial Public Offering. The first day the Fox stock appears on the market."

"Got it."

"Anyway, so you have ten thousand shares at a dollar a share, which is ten thousand dollars. But, what usually happens the first day or two is the stock shoots up as people invest. So, if the stock goes up to twenty dollars a share, your value goes up twenty dollars for each share you own." Chris's hands went up again. "So now you're looking at two hundred thousand dollars. Woohoo!"

I was starting to feel a little excited. "Wow," I said. "That really happens?"

Chris nodded his head quickly. "Oh yeah."

"Wow…" I said again. I left Chris and made the return trip to my office. I tried not to let this new insight distract me, but it was difficult because Chris had just explained how someone could make better than six times my annual salary in only two days.

The phrase "going public" took on a whole new meaning.

\*      \*      \*

Soon we had another reason to delay the Windows work. While we were all vacationing and daydreaming, a crop of bugs was found in 2.0. In fact, shortly after its release, reports of problems began to trickle onto the CompuServe Traffic and as time went on, we started to get them from Tech Support calls as well. Most of these problems were isolated or had an easy work around—but, the company policy of immediately addressing external bugs was still in effect for 2.0. If we heard about a bug, we had to fix it. Even after two years of development time, our product still needed more polishing.

The most remarkable thing—given the chaotic way in which our products were delivered—was how few heinous bugs were found in them at all. The public perception of Fox products was always one of speed and stability—and that was fortunate. We saw the effect the opposite perception could have.

Usually it went like this. A reporter from one of the trade magazines would find a bug in a companies' product while writing a review of it. As part of the review he would mention the bug he found, no matter how innocuous. This declaration served as a bit of blood in the water. What followed was a feeding frenzy. From then on, every review written would mention the bugs encountered and how unusable the product was because of them. The product would get labeled as 'buggy'. Soon after, sales would begin to slip.

That never happened to us, though. Reviews of FoxPro 2.0 would tout the amazing speed of Rushmore, the wonderful (of course!) design tools, and would make no mention of any bugs found. We were still perceived as an underdog of sorts, and even journalists like to root for underdogs.

\*      \*      \*

Outside of Sylvester Stallone's Rocky movies, it's difficult to stay the underdog forever, though.

At the start of the nineties, the days of a small company surviving on the revenues of a single product were rapidly fading away.

Companies were merging or being sold all the time. It wasn't hard to imagine a time when only companies like Microsoft and Lotus had the resources necessary to compete.

None of that escaped Dave's attention. Fox Software had the potential to grow into other markets, but we had few resources to foster that growth. We hoped to release a Windows product, a Mac product, and a UNIX product, and still make updates to the DOS product, but we had only a handful of developers.

We could hire more, of course, but recent history proved that throwing more programmers at a problem wasn't always the best solution. Ashton-Tate's team of seventy hadn't produced a product any quicker than our seven, nor had the final result been any better. (In actuality, it was a lot worse).

What we needed was a way to reach our goals using the limited resources we had.

# Chapter 22
# Unification

**DBMS: In addition to keeping your programmers for a long time, you've kept your team small. Why does it always seem that a small team of programmers will turn out a better product than a large team?**

FULTON: It's simple. If you put dots on a piece of paper, the number of lines it takes to connect those dots increases by roughly the square of the number of dots. So, if I double the number of dots, it takes four times as many lines to connect them. Now, if you think of the lines as interpersonal communications, you'll begin to understand why large groups fall apart. They spend most of their time communicating rather than getting the job done....

(Excerpt from "An Interview with Dave Fulton, DBMS magazine, October 1989)

\*        \*        \*

Since the spring of 1988, Fox had the only family of database products that ran on more than one operating system and worked seamlessly together. Using FoxBASE+/DOS (and later FoxPro/DOS) and FoxBASE+/Mac, each running on their respective operating systems, advanced users of our products could create applications that simultaneously shared the same data between the two platforms over a network. This allowed for systems where, for instance, the data entry personnel entered customer orders on a Macintosh while those in the shipping department viewed those same orders on a PC-compatible computer. None of our competitors had the same level of interoperability. We had the only true cross-platform story in the software industry. Period.

However, the breadth of the story wasn't nearly as wide as we would have liked. There was a fundamental problem in our process of software development that made it difficult to maintain our cross-platform strategy, and even more difficult to broaden it to include additional operating systems. The difficulties stemmed from the fact that nearly all the developers worked on the product on one platform until it shipped, and then switched to the other platform to work on the product there until it shipped. So, we'd spend a huge amount of time getting the DOS product finished, and then jump over to work on the Mac product until it was finished, and then move back to the DOS product again. At least, that's how the process originally worked.

Because the market demand for the DOS product was greater, and the amount of time we spent on it tended to be longer, the final result of this 'platform-switching' approach was a Macintosh product that consistently lagged the DOS product by close to a year. This diminished our cross-platform story because there were huge spans of time where our users lacked consistent products on both platforms. And the problem got worse as years went by. Because of the extended development time taken for FoxPro 2.0, by August of 1991, FoxPro 1.0 for the Mac still wasn't finished. The Mac product was now lagging behind the DOS product by nearly two years.

Of course, measures were taken to **try** to bring the Mac product to market sooner. Marty was never brought in to work on the DOS product so he could move (and adapt) the code we were creating to the Mac code base. He was diligent and made some progress, but with eight of us creating code for FoxPro/DOS (thousands of new lines by the product's end) it was a huge job for just one person to replicate that work for the Mac. It was like feeding a funnel from a fire hose. So, to increase the flow, Brian Crites joined him in that effort a year later. That helped, but ultimately that wasn't enough either. Finally two new Mac developers—Henry Seurer and Brad Serbus—were hired to shuffle over code as well. FoxPro/Mac still never shipped, though. It was real close a few times, but for various reasons, it never actually went out the door.

Now, with the forthcoming full-scale development of FoxPro for Windows, the problem was about to be compounded. We were either going to have to hire a lot more developers and risk the cohesiveness of our smallish team, or deal with continued lengthy lags between product releases. Neither of these solutions was well liked, but we'd soon be forced to make a decision.

\*　　　\*　　　\*

It was the month of September. I heard rumors that someone in the north end of the row had proposed a solution to our connect-the-dots problem. Curious, I went looking for facts. I sought out Brian Tallman first. If there was a good idea floating around, he was certain to know about it. He was probably even part of it. I already knew the name of the proposed solution. That in itself was intriguing.

"What's the Grand Unification Scheme?" I asked Brian, seated in his office. I knew what the "Grand Unification **Theory**" was. Astronomy was my favorite subject in college. The Theory is essentially a theory of everything. It's an attempt by physicists to explain all physical phenomena with a single underlying unity. It postulates that all forces—gravity, electromagnetism, and two others—are the same at some level. And at the instant of creation, they were indistinguishable.

"Well," Brian said, crossing his arms. "The Scheme grew from the fact that we have our own Fox API...."

I nodded. We had to create the API for the first version of FoxPro and it proved amazingly flexible throughout the development of the second.

"...and at a certain level we have most of the functionality that would be provided by an operating system. Our own routines to create windows, to draw menus, to handle text...."

We had all the routines necessary to write an event-driven application. Of that, I was well aware. I made extensive use of them for the better part of three years.

Brian nodded at his computer screen. "Like, I started playing with getting the windowing in the Windows product to work, and it seemed like the best way to get it up and running was to stick to our current architecture, keep our current windowing routines the way they were, and put the operating system specific stuff at a lower level somewhere." He moved closer to his desk and clicked a few keys. A couple windows opened to reveal listings of C source code. Brian pointed at one. "I used conditional compile flags to ensure the right code gets compiled for the right product."

I leaned in to study Brian's routines. It didn't take long to see the beauty of the Scheme. It was real cool.

An example might go like this. Take the scenario where both the Windows and Mac operating systems had routines to draw an imaginary thing called a 'widget', and in the FoxPro Screen Painter I wanted to allow our users to draw a widget as well. The low-level Fox API subroutine would look like this:

```
  void FoxDrawWidget(int x1, int y1, int x2, int y2)
#ifdef MAC
  {
        Point a, b;
        a.x = x1; a.y = y1;
        b.x = x2; b.y = y2;
```

```
        DrawWidget(a, b);
   }
#elseif WINDOWS
   {
        WidgetDraw (x1, y1, x2, y2);
   }
#endif
```

So, even though the specific Mac and Windows calls are radically different (DrawWidget() in the case of the Mac, and WidgetDraw() in Windows), from my Screen Painter all I would have to do is make this call:

```
FoxDrawWidget(5, 5, 10, 10);
```

And a widget would be drawn along a line from point 5, 5 to point 10, 10. I didn't have to worry about what operating system I was drawing the widget on at all. That was all taken care of for me at the (lower) Fox API level. The conditional compile flags (the '#ifdef MAC' and '#elseif WINDOWS') made sure the right version of FoxDrawWidget() was built for the appropriate product. The Grand Unification Scheme allowed most of the dev work to be done at a level where the operating system was irrelevant. It seemed like just the sort of thing we needed; the right idea at the right time.

"So, I told Dave about what I'd been doing," Brian continued, "and he got excited. In fact, everyone I've talked to so far has liked it."

"Me too," I said. If we could pull the Scheme off successfully, we could keep our smallish team and still make huge amounts of progress on any number of products. "What downside is there?" I asked.

Brian flipped his arms out, palms up. "Well, there's the Mac."

"The Mac?" I said, and then figured out what he meant. "Oh, yeah…." In order to fit in with the Scheme's "cross-platform" code base, the Mac code would have to be completely re-implemented. All the code-shuffling work Marty and his gang had done over the past several years would have been for nothing. I shook my head slowly. "Yeah, that's a problem."

Brian shrugged. "Well, maybe. But maybe not. In the long run it might be better for the Mac product. It would be integrated. Everyone would be working on it, to some respect."

"What do the Mac Dweebs think about it?"

"Well, I don't know. Marty seemed to be OK with it."

"I'll bet." Marty's complaints about coding "buck naked" echoed in my head. We already ignored the Mac product for close to two years. Any additional delay in its shipment should be more than offset by the advantage of having it part of the same code base as the other products. Subsequent shipments of the Mac product could theoretically occur simultaneously with the other products. Instead of working on a secondary product, the Mac Dweebs would finally be included in the big picture.

"Is that the only thing?" I said. "The Mac product?"

Brian caught his pants at the knees and scooted back in his chair. "Well, no one knows just how long the Scheme will take. Whether it would be quicker this way to produce four working products (DOS, Windows, Mac and UNIX), or to keep going the way we've been going. In the long run, the Grand Unification Scheme seems like a better solution, but for the short run..." Brian raised his shoulders. "Who knows?"

Brian brought an elbow to his armrest and caught his chin in that hand. "So, we're planning a meeting to discuss the whole thing. Get everyone in a room together and see what's what."

"When?"

"Tomorrow or the next day."

"Sounds good," I said, nodded once. We'll see...."

Brian smiled. "That we will."

*       *       *

A few days later, all fourteen of us gathered in the main conference room to chart the course of the product's future. Sitting around the large oval table was Amy Fulton, Bill Ferguson, Eric Christensen, Brian Tallman, Dave Heindel, Chris Williams, Sally Stuckey, and I who just finished work on FoxPro for DOS. There was also the Mac Dweeb team made up of Marty, Brian Crites, Brad Serbus, and Henry Seurer. Finally, there was the newly formed UNIX team of Jim Simpkins and Steve Shue. Dave, who rarely got involved in implementation details anymore, wasn't invited. The meeting was essentially a free-for-all for Unification issues with no specific leader. The better part of a day went by as we discussed the feasibility of the proposal and the intricacies of pulling it off. In a meeting that size— and with so much at stake—there is a tendency to get distracted by the details.

"How are we going to do child windows on the Mac?" someone asked. That was an interesting question, because our DOS product and the Windows operating system allowed for child windows— windows that lived within other windows—and the Mac OS most certainly did not.

"What about source control?!" Another good question. Previously the Mac sources were maintained using the source control system that was a part of the C language program the Mac Dweebs built their product in. If the source code was co-opted between four different operating systems, how would the checking in and out of source files be handled? And where?

"What will push buttons look like?" Buttons on every platform looked radically different from all the rest. Just one more interesting detail to solve.

"What about color schemes? Do we have to support those everywhere?" The definition of colors on prior versions of FoxPro for DOS had grown so exhaustive, it was almost too cumbersome for users to deal with anymore (like menus were before the Menu Builder). In addition, Windows had its own, more global, way for users to specify the colors of different parts of the interface, like windows and menus. Mac systems used colors only sparingly. And UNIX…well…most UNIX users were happy with two colors—black and green. Sometimes, black and amber.

It was Eric who tried to keep us on the big issues. "We have to bind the strong man," he said.

The first time he said it his comment was ignored. The conversation meandered off onto another design detail.

"We have to bind the strong man," Eric repeated.

Quiet returned. "OK," Chris Williams said, "what's the strong man?"

"Pixels or characters," Eric said.

Chris's eyebrows lowered. "Pixels or characters?"

"Yes," Eric said. "Pixels or characters. We have to decide what the native units for our routines will be."

Everyone was silent.

Eric wrenched his head forward, as if trying to pull-start the discussion. "We have to decide whether, if I'm calling the routine to create a window, the position and size information I send in is in pixels or characters. Or if I'm trying to draw a rectangle, do I send the rectangle information in as characters or pixels?"

Then we started to see it, and discussion ensued. It was an important question. Our DOS product, the only shipping FoxPro product, lived in a character-based environment. Because of this, everything about it—from the way windows were created, to the commands in the language—was geared toward characters. A character is actually a big thing. It is many pixels long and high. Forcing users on the Mac or Windows environments to deal with a measurement that imprecise would be like trying to force them to turn a screw with a shovel. Ultimately, the answer we arrived at—the right answer—was that pixels should be used internally for the graphic products (Windows and Mac) and characters for DOS and UNIX.

"What about the language, then?" Eric asked.

That was another problem. Using pixels for measurements on the graphic platforms would mean that xBASE code written on the character platforms wouldn't run without change when run on the graphic platforms. We didn't want that. We dealt with that issue with our FoxBASE+ and FoxBASE+/Mac products, but nobody really liked the solution we used then. Any code written on the DOS platform would run on the Mac platform, but the inverse wasn't true. We wanted no restrictions on the code our users could write this time. Code written on any and every platform should run on every other platform without change.

We had to come up with something else. One interesting solution—the idea of allowing for fractional characters (jokingly referred to as "foxels")—was proposed, but we realized it was pointless to discuss this aspect of Unification any further. Specific changes to the language always had to go through Dave first. So, we decided to deal with the subject of "foxels" later, when we were further down the road of implementation.

We were still left with one burning question, though. How long would the Grand Unification Scheme take us?

Again we weighed, deliberated, and discussed, and just when I thought we could discuss no further, we finally reached a consensus. We estimated it would take somewhere between a year and eighteen months to pull the whole thing off. That meant we felt we could produce three new Fox products: FoxPro 2.0 for Windows, FoxPro 2.0 for Mac and FoxPro 2.0 for UNIX from the same cross-platform code. All the while maintaining the viability of the existing FoxPro 2.0 for DOS product, and do it in less than two years. It was an ambitious estimate, but we were relatively confident we could swing it.

Then an even greater question arose. How were we going to tell Dave?

How could we tell him that we intended to sit and code for a year and a half before we had a single working product? How could we say the Mac product was going to be delayed at least another year? How would we break the news that Fox Software wasn't going to be able to release any products in all that time? We would need to be diplomatic.

We had just begun to formulate a plan of attack, when Dave walked in.

"Why are you all here!?!" he said, his eyes panning the room. "This decision doesn't take all of you! Why are you all here!?!" He paced the space near the door anxiously. "This meeting is costing me a year's salary!"

In an instant, the spirited sense of optimism that permeated the room left, only to be replaced by a sense of quiet nervousness. Fourteen pairs of eyes stared across the table at each other, begging someone else to speak first.

The room was silent for some time.

"Well, Dave," Jim Simpkins began, still as bold as ever, "we're meeting to discuss the Grand Unification Scheme and since it affects everyone, we thought it'd be best to have everyone here."

Dave dug his hands into his pockets and turned to look at Jim. "What's the consensus?"

"Well, we think it's a good idea," Jim said, absently bringing a hand up to support the side of his face. "We think we should do it." He was being gentle, feeding the words out slowly. "We were just trying to come up with some time estimates for our deliverables."

Dave was hungry for an answer. "So, what have you come up with?" he asked, still in motion. "How long will it take?"

Jim hesitated. "Well Dave..." He glanced around the table nervously. "We think it will take around a year and a half, maybe a year."

Dave stopped moving. "What?" he exclaimed. "It can't take that long!" He bowed his head and started pacing again, more animated this time. "A year...well, it can't take that long!" He looked around the room, and then frowned. "Listen! I want to discuss this some more. We don't need everyone here though."

With that, the meeting dissolved. Aside from the more senior members, we all suddenly had something more important to do.

The end result of our daylong meeting? We would pursue the Grand Unification Scheme—it just couldn't take us as long as a year.

And how would we do that? The conventional wisdom was clear. When confronted by one of Dave's impossible deadlines, just work on your project one day at a time. In the end, the deadline will change, and you'll likely have more than enough time.

So, we proceeded to do just that.

# Chapter 23
# Works of Art

One autumn day I was sitting in my office with the window slightly open. On my screen was a picture of our trademark fox head. The head itself was placed on a white square that appeared to have grown from a crossword puzzle-like background. I wasn't really certain of the meaning of the design, but I knew Dave liked it. I had the picture (also called a 'bitmap') opened in the painting program that came with Windows and had it zoomed in so I could see some of the individual pixels—the colored dots that compose the picture—as large, easily-changeable rectangles.

Using my mouse, I changed the color of one of the pixels, and then zoomed out the picture. It looked a little better. I zoomed in again and looked for another pixel to change.

I heard boom-steps walking in the direction of my office. The pattern of the footfalls was uneven. There were at least two people.

I squinted at the screen, and tried to ignore the clamor. I searched for the pixel I'd just decided to change.

I heard the steps pause outside my door. The door handle squeaked as it turned, and then I felt a rush of air hit my face.

"Kerry," a familiar voice said, "Could you show Richard the bitmaps you're working on?"

I looked up and smiled. "Sure, Dave. Bring him in."

\*         \*         \*

With the end of summer came a diversion from my usual set of tasks. Somehow, Dave found out that I took a course in Computer Art while in college and that I still enjoyed drawing on the computer in my spare time.

I'm not certain where Dave got that information, but if forced to guess I'd say it was Heindel. Heindel didn't think I got the credit I deserved, so he frequently did things to help me out. Sometimes he helped, other times, he ended up getting me more work to do—as was the case in this instance.

Development was in the process of creating two graphical products—FoxPro for Windows and FoxPro for Macintosh—so Dave decided we needed to have new background images designed for them. Making use of the knowledge that **someone** gave him, he thought I might like to create these works of art. Surprisingly, when approached with the idea, I said "Sure!"

These background images (bitmaps) were one of the most immediately noticeable features of the product. They resided on the background (desktop) window and featured an approximation of the artwork that appeared on the product's box, along with some script that identified the product version. They were visible the entire time a user was in the product—at least, until they did something to remove or obscure them.

And because they were such a highly visible part of the product, they were something Dave greatly cared about. What that meant for me was, by accepting this new assignment, I'd put myself in danger of being squarely on the hot seat again.

**That** would be a shame, because things had been laid back in Foxland recently. Even though the third DevCon was fast approaching, the stress on the development team was low because most of the products we were working on weren't complete enough to show. The UNIX product was the only product that was nearing any form of 'demo readiness', and that affected only two of our members—Jim and Steve. This left the rest of us in the easygoing stage of early product development, a place where there are few distractions and a lot of work gets done. It was a spot securely out of the limelight and a spot I liked to be in. Even though I readily accepted the 'using the computer as a brush' work, inside I was a little worried I opened up a 'whole new can of wombats'.

As the work progressed, though, my fears diminished. The bitmap project was enjoyable, a welcome break from coding. Dave's expectations were also lower. He wasn't nearly as critical of my artistic endeavors as he was of my code. I was able to work for many days without a confrontation—and most of the time—Dave was downright encouraging.

Of course, there was still the occasional impromptu showing for whomever Dave deemed worthy. In truth, though, those showings didn't bother me nearly as much as they used to. Over time I came to realize they showed Dave was interested in what I was working on. That wasn't all bad, at least he knew I was busy.

*          *          *

Then came the week of DevCon. It was a normal Tuesday night, at around eight in the evening, and I was at home. A commercial break had just come on, so I made my way to the kitchen for a snack. As I stood with my head in the refrigerator, contemplating the few options I had, the phone rang.

My nerves were immediately set on edge. Even though the atmosphere at work had been more casual since 2.0 shipped, my fear of the phone ringing hadn't subsided in the least. Call it a learned behavior. There were too many prior incidents to reinforce my fear.

*This couldn't be Dave, though,* I assured myself. *It's much too late. Every time he's called before it's been right after work.* I crossed the room to the phone. *It must be my parents or something. It can't be Dave.*

I was wrong. It was Dave and he was excited.

"Yeah, Kerry," he said, his voice slightly distorted. The car phone again.

"Yeah…?"

"Yeah, Tallman got the Windows product working today."

I knew that. I saw what Brian had done that afternoon. He got the product to a *limping along* state of functionality. This meant you could start the product and be presented with a Command window and you could type in a few commands. Things generally worked, and it didn't crash **too** often.

 If you did the right subset of things.

In the right order.

Most of the time.

However, it didn't look much like a Windows application. It looked mostly like a DOS application running in Windows. All of the interface elements, aside from the menus, looked wrong. It was partly functional, but not very pretty. Put simply, it was butt-ugly.

Dave thought I could help change that. "I'd like you to go in and help Brian get the bitmap into the product," he said.

I couldn't help but ask "Why?"

"Because," Dave explained. "I'm showing the Windows product as part of my closing session tomorrow."

*This is unbelievable,* I thought. *The product's barely working today and we're going to show it tomorrow? I know Dave likes to keep the customers informed, but this is going a little far. Even for him.*

Still, Dave's exuberance was infectious. "OK, I'll go," I said finally and hung up the phone. I ran to the garage and jumped in my car. *My first public art show since high school,* I though and smiled.

That night Brian and I worked until after midnight to try to get the bitmap into the Frankenstein-like Windows product. After I left, Brian toiled away another six hours on his creation, hoping to ensure that—

unlike the fictional monster—it would prove to be a positive reflection on its creator.

*     *     *

The next day found all of development dressed and present at the closing session. Unlike prior DevCons, this year we chose seats near the front, well within throwing range of the stage. We were a much larger and more relaxed group this time. Few of us had anything on the line. The only ones showing any nerves at all were Jim, Steve, Brian, and I—those whose children were about to take the stage.

When the time of the session finally arrived, the back doors swung open to admit a surge of attendees. Unlike the ho-hum year before, many of the attendees ran—and I mean **ran**—to find a seat near the front of the hall. Apparently, the word was out that something exciting was going to be shown.

Janet Walker ran the demonstration this time around. Seated at an onstage computer, the first thing she did was bring up—by all appearances—FoxPro for DOS. On the room's large screen, the familiar oversized 'FoxPro' letters blazed out from a blue background. She then entered a few commands, yielding typical results, and went on to run a small application—again providing the results one would expect from our DOS product. The response to this display from the audience was a collective "So what?" Janet exited the application to the operating system.

"I want to list out my files here," she said. She typed 'DIR', the command that—in DOS—would present her with a list of the files on her hard disk. In this case she received an error message for her trouble.

"That's odd," she said, looking confused. "Let me try again." She did, again bringing the same error message. There was a nervous silence for a few moments while Janet sat staring at her screen. Then a wave of 'oohs' and 'ahhs' rippled through the exhibition hall as some of the attendees began to realize what they'd seen. Janet's DIR command didn't work because it didn't exist in the operating system. She wasn't running the DOS version of FoxPro, it was the UNIX version. Janet typed 'ls'—the UNIX equivalent of DIR—and everyone became fully aware. The room erupted in applause.

From there, Janet continued her naive wandering act, eventually winding her way first into Windows and finally into our product. Brian's work flashed to life, adorned with the bitmap I created. On the big screen, the bitmap **did** sort of help. The product looked a **little** more like a Window's application.

At that point, the attendees were beside themselves. Janet ran the same dBASE application she ran on the UNIX product, producing similar—but more graphical—results.

Of course, a trained eye would notice that the results were a little strange. The graphical elements didn't appear quite like they should, and some of the items were a little misplaced. The attendees didn't seem to mind, though. They roared their approval.

Following Janet's presentation, Dave took the stage and spent some time talking about the future of Fox. He waxed poetic about our plans for the following year, outlined the Grand Unification Scheme, and detailed our road ahead, all in the 'lovable professor' style he exhibited at shows.

The crowd ate it up, cheering and applauding throughout. When the clapping subsided, Dave turned to look in our direction.

"And there are some people sitting in the front here who I'd like to recognize," he said, indicating us with a hand. "The Fox developers. They deserve a lot of credit for all the hard work and virtuoso stunts they've performed over the years."

The crowd applauded emphatically, ending in a standing ovation.

To the more reserved members of our team, this last bit was a little embarrassing. We took turns staring at the floor or each other—smiling and shaking our heads slowly.

Heindel was sitting a row ahead of me. He turned, looked at me, and smiled. "It's just a computer program!" he said. He was referencing a Saturday Night Live skit that featured William Shatner at a Star Trek convention. In it, he is asked one asinine Trek question too many and explodes. "It's just a TV show," he tells the room of socially challenged trekkers. "Get a life!"

Our users weren't **quite** that zealous in their dedication, but at times they could be close.

Just when we thought the spectacle was nearly over, Chris stood up.

*What is he doing?* I glanced at Sally, who just rolled her eyes and shook her head.

"And we owe it all to this man!" Chris yelled, pointing toward the stage. "To Dave!"

While the crowd politely applauded the admission, the rest of us let out a shared groan and more than a few stifled laughs. *Some things never change.*

\*        \*        \*

We had a meeting to discuss the whole event the following day.

"The demo was the highlight of the conference for me, boys and girls," Dave said. He was relaxed at his desk and noticeably happy. The rest of us were strewn haphazardly around his office.

"It was truly a virtuoso stunt," he said. He placed his pop can on the desk and tapped it softly as he spoke. "Sure the controls looked a little funny, and some of the positions of things were off. But those people didn't know." He looked at his can, pulled it closer. "Having something new to show—finished or not—well…it's important." He glanced at Brian. "Thanks again to Brian." He flipped a hand in my direction. "—and to Kerry, as well—for the last minute Windows product work."

I felt a little embarrassed. My work on the bitmap was in no way as crucial as what Brian did. The virtuoso stunt was all Brian really. *Still, I'll take the accolades from Dave when I get them.* "Thanks, Dave," I said softly, and Brian did the same.

That was **my** highlight of the conference.

\*     \*     \*

Yet, the winds of change were in the air. The computer industry was in a state of flux. Old enemies were becoming allies. Friends were now enemies. We were now positioned squarely in the middle. We had a lot to do in order to keep up.

So, those of us in development went back to our chores, some on the Windows product, some on the Mac, others on UNIX, and still others with smoothing out the edges of the DOS product we just shipped. My job was to get the graphical cross-platform Screen Painter working on both Windows and the Mac, and because it would be a proving ground for the Grand Unification Scheme—an idea I thought really cool—I couldn't wait to get started.

Life was good and almost predictable.

Then I heard the sound of desks in motion.

# Chapter 24
# Hints

Following DevCon, developer life got back to normal. Each of us toiled away at our respective Grand Unification task, pushing toward our indeterminate deadline, nearly oblivious to all that was going on around us

Meanwhile, our company was entering prosperous times. Early reviews of FoxPro 2.0 began to appear and they were extremely positive—most focusing on FoxPro's improved speed and data handling, made possible by the product's new *patent pending* Rushmore technology. They also frequently commented on the product's language and interface enhancements, while giving kudos to its new user-friendly tools.

Over time, the positive press started to have an impact on the bottom line. Sales of the product through the fall and winter of '91 consistently exceeded expectations. This left our production department, whose slogan was now "FoxPro—don't drop it on your foot," hard pressed to keep up with demand. It also led to the need for more people to test, sell, and support the product. Our infant Human Relations department moved quickly to address that need. By the start of 1992 the number of employees had grown to well over two hundred worldwide.

Space in our two-year-old building became a premium. The tech support office area evolved into a maze of ever confining passages surrounded by gray cubicle walls. Two of the building's three conference rooms were converted into offices. We even had one poor soul whose office was once a closet. It was a situation that couldn't continue.

To help alleviate some of the pressure, Fox acquired additional parts of the Country Charm shopping center where we were located. Initially we displaced only a radio station and a fitness shop, but now we were moving out a hardware store and a drug store as well.

But the space shortage continued. It finally reached the point where even the developers were forced to take notice; it's hard **not** to notice when another desk gets moved into your office.

The first to double up was Sally. Jadwiga Carlson, who was promoted from the testing ranks to development shortly after 2.0

shipped, became her officemate. Soon after, Henry and Brad doubled up in McClanahan's old office and rumors began to fly about who would be next.

The trend bothered me. I calculated that there were maybe one or two developers left to go before, I too, had a second desk in my office. I loved having my own space, and the solitude it allowed. I wasn't looking forward to sharing in the slightest.

*       *       *

Thankfully, there were positives to offset the anxiety over the cramped quarters. On Friday of Comdex week, 1991, Dave called development to the one remaining conference room for an important update. Until then, we heard little news from Comdex. Similar to the year before, Dave wanted none of us to be distracted from our Grand Unification work, and so decided that only he and Amy would attend the Vegas event. This meeting would be his way of filling us in.

I could tell by his demeanor that Dave had good news. He was serious, but a happy serious. "I just wanted you all to know," he said, scanning our faces, "and this should come as a pat on the back to everyone in the room," he then absently reached out to grasp the table edge, "FoxPro has won PC Magazine's Award for Technical Excellence this year."

*Another award is good, I guess.* We received a number of accolades over the years. Every magazine had an award. It was hard to keep them all straight, really.

Dave leaned back, and placing his arm on the armrest, shifted over to rest the back of his head in his hand. "This is a great honor, my friends. It's really the closest thing our industry has to an Oscar. You should all be very proud." He smiled pleasantly and glanced around the table again.

Eric and Bill were smiling and nodding. The rest of us were still clueless.

"FoxPro beat out some serious competition," Dave said. "Some of the most recognizable and widely used products out there. Excel, for instance."

That brought out the smiles—and a "Wow!" from Henry. Excel was an upstart Microsoft product that quickly became the darling of the industry. It was putting serious pressure on the other longstanding and popular spreadsheet, Lotus 1-2-3.

Amy smiled impishly. "You should have seen it. Bill Gates was there. He pouted when they announced the award."

Dave wiped the top of his head. "Yes, Bill did look a little distressed." He smiled and cackled softly. "Unfortunately, there's only one plaque. We have t-shirts for you all, though."

Amy looked at Dave and half-frowned.

"They're quite garish, actually," Dave said.

The t-shirts were handed out. They were black with a bright orange and pink design on the front. They weren't from PC Magazine, they were from PC Computing. Apparently, we won one of their awards as well. *Um...thanks PC Computing*, I thought. Still, the Technical Excellence award was cool. Our David-sized product had not only beaten down Goliath, it was going after his brothers.

Dave had more news though. He next told us that we had more in common with Operation Desert Storm than the nickname (MOAR) we had for 2.0's READ command. Dave had met someone named Brian Jones, contracted by the armed forces, who wrote a FoxPro application used for all the logistics for the desert war. Essentially, all the decisions on moving men, supplies, and armaments were relying on our product to do its job—and do it well.

This revelation changed the mood in the room considerably. There was stunned silence for a time, followed by expressions of disbelief.

*No way!* I thought. Memories of the bugs I knew that still existed in the product plagued me. FoxPro was a critical part of a major war. An uninitialized variable in the wrong section of code could have caused troop deployment from Iraq to Guam by mistake.

Dave had no such fears, though. He was cheery, talkative. He mentioned the possibility of our company going public. He told us lawyers had been pursuing that goal for some time and a decision would be reached shortly.

Since most of us saw dollars falling from the sky whenever the subject was discussed, we were all instantly in a good mood again—a mood that continued through the rest of the meeting, the rest of the month, and on into the holiday season.

*     *     *

The holidays at Fox were marked by an event called—appropriately enough—the Fox Holiday Party. At previous holiday parties my experiences wasn't altogether positive.

The first one I attended was the worst. The day prior I asked Heindel how to dress and he said, "Ah, it's no big deal. I'll probably just wear a sweater." So I'd worn a sweater, only to find that I was one of only two sweaters in the room (the other being Heindel, of course).

Every other man was wearing either a suit or a tux. Worse still, I was the only man in the room not wearing a date.

To compound my discomfort at being suit-less **and** dateless, a bully from my high school showed up as the date of one of our receptionists. It just doesn't get any better than that. It made for a memorable evening—but those aren't the sort of memories I usually seek out.

The following year was even more unremarkable. Since the previous year's event was a decidedly couples-only affair, I tried desperately to find a date. But, as frequently happened, I failed in the attempt. With the prior year's humiliation still fresh in my memory, I decided to skip.

The 1991 party was different though. I found someone to accompany me—an ex-Fox employee (who left for reasons I had nothing to do with)—and I had a really good time. The food was good, the company was pleasant, and the entertainment was unique—the highlights being Jim Simpkins karaoke version of "Walk All Over You" and Norm Chapman's rendition of "Down on the Bayou."

The one thing I couldn't help but notice, though, was the two ownership tables.

One table was clearly for the Fultons. Dave and Amy were seated there. With them were Amy's father Norm Chapman (our Vice President of Administration) and his wife. Also at that table was Dave's daughter from his first marriage. She spent a number of summers working for Fox.

The LaValley's table was equally stocked with Fox employees. Joining Dick and his wife were two of their daughters, Diane and Elaine. Diane was our Controller (She handed out the checks), and Elaine was an Administrative Programmer. Also at that table was "Marketing" Richard, still clearly a family friend.

However, little interaction went on between the two groups. Though side-by-side, they remained islands unto themselves; their conversations trapped within the bounds of their table.

That seemed weird to me. Although I'd seen hints of a rivalry before, Dave and Dick always appeared to be at least cordial around the office. They were partners in a successful software company, one that beat the odds on numerous occasions. I would think that, despite any personality differences, the two men (and their families) would be close. Usually surviving against long odds does that to people, brings them together, like soldiers in a war.

For the first time I began to suspect it wasn't just Dave versus "Marketing" Richard or Dave versus Diane, it was Dave versus Dick

LaValley—his longstanding partner. Briefly, I wondered whether it would affect the company over time.

I didn't think about it too long, though. On that night, I had a date, and I was enjoying myself. Everything seemed fine.

*        *        *

On the fourteenth of January 1992, much of northwest Ohio awoke to the results of a good-sized blizzard. Over the course of the night prior, and continuing on into the morning, ten inches of snow fell, covering Perrysburg and its environs in a blanket of white fluff.

It wasn't going to be a normal day for anyone.

Following breakfast, I got dressed and went out to clear the driveway. A half hour passed as I moved huge pillow-like clumps. When I finally reached the road then, I discovered it too was in the state the storm had left it. I looked to the south, the route I usually took to work. There were a number of cars already stuck or off to one side. My path was completely blocked.

*I'll head out sometime after the snowplow shows up*, I thought. I turned back for the house. Once inside, I pulled off my boots and tossed them aside. *What now?* I glanced down the hall, toward the center of my home. *Oh, yeah. Now I know.* I walked toward the small bedroom that served as my den.

In college I learned that video games are a great stress reliever. The University's Union building housed one of the computer labs where I spent much of my time. In that lab, I had to wait at least fifteen minutes (but sometimes an hour) for a printout to come back from the mainframe in order to see if my programs had worked. A bulldog of a man who discouraged student loitering guarded the printer. So, I usually spent my waiting time next door, at the Union's video arcade.

Now the Nintendo game system was my thing. It had been out for a number of years and I was well on my way to becoming an expert tester.

I switched on the machine. *Come on, Mario. Let's see what you can do....*

At nine-thirty the ringing of the phone roused me. I picked it up to find one of Fox's receptionists on the line. She had a question.

"Do you want a ride into work?" she asked, sounding way too chipper.

*How do I answer that?* I wondered. In actuality, I was happy doing what I was doing. "Huh?" was what I said.

"Dave bought a new 4x4 last night," she said, her voice still smiling. "He'll come and get you...if you want."

I frowned. I'd heard rumors about the four-wheeler Dave had ordered. He got it to haul around his telescope. His wife already christened it "the Star Truck".

It was supposed to be waiting for a hydraulic lift to be installed. *He must have gotten it early*, I thought. I glanced at the TV screen. Mario was stuck in mid-jump. I shook my head. *Well, now I know what my answer will be.* "Tell him to come get me," I said, turning off the game. "I'll be ready."

Fifteen minutes later, a white GMC sport utility rolled into the driveway. I was already bundled up, so I trudged out through the still-falling snow and opened the vehicle's back door.

Brian Crites was in the front passenger seat. In the driver's seat was someone I'd never met before. It looked like Dave, and sounded like Dave, but this person was **definitely** someone else.

"Get in! Get in!" the driver said excitedly.

Crites turned to look at me and gave a little uneasy smile. "We've had an interesting trip," he said.

Dave just chortled in agreement.

"I can bet," I said. If it were possible for a 4x4 to make a person intoxicated, Dave was soused. *I wonder if this is such a good idea...*

Dave giggled again as I got in. I closed the door and we were on our way.

I was told that Jadzia, who lived just to the east of me, was our next pickup. As we passed the trapped (and unoccupied) cars down my road, Dave waved and said "Ta-ta". He and Crites then shared a laugh.

I snapped on my seatbelt. *Who is this man?*

From there to Jadzia's home was relatively uneventful. The same could not be said for the journey back to the office.

"Where's the deepest part?" Dave asked, squinting at the road ahead. The snow that fell was powdery. At times it was almost fog-like.

Crites's eyes moved back and forth. "On the left, I think."

Any rational driver would have stayed right.

"Left it is," Dave said, cackling again.

I glanced at Jadzia. Her eyes were wide and she had a reserved, Mona Lisa-like smile on her face.

The truck steered toward the left side of the road, where a large snow bank lay. I felt the engine bog down. Snow flew up from the tires, and Dave laughed raucously.

*He's crazy!*

The rest of the trip was more of the same—a proving ground for my boss's new conveyance. The sight of a drift in our path brought gleeful laughter. Power on all four tires was Dave's opiate.

When we finally arrived at the office, many of the others had already managed (through whatever means) to make it in. The few exceptions that lived within range of Dave's new shuttling service were Marty Sedluk and Bill Ferguson. Calls were made to both of them. Marty, along with his wife Eleanor, naively agreed to be picked up. Bill categorically declined. "I have things to deal with here at his home," he said. I suspect he was just being wise.

Dave dressed and went looking for someone to ride along. Crites apparently had his fill of the snow adventure. "I've got to get some work done here," he told Dave.

Then Dave appeared at my door. "Do you want to go out again?" he asked.

It already felt like I'd been hauled into school on a snow day. I could barely concentrate. *And the trip to Marty's will prove more entertaining than anything that'll happen here.* "Let me get my coat," I said.

I was intrigued by the new side of Dave I was seeing. It was a little dangerous, but it was also a little fun. I had little contact with Dave beyond the office setting. All I really knew of him was the enigmatic stuff I saw at work. If I could understand more of 'peripheral' Dave, it might help me with the rest. *Maybe this trip will be my chance?* I had some form of friendship with nearly everyone on the team—why not Dave?

But any hope I had for building camaraderie was dashed about as completely as the drifts we plowed through. Between Dave's animated outbursts and my general unfamiliarity with talking to him about anything other than work, it was a lost cause. The only coherent conversation happened as we passed Bill Ferguson's neighborhood.

"So that's where Bill lives, eh?" Dave asked, with a nod in the direction of Bill's home.

I hadn't actually been to Bill's, but I knew approximately where it was. It was in one of the more exclusive neighborhoods just west of Fort Meigs. "I think so," I said.

Dave snorted. "That Bill doesn't want a ride into work today. He says he's got too much to do." He frowned and looked at me. "You know what I think?"

*I have no idea.* "No," I said. "What?"

Dave glanced back at Bill's neighborhood and gripped the steering wheel tightly. "I think he's just lazy!"

I smiled and watched the road ahead. Bill was frequently called "Eeyore" at the office because of his pessimism, but I never heard anyone call him "lazy" before. He'd written some important parts of the product. Many of them extremely complicated. As part of the original four, I thought Dave held him in high esteem. *I'm glad I agreed to be picked up.*

Dave spotted another drift and the conversation ended abruptly. Shortly thereafter we picked up the Sedluk's and shuttled them to work. We captives then split off to our offices. Less than twenty minutes later, though, I was standing next door talking to Jadzia. (Sally never made it in).

"...and then he said that Bill was lazy," I said, smiling. "The lesson for the day? If your boss offers you a ride to work, take it."

We shared a laugh. I glanced down the hall toward Dave's office. He had his jacket on and his laptop case in one hand.

"Hey," I said, wrinkling my brow. "It looks like Dave is going out again."

Jadzia raised an eyebrow. "Oh, really," she said. "I wonder who he's getting this time."

I watched as Dave made his way toward the front door. The laptop seemed like an odd thing to have with him. "You know what?" I said. "I think he's going home."

"What!" Jadzia exclaimed. She stood in time to see the front door swing shut behind Dave. "He's going home?"

I looked at Jadzia. "How are **we** getting home?"

"I don't know," she said excitedly.

I turned to look out the window. The snow still looked like fog. *Well, that's a good way to make sure work gets done,* I thought. *Strand your employees.*

Five minutes later we heard the voice of Howard, the Technical Support manager, come over the company intercom.

"Fox Software is closed for the day," he said. "Everyone please go home. And be careful."

"But our ride just left!" I said out loud.

"Any of you who need transportation," Howard continued. "Come see me. Dave told me to find you a ride home."

"I wonder if he mentioned developers," I said, smiling. "I bet Dave never specifically mentioned taking the developers home."

Jadzia pulled her coat on and went fishing behind the door for her scarf. "I don't know. But, let's go before the four-wheelers get away."

\*       \*       \*

The following day, after the storm broke and the roads were cleared, we returned to work to discover that Fox Software had been hit with another calamity.

"Did you hear?" Sally asked me that morning.

"Hear what?" I said. *What has Dave done now?*

"Glenn Hart died at MacWorld yesterday."

I was shocked. MacWorld was one of the premier trade shows for the Macintosh computer. It was held in San Francisco that week. Glenn was a marketing advisor for us in years past, but I didn't know he was still involved. "What happened?" I said.

Sally shrugged. "I guess he was having dinner with Janet and some of the other presenters and he had a heart attack. Just slumped down at dinner."

*Wow.* Even though I was corrupted to think of Glenn as "the Emphysema Poster Child", he was a real gentleman every time I met him. None of us wished him ill. He'd given FoxPro its name—for that alone, we owed him our gratitude.

Just a few short months later, events would occur that made us wonder whether Glenn's death may have, in fact, been a portent of things to come.

# Chapter 25
# Shock and Awe

"Someone is smoking in that restroom again," Marty said, making no effort to hide his displeasure.

It was another Kwong's day. The group this time was Heindel, Bill, Marty, and I. Our food had already been delivered, and in between light conversation, everyone was busy shoveling it in.

"That's gotta be against company rules," Heindel said. "Is our policy on smoking in the handbook?"

Bill sniffed. "It has to be," he said. "It should be standard for every company in the industry."

"Yeah?" I said, raising an eyebrow.

Bill skewered a piece of chicken with his fork and nodded. "Oh yeah, software and smoking is right out."

Heindel chewed hard. "Smoke particles are bad for the disks," he said, looking at me. "You know how they wear those white particle-free suits when they make silicon chips?"

I nodded. Most people had seen pictures of the particle free environments used in hardware companies like Texas Instruments and Intel. In fact, I had people (who didn't know any better) ask me if I wore one of those white suits at work. That would be a little worse than wearing a polyester suit all day...but just barely.

I had a hard time believing someone was actually smoking in our building, though. "Who is it?" I asked. "Do you know him?"

"He works in Tech Support," Marty said. "I think his name is Bill something."

Bill frowned. "That's unfortunate."

I grinned at Bill, and then examined my plate. Moo goo gai pan— one of my perennial favorites. I speared my own piece of chicken.

"They've got that d*** smoker's stairway," Marty said. "I don't know why they can't keep it in there."

Heindel shrugged. "I imagine its a little cold back there these days," he said. Since it was the middle of winter and the stairwell *wasn't* heated, that was a safe bet.

"Tough," Bill said. He and Marty shared a laugh.

The conversation stalled for a time as everyone went back to their meals.

Heindel pointed a fork in Marty's direction. "You know what would be funny?" he said finally.

Marty took a sip of tea and focused on Heindel. "What's that?" he said.

"To play with that guy a little."

Marty bobbed his head slowly. "How?"

Heindel smiled. "Well, say you and I were in the restroom when that guy was there."

"Yeah," Marty said.

"Yeah, and say I said something like 'Smells like someone has been smoking in here again'."

Marty hiccupped a laugh. "Oh, oh-kay," he said. "Then I could say something like 'Boy, I sure hope Dave doesn't find out'."

Heindel laughed hard enough to bring his hands to his face. "I got it…," he began, but his laughing stole his ability to speak.

I couldn't wait to see where we were going next.

Heindel calmed himself finally. "I could say 'Yeah, that last guy got fired'," he said.

Marty made an erasing motion with his hand. "No, no," he said. He then began to laugh deeply himself. Tears formed in his eyes. "It'd be better if you said 'Yeah, like he did with that last guy'." Marty pointed to himself. "Then I could say 'He would have been **better off** fired'."

The two of them then fell into a sea of shared laughter. Bill and I just watched them.

"That was a good one," Marty said, concluding the thought. The conversation then drifted in another direction.

Following lunch we returned to the office. Like I usually did, I went to my desk and fished out my toothpaste and brush. I then went to the men's room. As I entered, I noticed a hint of smoke in the air. *Maybe Marty's right*, I thought. *Maybe someone is smoking in here.* I crossed over to the sink. I glanced down and noticed a pair of feet in one of the stalls. *Hmmm.* I took the cap off my toothpaste; put a line on my brush.

Marty walked in, followed closely by Heindel. Marty had a toothbrush in his hand too. He tipped his chin up and sniffed the air. He then smiled at me before turning to look at Heindel.

*Oh, no…*

"Smells like someone has been smoking in here again, Marty," Heindel said.

Marty shook his head. Paused a moment. "Boy….I sure hope that Dave Fulton doesn't find out."

Heindel nodded. "Yeah, like he did with that last guy," he said.

Marty smiled broadly. "He would have been better off fired."

There was motion from the occupied stall and the sound of paper being crumpled. I saw the profile of one of our newer support technicians above the stall's wall. He was a tall guy, but I didn't know his name. He looked worried.

I felt the urge to laugh out loud, so I turned and walked toward the door. As I pushed the door open, I heard a loud flush. I glanced back to see Marty with Heindel following closely behind.

"Awesome," I said when we were safely outside. "You two were awesome."

And only laughter replied.

*          *          *

From my perspective the rest of the winter months at Fox Software were great. There were few times when I felt better about my job.

To start with, I was more than happy with the progress I made on the graphical Screen Painter. Using the code for our Mac Screen Painter as a starting point, I removed each line that called directly to the Macintosh operating system and replaced it with a call into our FoxPro API instead.

This process was slow at first, because there were a large number of holes in the Fox API. I'd attempt to convert a bit of code and find there was no Fox equivalent for the routine I needed. Then, because the rest of team was up to its neck in conversion work as well, either Marty or I would have to fabricate the missing API routine and test it on both graphical platforms (the Macintosh and Windows). When we were confident it worked, we'd check it in, and I'd go back and make use of it.

The forward momentum was steady though, and by March, some semblance of the Screen Painter was working on both platforms— proving in practice that the whole Grand Unification thing would work. In all honesty, it was really cool to see the same code running in two places. *Why hadn't we tried this before?* It was like helping the Wright brothers build their first plane.

In addition to this coding success, my working relationship with Dave had—for the first time in nearly four years of employment— grown almost comfortable. It was easier to talk with him at a professional, non-reactionary level. I also started to see a change in Dave too.

*          *          *

I was in Brian Tallman's office one morning discussing a bug. This time, like so many times before, Dave bustled in and directed me to his office with a hand wave.

As I followed, I fought with responding the way I always had. I couldn't think of a reason why I'd be in trouble, but that was usually what The Walk meant. *It's going to be OK though*, I reminded myself. *Even if I did something wrong, it's OK. I've survived this many times before....* When we reached his door, I painted on a look of professional interest and gave my usual, "Yeah Dave, what's up?"

"Have a seat," he said, and then nodded at his computer screen. "Which of these do you like better?"

I looked at the screen. I saw three small icons, each with our trademark fox head as part of their design. They looked like potential icons for our Windows product. *Wait a minute*, I thought, glancing at Dave and back at the screen. *I think he's asking for an opinion.* My brain froze for a moment. *I'm not sure how to deal with this.*

I studied the designs closely. All three were nice, but one clearly seemed better. It was a purely aesthetic choice, though. "I like that one," I said and pointed.

"That one...?" Dave said softly, squinting at the screen. He mused for a moment, cradled his chin. "Yeah," he said finally, "that's my favorite too." He gave me a short nod. "Thank you." The decision was made.

I stopped myself from grinning. *Dang!* I thought as I left. *I could get used to this. Things are going to be alright....*

*       *       *

A few weeks later, near the end of March, Dave called the developers to the conference room.

It was a Friday afternoon and I suspected it was going to be another "body parts" talk. Whenever we had a long, relaxed lull and Dave wanted to re-motivate us, he'd give a speech with the phrase "a\*\*holes and elbows" as part of it. The phrase was apparently gleaned from the motivational repertoire of a drill sergeant Dave once knew. The sergeant would order his charges to get busy scrubbing the floor and remind them that "All I want to see are a\*\*holes and elbows until it's done".

FoxPro was the developers' floor and Dave was our sergeant. We'd been comfortable for close to nine months and that seemed past due for change. There must be a reason why the products needed to ship right away, a reason for us to work harder.

As I entered the conference room and found a seat, I sensed something different. The people who were invited to the meeting were an unusual assortment for the "body parts" talk. Everyone in development was present, as expected, but also the test manager and the two youngest testers, Matt and John. *Why not the whole test team?* If we were gearing up again, they should be there.

Janet Walker was present. *Not unusual.* A couple of the writers were there as well; Crites's wife was one, Janet's husband the other. The writers had worked like slaves since the bank building days. Could they possibly need more motivation? It just didn't make sense.

There was also a feeling in the air; something not quite right. I couldn't put my finger on it precisely. Apprehension? A touch of uneasiness? *Something.* In truth, the entire month had a touch of strangeness. Dave's new approachability was a welcome change, but there were also gatherings in offices that broke up when I drew near. Something was definitely different, but every meeting with Dave had its own character. Strange feelings and behaviors were not uncommon. *Maybe this is just more of the same.*

"Alright, is everyone here?" Dave asked, glancing around the room. "OK. OK. Good! The reason you all are here is to inform you that a letter of intent has been signed between Fox and Microsoft to begin proceeding toward a merger of the two companies…"

*A letter of intent!?* I exclaimed silently. *Merger!? Microsoft??* I hadn't even heard rumors of such a thing. I couldn't believe Dave was going to give up control of his company. It just didn't make sense. Especially after all we'd been through.

*Still,* I rationalized, *it might not be so bad.* Microsoft was nearly a hundred times our size. Working for them might bring a little more stability to our schedule.

I knew we'd stay in Perrysburg, though. There were people in the group who'd never move away. We had strong ties to the area. It was part of the reason Dave hired us; he wanted developers who weren't going to run away. So of course we'd be able to stay. *Now what was Dave saying…?*

"There was a time earlier when Microsoft talked about buying us, but they wanted us to relocate, and no one wanted to do that. So, the whole thing sort of fell through." Dave paused and the room caught its breath. "Well, this time it was one of Bill's first conditions that the development team move to Redmond. They've promised it would be like a helicopter just picked us up and moved us…"

My heart dropped. *Come again? Move? A helicopter?* The "How will this effect me?" questions started to be answered in my mind, and I didn't like what I was getting. *I'm not gonna move! I grew up in Ohio.*

*My parents are here. My best friends are here. My church is here. My
college is here. My high school is here. All the girls I'd ever dated are
here.* I thought about the large purchase I'd made two years earlier.
*And yeah, my house is here too. No way was I going to be able to
unload that at the drop of a hat. So take that ya merging so and so...*

"For those of you who have houses, Microsoft has promised to
arrange for them to be bought by a relocation company so you don't
have to worry about them. See, it will be just like I said—like a
giant helicopter."

Dave went on to say some of the more senior team members were
aware of the intent for a couple of weeks (which explained the
developer meetings that ended when the participants saw me).

He turned slightly to look behind him, where the testers stood
blocking the windows. "And for our young testers, Matt and John," he
said, smiling slightly, "you may consider this your *apotheosis*."

Matt and John exchanged confused looks. They'd seen Dave in
action. They probably thought they were about to be castrated.

"Apotheosis roughly means 'ascension to godhood',"
Dave explained. "When the merger is finalized you two will
become developers."

"Oh," Matt said, giving a little sheepish grin. He stepped back and
his face got serious again.

John smiled broadly. "That's fine with me," he said. "I have
a brother in Seattle...." His head bobbed a little. "This is all fine
with me."

He was alone in his joy. Dave asked if there were any questions.

Stone silence answered him. I felt like sobbing—or punching the
wall. I was conflicted; laid waste inside. The rest of the team just stared
absently at the floor or at each other. Our new reality was hard to face.

"Also," Dave continued, "since this information isn't general
knowledge yet, you aren't allowed to tell anyone until it is released to
the public. We'll have an announcement to the rest of the company
early next week."

*Oh, that's just great,* I thought. *The biggest news of my life, and I
can't tell anyone either.*

The meeting ended and Dave abruptly left the room. All present
slowly coalesced into small groups and discussion ensued. Heindel and
Brian Tallman were in one corner of the room, so I walked over to join
them. As more senior members, I figured they had a couple more
weeks to think it through.

"What do you guys think?" I asked.

Brian smiled a little. "It's a big change," he said.

"Yeah, a big change," Heindel echoed.

I knew that. *Come on, guys, help me out.* "So what do you think about moving?" I asked.

Brian shrugged. "We'll see. I've read things about the area. Well...it's real expensive."

Heindel looked at the floor. "Yeah, I don't know..." He looked back at me. "I wanted to tell you." He frowned. "We don't have it worked out either, really. We only heard last week." He shook his head slowly. "It's going to be a big deal. I just don't know yet."

Apparently, the additional lead time in knowing hadn't helped them much. How could it? I stepped away, and then aimlessly left the room. *What a shock,* I thought, shaking my head. *And just when I thought life was easy.*

*    *    *

I slunk into Sally's office and sat down. Jadzia was present, but absent.

"Did you know?" Sally asked

I shook my head. "No. No idea."

Sally was holding her hands together in her lap. "Wow...I watched you. And the way you sat there, I thought you knew."

She'd never seen me in shock before. "I didn't know," I said and paused. A dozen seconds went by. "What do you think?"

Sally shook her head slowly. "Dave's screwing us again. Move or resign—it's just like him."

One detail I overlooked from Dave's speech was the fact that the developers had two options following the merger. Either we moved or we resigned. I didn't know what other alternative there might be, though. "Yeah...but what else could he do?"

Sally sniffed. "Usually in a buyout like this the employees would be offered severance. Some money—maybe a half-year's salary. Enough to get by until you find another job. But we aren't getting any." She shook her head again. "Just move, or resign."

"Yeah, that's sorta weird," I said. It seemed almost cruel to do such a thing to people who'd worked so hard for you. "I wonder why Dave's doing that?"

Sally raised her hands. "Because we're part of the deal!" she said. "Microsoft doesn't just want the code. It isn't nearly as valuable without us. They want us!"

That made sense. No one knew a child better than its parents. Of course they'd want the developers. *Nice to be wanted, I guess.* I stared at Sally quietly for a few moments.

"What are you going to do?" she asked.

I looked out the window at the adjoining building's tarpaper roof. Crows played in a puddle there. "I don't know," I said, standing up. "I think I'm going home."

*       *       *

There was no easy way to get my arms around the enormity of what had just happened. As I left the office, all I felt like doing was going home, sitting on the floor, and petting the dog. So that's what I did.

But, as it turns out, dogs take devastating news about the same way they take everything—friendly consolation with little actual advice. That's not what I really needed. I needed someone to share my pain. I heard Dave's voice: "You aren't allowed to tell anyone until...."

*Screw it. If all the guys at work can tell their wives, then I can tell my folks.*

I phoned my parents, but they were about as much help as the dog. Though equally shocked by the news, their advice was completely divergent.

"You could find a job around here, couldn't you?" Dad asked. "You could at least look around."

"It'll be alright, dear," Mom said. "Maybe you should try it out there. You can always come back if you don't like it."

Together, though, they encouraged me to do what I felt best.

The only thing I felt "best" was to sit on the floor and pet the dog.

*       *       *

A few days later the rest of the company gathered in one of the special event rooms of a nearby hotel. It was another strange experience. Similar to the developer meeting, the tension in the room was considerable. It was the first 'whole company' assembly since the lawsuit meeting four years before. That alone was enough to make the attendees edgy.

Dave began the session with a little speech detailing the history of Fox Software. He then segued into what he saw happening in the software industry in the future. "The computer market will tend to condense into larger and larger companies," he said, "and smaller companies will be forced to sell out or fade away."

He talked about finding the right company to merge with and theorized about who the eventual winners would be. He then outlined the planned merger with Microsoft and introduced the Microsoft people who were present, but still near the back of the room.

That too was weird. Six or seven Microsoft employees marched down the center aisle to join Dave at the podium. As they did so, the temperature in the room dropped a few degrees and the Imperial March from Star Wars started to play in my head. It was as if Darth Vader and his storm troopers finally found our rebel base.

Dave surrendered the podium to Mike Maples, a Microsoft VP. The large, sandy-haired man then gave what would normally have been a good speech. He talked about "amazing changes" and "bright futures," about "Fox's success" and our "wonderful products". In the context, it was too much like one of the pep rallies I was forced to go to in high school. Except there were no skirts and no cheering. The employees had just had their world destroyed; you can't comfort them by telling them "we're headed for a wonderful tomorrow."

It was hard to imagine what Maples could have said that would have sounded better though. Anything more than an "I'm sorry" was too much.

Following his speech, there was a short question and answer session, and then the meeting adjourned. As the crowd cleared out, Dave beckoned the developers to the front, where the Microsofties lingered. He introduced us, one by one, to Mike Maples and a handful of other people, all who appeared to be named "Mike," as well.

One of the Mikes was Mike Murray, Microsoft's Director of Human Resources. He was a short person with brown, feathered hair. He reminded me a lot of the actor Dudley Moore. Following the initial round of introductions, he threw out a typical HR question: "What do you think of when you hear the name *Microsoft*?"

I turned to look at the others. The only 2.0 developer not present was Sally. I expected either Bill or Eric to answer.

"I think we'd all say 'Quality Products'!" Chris said.

I swallowed a groan. I checked the faces of the other developers and saw I wasn't alone in my feelings.

"Do you all work on the Macintosh product?" Mike Maples asked, trying to steer toward more technical subjects.

"I'd say we all swing both ways!" Chris shot back.

I pinched my leg through my pants pocket. I really wished Chris would stop speaking for us. *Good grief,* I thought, *you've never even compiled the Mac product, Chris! And even though I have, I wouldn't have described it as **swinging both ways***!

I shook my head and looked toward the back of the room. It was getting pretty empty. *I've had enough of this.* I excused myself and made my way to the door.

*       *       *

The remainder of the week was horrible, the atmosphere heavy with emotion. The usual morning meetings in Sally's office were both poignant and exciting at the same time. We now had something to discuss that overshadowed anything we ever talked about before, yet it affected us more profoundly than anything before had the potential to. The participants' feelings were decidedly mixed.

Sally was pretty negative. She hated the thought of relocating, but mostly she was upset with the way the merger was handled. The "move or resign" ultimatum bothered her the most. "It's as if their saying: 'Thanks for the hard work and have a nice life!'" she said, and I had a hard time not agreeing. To rub more salt in the wound, we found out the rest of the company (anyone who hadn't been in that first meeting) would be offered a generous severance package should they decide not to join Microsoft. "Dave screwed us," Sally said again.

Another thing she took issue with was the "signing bonus" we had waved in our faces. Microsoft was desperate to know how many of us would be going, so they offered a monetary bonus to any developer who signed before a certain date, less than a month away. This served only to divide and confuse our team more. Ten thousand dollars would be given to any "senior" member that signed and five thousand to the rest, but the definition of "senior" was arbitrary. It had nothing to do with time served or products shipped. It was just anyone in the pecking order higher than Sally and I. "They can take that money and stuff it," Sally said, and once again, she had a point.

Sally had more potential employment options in the Toledo area than most of us though; she'd retained a number of connections from her time at Chris's company and would have no problem using them. I figured her for a 'no go'.

Jadzia didn't like the way things were handled either, but that wasn't her main concern. She wanted to be a coder, and if that's what you wanted to do, Microsoft was a good place be. In her heart, she really wanted to sign up.

However, she had other difficulties with signing. Her husband had just achieved tenure at the University of Toledo, and understandably, he didn't want to give that up. Their situation was further complicated by the fact that their first child was on its way. The due date was just a short time after the merger was to take place (in late June). Jadzia wasn't keen on doing a Madonna-like trek across country while pregnant. I figured her a 'no go' as well.

Marty was standing on the opposite side of the fence entirely. He was the most pro-merger person on the team. Part of his excitement came from the area of the country we'd be moving to. He loved biking and hiking—anything to do with the outdoors actually. With its moderate weather and beautiful scenery, the Pacific Northwest offered many possibilities for him to express that love.

Marty also liked the variety of software opportunities Microsoft would offer. After coding 'buck-naked' in his office for years, the thought of having other outlets for his skills intrigued him. He needed a change. He was a 'go-go' for sure.

For myself, I barely knew what to think yet—much less what to do.

# Chapter 26
# Valediction

From a fifty thousand foot view of the software world, the merger made good sense. It was a "pooling of interests" that appeared to have nothing but benefits for both companies.

The benefits for Microsoft were obvious. They had no real presence in the database market—and at close to a billion dollars—it was a market too large for them to ignore. They'd struggled for years trying to produce their own database product—but in the spring of 1992—that product (code named *Cirrus*) was still at least half a year away. An additional six months surrendered to the competition could be decisive, because the competition was already well ahead. The purchase of Ashton-Tate positioned Borland to dominate the market. They now owned two of the most popular database products for the PC—dBASE IV, and Borland's own, Paradox. Joining with Fox would not only get Microsoft into the game, it would get them a marquee player—FoxPro.

The merger would also give them the means to ensure their future database products were successful. "The merger...will provide Microsoft with great development talent," Bill Gates said in the initial (March 24th) press release, "as well as leading-edge database technology." In a later release, he said the Microsoft plan was "to integrate the individual strengths of the Microsoft and Fox development teams." The Fox developers were a crucial part of the transaction. Aside from continuing to produce quality Fox products, we'd bring knowledge that could be integrated into future Microsoft products.

There were many benefits for Fox as well. First off, it would solve the problem of not being a publicly traded company. As soon as FoxPro was a Microsoft product, we could begin to sell it to all those companies who'd been hesitant before because of our "privately owned" status.

The merger would also give the Fox team access to more resources than our company could otherwise support. Microsoft's productive sales and marketing force would now be available to us. We'd be able to use their recruiting to find promising developers, testers, and writers. Many of the day-to-day hassles of running a software company would become infinitely easier. Dave publicly hyped this benefit the most. "I am thrilled to have the vast resources of Microsoft at my fingertips," he said in a press release. "I feel like a kid with the biggest train set in the world."

On a more personal level, it gave Dave a way to sever his ties with the LaValley family. As subtle episodes during my employment had suggested, the relationship between the two families was no longer amiable, nor had it been for some time. Dave's method of resolving personal difficulties was clear—he terminates them. The partnership with LaValley was a divorce waiting to happen. Microsoft would play the part of the rich paramour, allowing for a clean break.

*       *       *

Though the merger was a match made in heaven for the companies— for the developers, it seemed a small taste of hell. We had our own version of Dave's train quote. "I feel like I've been **run over** by the biggest train set in the world," was how it read.

After the merger was announced, all development work came to a halt. It was *impossible* for us to do anything but discuss the implications. There were constantly new tidbits of information to absorb. Crites and Heindel traveled to the Pacific Northwest and reported on what they saw. Everyone was making phone calls or making trips to the library. The quest for knowledge was paramount. Impromptu meetings were held in every office to weigh the pros and cons.

There appeared to be many positives. The Microsoft campus was a near ideal working environment. We would be trading our views of rooftops and dumpsters for those of mountains and fountains. Instead of a lunch outing to Burger King or Pizza Hut, we would be able to dine at a company-subsidized cafeteria. Instead of an occasional snowball fight in the parking lot, we could play basketball, volleyball, or soccer on one of Microsoft's sport courts.

Additionally, the Greater Seattle area offered a plethora of new activities. There were professional sports teams for the sport lovers, trails to hike for the Marty-types, and skiing, diving, boating, and beautiful scenery for everyone else. It was a welcome change for our country-Ohio eyes.

But, there were negatives too, and the negatives were what fueled our discussions.

*       *       *

A few weeks after the announcement, Dave sent Amy and another woman to "do some leg work" for us. Their stated goal was to research the cost of living differences. However, when their information was actually presented, I suspected their trip was more of a shopping outing than anything else. They giggled as they told us things we didn't want to hear.

The one important bit of information we got, though, was that nearly everything in Seattle costs more. In fact, the only utility that wasn't twice as expensive was electricity. (The local electric company, Toledo Edison, has a nuclear power plant. They use it to generate power from uranium and money from consumers.)

The most alarming difference was the cost of housing. Nearly all of us had homes, and even though a relocation company was hired to buy them, it wasn't clear we could buy replacements on the other side. Brian Tallman's wife had called the Redmond city offices (the city where Microsoft is located) and asked what sort of place she could get for a hundred and twenty thousand dollars. The answer was "a shack."

In contrast, the house I purchased two years before cost me $73,000. Granted, it was only 1200 square feet, but it was all brick and on close to an acre of land. It was also in a pleasant neighborhood on the edge of town.

If I were to buy a house, I would need every bit of the signing bonus I was offered.

\*       \*       \*

Another large source of worry was the rumored number of hours the average Microsoft employee worked. We heard a typical workweek at Microsoft was somewhere on the order of sixty to eighty hours. During the busiest weeks of a shipping cycle, our team might have touched those hours, but it wasn't the norm. Most of us had some semblance of a normal—though highly interruptible—life outside of work. None of us wanted to lose that.

But, we couldn't get a definitive answer. When asked, the Microsofties usually waffled, saying things like "in development it's expected you'll work some extra hours." That wasn't very reassuring.

I finally decided to ask Dave about it. I strolled into his office to find him seated at his table with marble tile samples arranged in front of him. He was picking out the floor of his new Washington home.

Dave held a tile up to appraise it, but still managed to see me at the door. "So, Kerry," he said, "do you have any questions left about the big move?" He squinted at the tile. It was white with black specks. Like gnats on soured milk.

I frowned. "Well, I do wonder about Microsoft some," I said. "I heard they work a lot of hours."

Dave put the tile down, grabbed another. "You'll be working for me," he said, "just like here!" He shifted a little and I saw a glint of light on the tile's surface. "We'll be working just like here."

That wasn't much comfort either. I paused, unsure of what to say next.

Dave looked at me intensely. "Look Kerry, life's a banquet."

I wrinkled my forehead. *Life's a what?*

"Life's a banquet," he said, slowing his inflection. "You've got to sample it." He turned back to his samples. He picked up a shadowy pattern and studied it closely.

I waited for a few moments, wondering if he'd say anything more, but there were no further reassurances.

I shook my head and left for my office. I fully understood the concept of "nothing ventured, nothing gained," but some of us were clearly taking a bigger risk than others.

That was the last question I asked Dave Fulton. Marty's hope to work on another product was starting to seem wise.

*      *      *

To add to the confusion of the times, Dave soon decided we should ship FoxPro for Windows as soon as possible. In an effort to focus our exceedingly divided attentions, he dropped development on every product except Windows and made Chris our lead (and unofficial whipping boy). For one last time Dave tried to rally the troops, scraping for a reason why we needed to ship right away. We'd seen the song and dance many times before.

The rallying cry was different, but the objective was always the same. FoxBASE+ had to ship because the company needed the money. FoxBASE+/Mac needed to ship because we lacked a cross-platform story. FoxPro 1.0 needed to ship because it was our "response to the lawsuit." FoxPro 2.0 had to ship because we were in danger of losing market share to Borland. Now FoxPro for Windows had to ship because it would be our "calling card to Microsoft." We had to make a good impression on our new owners, and that would be our way.

We were told to push until it hurt. We couldn't, though, because we had no emotional energies left to commit to another development push. Those of us who had been through shipping cycles before, simply ignored Dave's gyrations. We worked, but we spent as much or more time discussing aspects of the merger.

That left Dave with a lot of management energy to burn. He spent it on the easy targets.

"Shamu!" he yelled from his office as Chris Williams went by. "Get your mighty flukes in here!"

Chris hustled into Dave's office, a harried look on his face. "Yes, Dave?"

"I want the person responsible for the Index dialog and the Modify Structure dialog in here, right now!"

"OK, Dave." Chris rushed to the far end of the building, to where Brad and Henry shared an office.

Just after the merger announcement, an effort began to make the dialogs in our product look *precisely* like those in other Microsoft products, like ones found in Word and Excel. As part of this effort, Janet studied these products in excruciating detail and came up with a multi-page description of what she perceived to be Microsoft's standards for dialog design. It bore drawings of dialogs and instructions like "if configured horizontally, the OK button is 6 pixels from the bottom of a dialog and the Cancel button is 6 pixels from the right...."

Brad and Henry's job was to make every dialog in our product match those exacting standards. The rest of us lovingly referred to their task as "asinine dialog scootching."

"Dave wants you guys in his office," Chris told the busy youngsters. "Right away."

The two followed Chris back. After they seated themselves, Dave flew into a rage.

"MODI STRU is all f***ed up!" he said, pacing the office. He moved closer to the room's table and kicked one of its chairs Bobby Knight style. "Do you two even know what you're doing?!" he said, thrashing about. "Don't you test this sh**?!" The tirade continued for some time. When Dave was done, Brad and Henry left the office looking as if they'd been hit.

As soon as they were beyond audible range, Dave looked at a wide-eyed Chris and smiled. "That was a good one, wasn't it?"

Dave's heart wasn't really in it either. At least, not the way it used to be.

*        *        *

My biggest concern was whether there was any real gain for me in joining Microsoft. I'd have a job—that was certain. Aside from the potential signing bonus—which made me feel no more wanted than the guys who'd just been "apotheosized"—there seemed to be few monetary incentives.

Dave had given us each a spreadsheet that showed what our salaries would be and the options we'd be eligible for the day we walked into Microsoft.

My salary didn't look that great. The prior summer I was given a raise that put me just over thirty thousand a year. That was respectable pay for northwest Ohio, but a bonus program started after 2.0's release, and because of that, my salary nearly doubled in '91. Sales had been good.

The salary in the spreadsheet was only a thousand dollars more than my current salary, though, before the 2.0 bonus. In a meeting I had with some of the Microsofties, I quizzed them about my pay. Again, they waffled. When I finally pressed them, they caved a little. "Listen," they said, "Dave set the salaries. Ask him."

I saw no reason to ask Dave, though. His mind was on the plans for his new Washington home, and I hadn't seen much to show that he valued me as a developer. I didn't get the early "heads up" on the merger. I wasn't offered the larger signing bonus. Now it looked as though he'd given me a salary that I could barely live on. What was the use?

There was another portion of the spreadsheet though. The stock options portion. Aside from the mini-lecture Chris had given me months earlier, I still knew little about the market. However, I was becoming an expert on stock options.

An "option" was really the right to buy a certain number of shares at a low price, usually the price for the stock at the time the option was offered. These stock options could be "exercised" (i.e. purchase the stock at that lower price) at some later date. In my case this later date was roughly four years from the day of the merger. The four years of waiting is called the option's "vesting period" and the reason a vesting period is usually attached to options—at least, from the company's perspective—is to encourage the employee's commitment. When that vesting period has passed, the employee is free to exercise (or not) the options. Once exercised, the purchased shares of stock can remain in the employee's possession—giving him a sizable investment in his company—or he can turn around, sell the shares, and pocket the profits (i.e. the difference in the share price on the day of exercise versus the day the options were received). It cost companies little to offer these options to employees, so an average option offering may be thousands of shares. Sometimes even tens of thousands.

My spreadsheet specified the amount of options I'd be eligible for and Dave had plugged in some growth rates to make them look like they could be worth something…someday. His estimates assumed the stock would go **up** during all those vesting years, though, and there were no guarantees of that. The stock could just as easily go down.

One day—as I scowled and closed the spreadsheet—Marty walked in. "What are you looking at there?" he asked.

"My spreadsheet."

He smiled. "Well, don't be plugging in any Chris Williams-type numbers. Microsoft's stock won't do that."

I returned his smile. Dave's default numbers were projecting the kind of growth that Microsoft had over the last few years—nearly doubling every year. In Chris's world, the stock would be doing four times better. "Don't worry," I said. "I won't." I turned my chair his direction. "In fact, I'm wondering if I can survive."

Marty crossed his arms. "Oh, you'll survive. Just don't count on those options. They'll go up. But not like that Chris Williams thinks."

"But what if they don't?" I said. "How can you be so up on moving?"

Marty raised his shoulders. "I've done research. Microsoft's a good place to be. And if Fox doesn't work out, I can go somewhere else. To another product."

I couldn't get over someone who had been such an Apple-fanatic, now being so pro-Microsoft. The two companies had been locked in a lawsuit of their own for years. And I hadn't given much thought to working on another product. I had a lot of time and energy invested in Fox. I didn't want to think about another change.

Marty raised a hand in a calming motion. "It won't be like here, where Dave can fire you if he wants. It takes a lot longer to get rid of someone." He lowered the hand and shrugged. "And if not, there are other companies out there. Just having Fox and Microsoft on your resume is enough." He then echoed my mom. "And if all else fails, you can always come back."

He was right, but I still wasn't sure.

*     *     *

As the "signing bonus" deadline approached, I had a pretty good feel for what the other team members were doing. Eric and Bill had essentially signed on since the beginning. They were consulted before the deal was even announced, I assumed. Chris took the development lead position, so he was apparently onboard. Marty was a sure thing.

Heindel was surprised to find his wife was OK with whatever he decided. He was one of the first to fly out to look around and he came back pretty convinced. He saw a few houses, talked to a pastor or two, and toured a school for his kids. "I think we could be blessed in this," he said.

Sally had stuck to her word on the signing bonus. She was going to make her decision at the last possible moment (in late May). She was still really fearful. "Sheep!" she said. "Everyone here is acting like sheep." She scowled and shook her head. "Dave hired sheep."

\*     \*     \*

Tallman was the one senior developer I wasn't sure about. He stayed in his office and out of the sea of conversation that flowed over the company. I decided to take the sea to him.

"So, are you going?" I asked, getting right to the point.

Brian swiveled his chair toward the door. He crossed his arms and gave a little smile. "Oh, I reckon so," he said.

"Really?" Brian had probably done the most moving in his life of any of us. He relocated from Florida to work for Fox, so that aspect of the merger probably didn't bother him much. He seemed really concerned about finding a home, though. "Even with the cost of everything?" I asked.

He frowned. "Yeah, it may be a little tight for awhile. But we'll survive."

I told him of my conversation with Dave about work hours.

He shrugged. "Hard to know until you're there, I imagine. But it's like that Psalm."

"What one is that?"

Brian shifted in his seat and straightened his shirt. "Thirty-seven, twenty-five," he said after he resettled. "It says something like 'I've never seen the righteous forsaken, or their children begging for bread'."

I nodded. I probably read that at some point in my life, but it wasn't hardwired. I could see the connection. Leave it to Brian to boil things down to their essence. "True enough," I said. "Things'll be all right."

"Yep," he said with a nod. He was floating on a raft in the eye of a storm.

I returned to my office and sat down. Brian had made his decision and now I had to make mine.

\*     \*     \*

I'd taken my first trip to the Seattle area with my dad a short time before, and we enjoyed the experience. We got a tour of Microsoft and saw some of the sights. We even checked out a few houses.

I figured with the equity in my Perrysburg home and money I'd saved, I should be able to swing the down payment on a similarly sized home there (on land the size of a postage stamp). In the meantime, Chris found a bank officer that would take our stock options into account when offering us a loan. That would help.

Things would still be tight. My salary was low, and there was really no one I could talk to about it. If I went to Microsoft, I'd just have to live simply for awhile.

There were **many** unknowns…

As there had been when I started working for Fox. I took that earlier opportunity as a blessing, an answer to prayer—God working in the circumstances—and much happened. True, much of it was difficult. I even nearly quit a few times. But, I was shaped in the process. I was more confident, knowledgeable—an asset whether Dave realized it or not.

And, if nothing else, the last four years had been **extremely** interesting.

I had a decision to make, but ultimately it was one between fear and faith. *A 'sheep' I may be, but Dave ain't my shepherd…*

I knew what I was going to do.

\*       \*       \*

Through April and May the number of developers taking trips to Washington continued. Most of us took two trips—one to "sell" us on the area and another for us to "buy" a new house. As the list of those taking "buy" trips got longer, it became clear that most of us would be joining Microsoft. That meant we all had a lot of planning to do and plenty of "good byes" to say.

My personal goodbyes were tough. I was leaving my family and the friends I'd known since childhood. In some ways it was fortunate I still (due to what my friends and I were now calling "the Curse") had no 'significant other'. It was one less emotional trauma to deal with.

I was hopeful on that score, though. Having exhausted the possibilities in Ohio, I now had a new state **full** of women who had never even met me.

In the end, there was only one Fox developer to say goodbye to. Out of all of us, only Jadzia stayed behind. No equitable job could be found for her husband—and with a child on the way—the security of his recent tenure was important.

The rest of us were on our way to Redmond. Plenty of familiar faces would be joining us. Over a hundred Fox Software employees found work at Microsoft somewhere—some in Washington, some in the Carolinas, and some in Texas.

The swift and wily Fox was well on its way to becoming a part of Microsoft. It was inevitable. The development group moved in waves throughout July. The eager (Chris and Marty) left immediately, the bulk of the team moved during the middle part of the month, and the willing-but-wary (Brian, Sally, and I) left just as July was coming to a close.

One by one, we packed up. One by one, we moved on. One by one, we let go.

*        *        *

On June 26, 1992 I had two souvenirs to remind me that the merger was a reality.

The first was a small square of Lucite I got the night before. The Lucite had the Microsoft and Fox logos on it and a small script to say that Fox was acquired for 2,033,855 shares of Microsoft stock. Those shares would be divided equally between the two owners. After a recent split of the stock, it amounted to around ninety million dollars a piece. *No problem buying a house there.*

The second was an interoffice memo that all Fox Software employees were given. It was written by Dave Fulton and the subject line said "The Merger's Complete!" The text was as follows:

I am very pleased to report that the Fox / Microsoft merger was completed yesterday. Fox and Microsoft are now one and the same.

The Fox Story is surely one of the most remarkable success stories in the software business. Who'd have thought that we could start out humbly as one of many dBASE work-alikes, then survive Ashton-Tate itself to become the acknowledged leader in database technology? Now we are a significant part of Microsoft, the one true "class act" in this business.

You've all been part of this story. For your loyalty, your support, and your hard work please accept my profound thanks.

Many of us will continue as part of Microsoft. This means we'll have the opportunity to do what we do best—building, selling and supporting world-class software—on an unprecedented scale. The challenge is exciting, and more than a little intimidating. Nevertheless, I'm certain we will succeed.

For those who won't be joining Microsoft, this may be a melancholy time…good-byes are never fun. I hope you will look back on your time with Fox as a period of personal growth, learning and perhaps even some fun. I think your experiences at Fox may serve you well in your future careers.

My personal best wishes to each one of you as you enter upon a new career at Microsoft or pursue other opportunities. Thanks again for your efforts!

So ended the story of Fox Software. If I had written the story myself I would've written a different ending. I would have Fox grow to ten times the size, our product catalog increase, and the developers become wildly rich. But life wrote a different story. A success story? Sure, but a different kind of success story.

In some ways the growth of the company paralleled my own. I went from a kid out of college to being one of Fox's perceived cracker-jack developers. I watched a company of only a handful of people grow to hundreds. I was berated, scolded, applauded, and cheered. I saw the best and worst the software industry had to give and lived to tell about it.

The last Friday of the last week of July, I packed my office, turned in my ID badge and walked out of Fox Software for the last time. There was a summer breeze blowing, and with it came a strong feeling of melancholy. Left behind was a wealth of experiences—some good, some bad—but all interesting. What lay ahead, God only knew, but I had a feeling He was there, working in the circumstances again….

And without a doubt, I'd have a tale or two to tell.

# Epilogue
# There and Back Again

What happened next is full of ironies. The irony for me is that I'm
headed back again. As I write this, my house in Washington is sold, my
stuff is in boxes—and within a few weeks—I'll be back in Ohio. I
guess it's as they say: You can take the boy out of the country, but
never the country out of the boy.

It's been nearly eleven years since the merger and much has
happened in every way. Ashton-Tate is a far distant memory. Borland's
market presence is virtually nonexistent.

Microsoft, on the other hand, has been wildly successful. There is
no part of the software industry where their influence isn't felt. Their
*Cirrus* database product is now a part of Office XP—it's called *Access*.

However, with all those changes, one thing remains. The product
that was the central focus of my life for eight years—FoxPro—
survives. The latest version, Visual FoxPro 8.0, was released just this
year, and the gurus love it. Few products that started in the eighties are
still viable. None of Fox's competition is still around. Yet FoxPro
remains. I am still a relatively young man, but sometimes I think
FoxPro will outlive me....

As for the characters in the story—the astounding Fox team—their
stories diverged shortly after we relocated. Ironically, many of those
stories also passed through the exact same checkpoint a few years later.

One perk of joining Microsoft in the early nineties, though perhaps
only Chris saw it, was the company's stock options program. Few
would have imagined that the growth of Microsoft's stock would be
such that a person given options for only a few thousand shares in
1992, would see those options grow to be worth over a million dollars
just six years later. Because of that unparalleled growth, many of the
Fox group found themselves with the ability to pursue other interests
(and dreams) when they finally grew tired of programming (which
many did).

I'll tell what I know starting from the top.

Dave Fulton created quite a stir at Microsoft. As suspected, he
didn't take well to being employed by someone else. He lasted at Bill
Gates's company about a year. In that time he managed to oversee the
shipment of FoxPro on all four platforms—Windows, DOS, Mac, and

finally UNIX. He also tried to fire a handful a people, mouthed off to a couple key executives, and started—what's reported to be—an outstanding collection of rare musical instruments.

The last time I saw Dave was at the party thrown for his retirement from Microsoft. The highlight of that gathering was a reenactment of "a day in the life of Fox Software" that included some of the scenarios described in this book. The members of the original development team were the performers, and Heindel played the part of Dave, complete with a fake bald head and a full length fur coat. Following the presentation, Dave Fulton's comment to the group was: "How did you remember all that stuff?" My unspoken answer was: "Weren't you there? How could we not?"

Dave's wife, Amy, was present at the performance and smiled from ear to ear. At Microsoft, she worked on FoxPro for Windows until it shipped. Then—when Dave left the company—so did she.

Eric Christensen began his Microsoft career in an unenviable position. The company didn't allow husbands to supervise directly their wives, so Eric was made Amy's direct supervisor and Dave was still his. *Rock and a hard place.* Rumor has it his first review period was quite interesting.

As the development of the Windows product continued, and then the Mac product, Eric became less and less a Fox commodity and more a division-wide resource. He subsequently left to work on SQL Server, where he still works today. The last time I saw him he was in a production of "the Pirates of Pensanze" with two of his children (now much older than I remember). That guy is still a genius.

Brian Tallman stuck with the Fox group for quite a while. At the start of Visual FoxPro 3.0 for Windows, Brian became the development lead and was arguably the best supervisor the Fox team ever had. His talent, patience, fairness, and faith were the hallmarks of his leadership. After 3.0 shipped, Brian stepped down from his lead position, and then moved over to the Windows OS team. A short time later, he retired from Microsoft. He now lives the life of a farm boy with his wife and children.

For all the jokes about being "Eeyore", Bill Ferguson was a solid developer and an even better architect of software solutions. Good ideas were his forte. After a few years with Fox at Microsoft, he transferred to the C/C++ group. He then left the company to pursue other interests. Last I knew he was heavily involved with his family, his church—and somewhat surprisingly—his music. (At Fox, Eric, not Bill, had always been the musical one.)

My friend—the Heindel-man—hung with the Fox group through the shipment of the 2.5 Mac product and on into the development of the 3.0 Windows product. The idea of finally bringing "Objects" to FoxPro (a principal part of 3.0) really torqued him though. He was convinced the idea was killed years before for the right reasons. "This is not what our users want," he said, echoing Dave's earlier sentiments. Still, he begrudgingly did the work of converting READ to use objects. In the process, he cleaned up the mess that always seemed to plague that code. *We have met the enemy, and they are ours.*

After that, Heindel moved to a new group Microsoft started, one that centered on travel. This group eventually evolved into the online travel site, Expedia. He was there for a few years, and then went to a group working on online bill payment and presentment. Shortly after its technology was proven to work, that group—called 'TransPoint'—was sold to another company (CheckFree, originally from *Ohio*). Before that transaction took place, however, Heindel left Microsoft. He is now active in various ministries at his church, one of which is a 'no cost' computer training course for the unemployed and computer illiterate. *Still helping those who are a little misplaced...*

Marty's Microsoft career was full of ironies. As his part of the Windows product, he was put in charge of the Report Writer. This brought him the attention he so desired, but...well, I think I've illustrated the downsides of that. Marty was one of those Dave threatened to fire—and not surprisingly—that bothered him.

"Move me two thousand miles and then threaten to fire me?" he said one day in my office. "No way." He pointed a finger toward that troubling corner office. "After this product ships, I'm outta here!"

During our first Microsoft review period in December, (which was when transfers were allowed) Marty left the group. He joined the Works team and worked on that product for a number of years. He then worked on mapping tools for a time before ending his Microsoft career as a well-respected lead in the Natural Languages group. Marty then claimed another first. He was the first to move back to Ohio. He and his family returned less than two years ago.

Chris stepped into Microsoft and grabbed tightly the handrail of the "up escalator." He left the Fox group shortly after the first Windows product shipped, and took a management position with the C group. Shortly thereafter, he got the enviable title of "Director of Product Development." Over the course of the next few years he moved around a lot (but always in the 'up' direction) until he landed in Microsoft's Human Resources division. While there, he reached the pinnacle of success for the upwardly mobile at Microsoft: Vice President. I guess the "up escalator" works best for those who wear monogrammed shirts. He served only a short time as a VP before he too left the company.

Jim Simpkins seemed to have found the "up escalator" as well. After the UNIX product was out the door, he became a Program Manager for Fox (chiefly a design position), and then hopped over to Microsoft's other database product—Access. If Jim found an escalator, it was one that got off at a different floor. He was the first non-Fulton developer to leave Microsoft. He stopped short of calling it retirement though.

"I tell people I work for Microsoft," he said when I saw him at the gym. "It's easier to explain."

I smiled. "OK. So what do you do with your day?"

Jim shrugged. "You know those things in your life you stop doing to go to work?"

"Yeah…"

"Well, you just keep doing them."

I always liked Jim.

Brad Serbus and Henry Seurer were kind of short shifted by this narrative—and in fact, short shifting was a part of their Fox career. They were rarely given significant projects to work on, and so they rarely got significant credit. In either case this was unfortunate, because they're both interesting characters. They fit well into the Microsoft experience. We three even played together on a Microsoft-sponsored whirlyball league together. *Team D, forever, fellas!*

Henry, a South Dakota native, was a big part of both the Mac 2.5 and 3.0 efforts. Following that, (and partly due to my urging that he'd get pigeon-holed) he moved to the mapping group at Microsoft. He eventually wound up as a part of the Expedia spin-off company. The last I heard he was trying to rejoin Microsoft again, though. I hope he found a place where he enjoyed the work and his efforts were finally appreciated.

Brad, originally from Michigan, also left the Fox group after the Mac version of 3.0 shipped. Last I heard he was in the Windows team. Brad is a fun-loving and personable guy. I have no doubt he eventually found success.

Another notable character in the Fox story was not only short-shifted by my narrative, but he was left out entirely. His name is Walt Kennamer and in 1990 he joined Fox from the accounting firm Ernst & Young. Walt was hired to be Fox's Chief Operating Officer, but even before that he was well known in the dBASE community. After the merger with Microsoft, he too was apotheosized (if that is possible from the position of COO). He became a developer and worked side-by-side with the rest of the Fox team. (I even got to teach him a few coding tricks myself. <grin>) Walt has a rapier wit that hides within an unassuming facade. He was a welcome addition to our team. He worked with the Fox group for roughly five years and took on many interface chores in all the FoxPro products up to—and including—5.0. He then left the group to work on a number of Internet projects (the most visible being the Microsoft Investor site) before eventually retiring from Microsoft.

Brian Crites was the captain of the 2.5 Mac effort. After that, he went to a team that was working on "demand video." The system he and his team developed got limited utilization in an apartment building near Microsoft and was also implemented somewhere in Japan. He and his wife, now parents, are both still hard-at-work for the company. Joan is the head of Tech Writing for a whole division and Brian is a lead on Windows Media Player.

Matt Pohle (another of the 'apotheosized') stuck with Fox through the 3.0 Windows effort, and worked primarily with OLE. OLE knowledge was a hot commodity then and Matt used his skills to get a position with the Access group. After that, I (beyond hearing about a marriage and a house on the lake) lost touch with him....

John Beaver (primarily known as "Beave") became a good friend, though. I was even one of two best men in his wedding. Career-wise, Beave blossomed at Microsoft. After close to five years at Fox, he moved to the TransPoint effort with Heindel, and then left to join a group constructing tools for monitoring web traffic and presenting online advertisements. That group was run by a former Fox guru, George Goley. Beave's still at Microsoft, and surprisingly, still has a lot of hair.

In the end, Sally was the biggest Fox diehard of us all. She stayed with the ever-shrinking Fox group until she left Microsoft, less than a year ago. She was responsible for numerous key areas of the product. In my time working with her, her most notable contribution was the Object Manager, a pivotal part of Visual FoxPro 3.0 and its successors. She too is on her way back to Ohio. She'll beat my wife and I by a week or two.

As for me, I worked on both the Windows 2.5 and Mac 2.5 products until they shipped. I was then brought over to work on the Windows 3.0 version where I got to write—for the third time—a Screen Painter. This time it was actually called a "Form Tool" and it was much more sophisticated than my earlier efforts. It was undoubtedly some of the best code I ever wrote. *Third time's a charm!*

After that, I moved over to the 3.0 version of the Mac product and eventually became its captain. When the development of that product was winding down, the rumor swept through our division that the Fox group and its products were about to be dropped. With the help of another developer (named Greg Smith) I composed a song to commemorate the occasion. The melody went something like this…

Hi-ho, hi-ho, it's off to Consumer (division) I go,
Our product's dead, that's all they said,
Hi-ho, hi-ho, hi-ho, hi-ho…

The supposed death of the product, and the short shifting my team (and I) subsequently got, was enough to motivate a change. I followed Heindel to Expedia and stayed there about a year. Aside from what I learned about the inner workings of the travel industry, that experience just wasn't very fun for me. I never felt like I really belonged, and I was starting to question whether I wanted to program anymore. So, shortly after Heindel left for TransPoint, so did I.

The TransPoint group was great and I found some enjoyment in programming again. Still, a part of me was growing restless. *I can't possibly write another 'for' loop….*

Just when I reached that point, I wound up sitting beside an elderly man on a plane.

"What do you do?" I asked him. That's the normal way to initiate conversation on a plane, after all.

The man glanced at his wife and smiled. "I'm a writer," he said and straightened himself in his seat. "And I'm that most uncommon of creatures—I'm actually a **published** writer."

"Really?" I said. "I've always wanted to write."

The man sniffed. "Well, start early," he said. "You might get published before you die."

I took that as a sign. A little over a year later I left Microsoft, purchased a laptop and started "dinking around" with this text.

Over the course of the next three years, I wrote a couple novels (yet to be published) and gave some time to ministry opportunities myself. In that time I also met someone who appeared to like listening to my stories nearly as much as I liked telling them. There was only one way to guarantee she'd remain a captive audience, so I married her.

Then, on a whim, I searched for my name on the Internet. I found a website that detailed the history of Fox and its products. Many of the contributors were names I recognized from my days in Perrysburg. *Dang,* I thought, *someone might actually care to read my stuff.*

I dug out my Fox scribblings. And now—less than a year later— you hold it in your sweaty little hands. *Looks like I found someone else who cares.* Many thanks to my publisher, Whil. Thanks also to you, fearless reader! You hold the first of what I hope to be many published works. (But I never know for sure what circumstances will be next.)

So there you have it. Some tales just deserve to be told—I hope you enjoyed mine.